Walking
with God
in the
Classroom

Second Edition

Walking with God in the Classroom

Christian Approaches to Learning and Teaching

Second Edition

Harro Van Brummelen

Alta Vista College Press
Seattle, Washington

ISBN 10: 1-886319-07-3
ISBN 13: 978-1-886319-07-3

Published by Alta Vista College Press
P O. Box 55535, Seattle, WA 98155, U.S.A.
(206) 524-2262; fax (206) 524-1837

Scripture quotations are taken from The Holy Bible: New International Version. *Copyright 1973, 1978, 1984 International Bible Society. Used by permission of Zondervan Bible Publishers.*

Table of Contents

4   PLANNING FOR LEARNING   92

5   SHAPING THE CURRICULUM   126

Preface

This book deals with Christian approaches to learning and teaching. The Bible has much to say about our view of persons and their relationship to God, each other, and God's created reality. It also gives guidelines for nurturing children, guidelines that have implications for the classroom. Yet the Bible is not a sourcebook for specific teaching strategies or discipline procedures, and we should not use it as such. This book shows how some of the underlying Scriptural norms may be applied to contemporary classrooms.

I do not claim to present *the* Christian approach. God has created humans in such wondrous ways that no one individual can begin to exhaust the complexities of human learning and classroom teaching. Besides, students and teachers all differ in personality, learning style, range of abilities, community context, and even tolerance for noise, open-endedness, and tiredness. All these factors influence the context and practices of specific learning situations.

The second edition of this book, like the first, is intended for a fourfold audience. First, the book serves as a textbook for courses that introduce teaching and learning to Christian college and university students. Second, prospective and current Christian school teachers may use it to think about what it means to walk with God in their classrooms. I have been gratified that many Christian school staffs used the first edition as a discussion guide. Third, the book encourages Christians teaching in public government schools to consider how and to what extent they can teach Christianly. Finally, board members and supportive parents have also read the book to gain further insight into Christian schooling. The translations of the first edition into Hungarian, Korean, Polish, Romanian, and Russian have also been used in these ways.

After ten years, a second edition of *Walking with God in the Classroom* was needed. The principles of the first edition have not changed. However, we face new social and educational trends and issues. In this edition, I have included a number of significant ones such as conflict resolution and constructivism, together with my reactions. At the request of a number of Christian teacher educators,

I have also included a chapter on being a Christian teacher in a public school. This chapter is a slightly edited version of a booklet prepared by the Evangelical Fellowship of Canada's *Task Force on Education* of which I have been a member.

Many persons helped me write this book. First and foremost, I am indebted to John Vanderhoek, presently principal of Penticton Christian Community School in British Columbia. John co-authored Chapter 4 and several sections of Chapter 9 of the first edition. Many of his ideas still pervade sections of Chapters 3 and 7 of the current edition. Elaine Brouwer of Alta Vista College Press in Seattle carefully read drafts of chapters of this second edition and her reactions improved the manuscript. Others, from five countries around the world, made concrete and helpful suggestions for this edition: Robert Bruinsma, Tony Hawkins, Joy McCullough, Denis O'Hara, Herman Proper, John Van Dyk, John Vriend, and Wesley Wentworth. Finally this book would never have become a reality if it weren't for the many teachers and prospective teachers whose classroom practice and expertise deepened and extended my insights. To all who have given their input, my thanks for supporting what has truly been a community effort.

Glen Van Brummelen drew the book's diagrams for me; as usual, the son's computer skills outshone the father's by several magnitudes.

I dedicate this book to Geraldine Steensma. In 1972, as a young teacher unexpectedly plunged into becoming a high school principal, I was inspired by her little but incisive book, *To Those Who Teach*. A few years later, we co-edited *Shaping School Curriculum: A Biblical View* (1977). I benefited a great deal from her vision, a vision that so obviously stemmed from her love of the Lord and for children. My work continues to reflect some of her basic insights.

Harro Van Brummelen
Trinity Western University
Langley, British Columbia
e-mail: vanbrumm@twu.ca

Chapter 1

THE NATURE AND PURPOSE OF SCHOOLING

*M*s. *Jones starts her grade 11 world history class when the bell rings. After quickly reviewing the concepts of the previous day, she continues to present a clear, detailed outline of the causes of World War II, using overhead projections of computer displays she had prepared beforehand. The students take careful notes, realizing that they have to "know their stuff" for the weekly quiz. Ms. Jones welcomes questions for clarification, but little discussion of underlying issues takes place. The students implicitly accept that the interpretation Ms. Jones presents is the correct one.*

Across the hall, students in the same course rearrange Mr. Wong's classroom desks into groups representing Germany, Poland, France, England, Russia, and the United States. Quick final group strategy sessions take place. Students review their research notes. Do they know their assigned roles for the simulation session that will focus on the causes of World War II? They realize that Mr. Wong will evaluate them not only on factual accuracy, but also on how well their team has worked together, the thoroughness of their research, and the force of their argument.

Next door, Mrs. Jensen's students come to class well prepared. They have read the textbook section on the causes of World War II. They respect Mrs. Jensen's ability to ask penetrating, thought-provoking questions. They don't want to be embarrassed not knowing the concepts that form the basis for class discussion. Mrs. Jensen makes you think. She constantly elicits, challenges, gives counterexamples, and has you con-

sider different points of view. She forces you to look behind the facts at the motives, the root causes and the consequences of the actions and decisions of leaders.

Ms. Jones, Mr. Wong and Mrs. Jensen all believe they are implementing their school's mission statement, its aims, and its social studies goals. They use the same curriculum guide. Yet, if these lessons are typical ones (and always be cautious about drawing such a conclusion!), then each has different implicit beliefs about the nature and purpose of schooling. Students in each class will experience learning quite differently. They consider the same topic but learn different content. They practice varied cognitive skills. They acquire diverse views of the goals and processes of history. Through the structure of each classroom they implicitly develop distinct views of what kind of knowledge is important.

◆ ACTIVITY 1-1

The differences in the three classes described raise important questions. *What should a history course accomplish? How should we implement it?* Assuming that the lessons described are representative ones, outline how Ms. Jones, Mr. Wong, and Mrs. Jensen differ in their views of the nature and purpose of schooling. Before reading the rest of the chapter, write down what you believe to be the key purposes of schooling and how teachers can attain them.

This chapter presents one possible view of the nature and purpose of schooling. As you read, keep your sheet handy and jot down points that indicate your own view. This will help you develop a statement of your own approach to schooling, teaching and learning. Remember that this book's aim is to help *you* walk with God in your classroom in new, responsive, and deeper ways.

I believe that, as much as possible, the function of schooling should be to educate children and young adults for a life of responsive discipleship in Jesus Christ. However, like any compact statement, that leads to many questions. Isn't this true of nurture in the home and in the church as well? If so, how does the role of the school differ from that of the home and the church? What do we mean by "responsive discipleship"? Is this phrase just a platitude or can it truly enhance what happens in classrooms? Is it meaningful to talk about responsive discipleship when we teach mathematics or Spanish? This chapter begins to discuss these questions, while later ones will look at particular issues in more depth.

As a practicing or prospective teacher, you need to define and constantly refine what you believe about the nature and purpose of schooling. That does not guarantee that your teaching will reflect the view you have developed: the interaction between theory and practice is complex. But having an explicit conception helps you reflect on what is happening in your classroom. You can then plan and implement appropriate changes. That, in turn, will deepen your insight into how you view learning and teaching.

◆ ACTIVITY 1-2

Several years ago I participated in writing *A Vision with a Task* (Stronks & Blomberg 1993). There we described *disciples* of Jesus Christ as persons who acknowledge and trust Christ's trailblazing, using his power and directives to nurture the potential in themselves, in others, and in the rest of God's creation. They *respond* to God's calling with wisdom and knowledge, with discernment and creativity, with playfulness and perseverance, and, above all, with love and compassion.

We also listed three basic characteristics of *responsive discipleship*. First, we said, it means that schools help to *unwrap students' gifts* so that they use their God-given talents to develop their unique potential (Mt 25:14-30). Secondly, students learn to *share each others' joys and burdens*, developing their individuality in order to offer their unique gifts to their neighbors and to society (Ro 12:3-8). Third, schools *promote shalom*, the biblical peace and justice that heals brokenness and restores relationships (Lk 1:51-53). In all these ways students learn to respond to God's call in obedient and responsible ways.

Consider once again the classrooms of Ms. Jones, Mr. Wong, and Mrs. Jensen. In what ways do they bear out these three characteristics? Can you think of other important elements of *responsive discipleship*? Think of examples of how you could include each component of responsive discipleship in your classroom.

In the first edition of this book, I used the term *responsible discipleship*. Which phrase do you prefer? Why?

Agencies of Christian nurture and education

The nurture and education of students involve many institutions. The traditional ones are the home, church, and school. Today, the media, businesses, community agencies, and sports leagues also play important roles. Neil Postman, for one, has shown how television's emphasis on immediate gratification and quick emotional response can undermine listening and writing skills as well as logical thought. He adds that personal computers foster self-centeredness and a lack of commitment. Therefore schools, he claims, must give youth a sense of coherence and meaning (Postman 1993, pp. 16-17, 186).

Christians, of course, oppose television's superficial hedonism and technology's underlying faith in its ability to provide happiness for all. However, our starting point for thinking about Christian approaches to education may not be reactionary fear. Our positive point of departure is that the key agencies of nurture ought to help children live and become committed to bring glory to God's name.

Note here the distinctions among nurture, education and schooling. Nurturing children means bringing them up and cultivating their capacities in supportive, encouraging and compassionate ways. Educating them involves deliberately stimulating and developing their perceptions, insights and abilities. Schooling refers to educating students in a formal institution set up for that purpose. Ideally, education and schooling both embrace nurture based on the Great Commandment to love God and each other. Such nurture does not exclude discipline. Biblical nurture directs and redirects people to follow God's paths of integrity, righteousness, justice, and mercy.

The most important agency of Christian nurture is the *family*, the basic building block of society. God first of all directs injunctions to nurture children to parents (Dt 6:6-9; 11:18-21). Paul adds that parents must bring up children "in the training and instruction of the Lord" (Eph 6:4). Ideally, children experience and develop their ability to live the Christian life within a secure family environment based on a Christian atmosphere of love, support and discipline.

How parents model their convictions and lifestyle is crucial for children. More than anyone else, they can communicate to their children how the insights gained from an obedient listening to God's Word should govern the Christian life. Most of the home's education is informal. It takes place through daily interaction and discussion, devotions, provision of toys and games and books, sharing chores, going out together, and so on. Children learn most from the way parents structure everyday family life and from their personal modeling.

The second agency of Christian nurture is the *church*. The book of Acts emphasizes the teaching ministry of the church. Both Peter and Paul taught how God works through history and has fulfilled history with the Good News of Jesus Christ. In Corinth and Ephesus Paul stayed for lengthy periods, teaching people the Word of God (Acts 18:11; 19:10; 20:31). Similarly today, the church must teach youth the Good News and how they can take up their full responsibilities in the fellowship of believers. The teaching function of the church does not stop after conversion or profession of faith. Rather, the church continues to guide people from the more elementary truths of God's Word to its more in-depth implications (Heb 5:12-14). The church's educational programs emphasize what we believe, how we apply that to life, and how we function as part of God's church.

The injunction to nurture children in the Lord goes beyond the family and church, however. Both Deuteronomy 6 and Psalm 78 also address the people of Israel collectively. Telling "the next generation the praiseworthy deeds of the Lord, His power and the wonders He has done" (Ps 78:4) is a responsibility shared by the whole Christian community. In Biblical times, "schooling" took place within the extended family and, to a limited extent, in the synagogue.

Today, society has become so complex that few homes and no regular church education program can provide adequate general education. Besides, society provides few meaningful full-time roles for adolescents and young adults outside formal education. Schools and colleges therefore have become necessary and influential. Indeed, with widespread family breakdown and low church attendance, schools are sometimes forced to take on some roles that used to belong to the family or church.

I am personally convinced that Deuteronomy 6 and Psalm 78 imply that in today's society distinctly Christian schools are desirable. The Christian ethos that at one time undergirded North American society has all but disappeared. Children must develop thoroughly "Christian minds" if they are to be ambassadors of Christ in a secular society. That is difficult for the family and the church to accomplish by themselves with so many counteracting influences in society. We shortchange children's nurture in the Lord if their schooling does not openly proclaim that "the heavens declare the glory of God," and that "the precepts of the Lord are right, giving joy to the heart" (Psalm 19:1,8). At the same time, we need Christian teachers to be salt and light in public schools. If you are or plan to be a public school teacher, you will, by God's grace, still be able to implement much of what this book says about learning and teaching in that setting.

The home, the church and the school ideally form an educational tripod standing firm on the base of the Word of God and the flame of Christ's Spirit. All three need to work together to prepare children for the Christian life. If the school "leg" of the tripod rests on a different base, children will have difficulty staying in balance as they respond as Christians to the secular world around them. At the same time, the school can neither replace the family nor the church. The home in particular provides an essential base for the school's more formal education task.

◆ ACTIVITY 1-3

On the basis of several Scripture passages and a brief look at the state of today's society, I conclude in this section that Christian schools are desirable. Debate the pros and cons of Christian schools. Do so in terms of potential benefits and drawbacks for students and the Christian community. Under what circumstances would you favor Christian schools? Public ones?

Some jurisdictions in Canada operate Christian public schools. These schools must follow the state curriculum but their Christian teachers promote Christian values. What are the advantages and disadvantages of such arrangements?

Promoting a vision of the Kingdom of God

◆ ACTIVITY 1-4

The mission statement of a school summarizes its central purpose and the type of learning community it wants to be. Below are two typical mission statements for a public and a Christian school. In what ways do you agree with each? How would you change each to reflect your own views?

The school will help students to acquire knowledge, skills and attitudes needed to function in a culturally diverse society and to become respectful and self-directed citizens who contribute to a sustainable economy.

The school will be an encouraging learning community that stimulates its students to be and become followers of Jesus Christ by developing and using their gifts and God-given resources responsibly and creatively to serve God and their neighbors.

Almost no school today functions without a mission statement. It is much easier to design such a statement, however, than to ensure that it guides the school's overall program. Nevertheless, mission statements underscore that education is never neutral. Schools give form to concepts and ideas. They shape attitudes, values and dispositions. They teach about the past, attend to the present, and consider possibilities for the future, both on a personal level and for society (Groome 1980, p. 21). Schools use basic beliefs (often implicit ones) to set out an overall educational direction. Teachers' views of human beings and of the purpose and meaning of life influence how they interact with people and what and how they choose to teach. Education is always religious in the sense that it cannot but lead forth on the basis of faith commitments and ideals.

Basic beliefs underlie the public school mission statement given above. These include that our society should accept diversity and not seek to be a "melting pot." Also, schools ought to prepare students in the first place for employment in the marketplace. While these may be worthy purposes, by themselves they are limiting ones. The sample Christian school statement is much broader. Unless you are familiar with the Christian faith, however, you may not know the meaning of phrases like "followers of Jesus Christ" or "to serve God and neighbor." Mission statements need to be fleshed out.

An important theme that is central in the teaching of Jesus Christ and that undergirds the Christian school mission statement is that of the Kingdom of God. The vision of the Kingdom of God points

Christians not only to the redemption of God's people but also to the realization of God's intents and promises for His whole creation and for His people (Ridderbos 1962, p. 23). The Kingdom of God is a symbol of God's liberating or re-creating action. The whole of life and reality are to be transformed by God's grace and power.

The fulfillment of the Kingdom of God began with the death and resurrection of Jesus Christ. Its final significance will be revealed with Christ's return. The great gift of God is that, despite our short-comings and sinfulness, the seed of the Kingdom is already here. Christian schools may therefore challenge and prepare children to be and become citizens of the Kingdom of God. On the one hand, Christ has already established that Kingdom. On the other hand, it will not find its ultimate fulfillment in this present life (Lk 4:18-21 and 17:21; Rev 21-22).

Helping children become Kingdom citizens has a number of educational implications. First, to be part of the Kingdom calls for conversion (Mt 3:2). A school has a much broader educational task than the church. Nevertheless, the Christian school's instruction must proclaim the necessity of heeding God's call to repentance, conversion and obedience. Personal submission to Jesus Christ as Savior and Lord of Creation is a prerequisite for being co-heirs with Christ. Our commitment affects our whole way of life, including our academic endeavors. Christian school attendance can benefit children who are not Christians. Only those who devote their lives fully to Jesus as Lord, however, will personally grasp the fullness and joy of the responsive discipleship that the school fosters.

Secondly, Kingdom citizens are not individual imitators of God (Eph 5:1) but also members of the Body of Christ (Eph 4:1-16). God calls us to use our unique talents in service to the whole Body. Christian schools must be training grounds for such communal action. They must help children be "fellow citizens with God's people and members of God's household . . . being built together to become a dwelling in which God lives by His Spirit" (Eph 2:19, 22).

Thirdly, Kingdom citizens have a mandate: "Go make disciples of all nations . . . teaching them to obey everything I have com-manded you" (Mt 28:18-20). Significantly, this injunction comes at the end of Matthew, the gospel of the Kingdom of God. Christian teachers must study and understand Christ's teachings so that they can apply them in the school situation. They need to develop the implications for various areas of life with their students. They must encourage their students to take up their calling, not just on the future, but here and now. They must help them to reach out to others whom God similarly calls to obedience. The classroom must be a laboratory for practicing the central love command. Here students learn to accept and use God's gifts of life on earth while at the same time not setting their hearts on earthly treasures. Here students learn what it means to live a life of surrender to Him and of love to others. Christ had much concern for the widow and the orphan, the disadvantaged and the oppressed, the hurt and the sick. Promoting righteousness and justice is part of obeying Christ's commands and must be an integral part of schooling.

In the fourth place, Kingdom citizens live the fruit of love, service and truth in response to God's mandate. "All over the world," says Paul, "this gospel is producing fruit and growing, just as it has been doing among you since the day you heard it and understood God's grace in all its truth" (Col 1:6). The school's educational programs must provide constant opportunities for students to put faith into practice. Furthermore, discipline unto discipleship, also in the school, "produces a harvest of righteousness and peace for those who have been trained by it" (Heb 12:11).

Finally, a Christian school itself must be a signpost of God's Kingdom to the world. By its very existence in a secular society and by actively promoting a vision of God's coming Kingdom through its programs, the school is a witness to the fact that God is Sovereign and that Christ is Redeemer and Lord. A Christian school stands in the community as a monument to the fact that Christ claims *all* of life, including education in the school.

Christian schools and Christian teachers are far from perfect. Sin captures all people to a lesser or greater degree. That is also true in institutions that take hold of God's promises and proclaim a vision of God's Kingdom. Yet, God will work in Christian teachers "to will and to work according to His good purpose" so that they may "shine like stars as [they] hold out the word of life" (Php 2:13, 15).

◆ ACTIVITY 1-5

Some educators urge Christians not to try to answer whether a school is Christian or not, but, rather, to find out to what *extent* it is Christian. In view of God's calling for Kingdom citizens, do you agree? Why or why not? Can you see characteristics of public schools that might be termed "Christian"? Characteristics of Christian schools that are "secular"?

Two classroom examples

Perhaps the last section seemed theologically sound but left you wondering how the concepts would affect what happens in classrooms. Here are two classroom examples.

♦ *Ms. Kovacs begins her kindergarten year with teaching a unit about creation. On one wall she outlines a large circle divided into four equal parts. She labels the four parts things, plants, animals and people. She discusses these four "realms" with her students and asks them to draw pictures for each category. She helps the students paste their pictures in the right quadrants.*

Ms. Kovacs also has a picture of a huge hand above the circle. "Who looks after our world?", she asks. She elicits from the students that God created and sustains the world, and that God's hand is in control. She stresses that God made people special. They form a separate realm and are not just part of the animal realm. God gave them a special task to care for the earth and to praise God. The pupils trace their own hands, cut out the shapes and paste them between the people "quadrant" and God's hand to symbolize that God has given them, too, a special calling.

Then Ms. Kovacs asks her pupils how we can praise God (singing, go to church, pray to God, love others). How can we care for the earth? (look after animals and plants, don't waste food). She explores how God has given us a beautiful creation but that often people mess it up. She then asks the students how they can serve God and neighbor inside the classroom (clean up, obey the teacher, be kind to others). In this way, Ms. Kovacs helps students realize, young as they are, that they can already take up their calling as disciples of Christ in a responsible and responsive way—and thus participate in God's Kingdom.

♦ *Now let's look again at the World War II example at the beginning of this chapter. If we are to promote a vision of the Kingdom of God as we teach this topic, we will first of all need to explore the motives of the decision-makers leading up to and during the War. We trace the sinfulness that led to the incredible destructiveness of the War. We explore how the War affected politicians, soldiers, and innocent bystanders. We are truthful about the inhumanity committed on all sides: the atrocities of the Holocaust, but also the forced internment of Japanese Canadians. We review how Christians responded. Some passively accepted Nazism. The theologian Bonhoeffer forfeited his life in an unsuccessful plot to assassinate Hitler. Many Dutch Christians risked their lives to save Jews from the gas chambers.*

The unit's focus becomes a responsible Christian attitude to war. Should Christians be pacifists, as is true for the Quakers and Mennonites? If not, when is a war "justifiable"? To ensure that students do not just think that the issues of World War II are ones of the distant past, we also discuss questions such as, What role should Western and other nations play in fostering peace around the world? Is it right for Western nations to profit from supplying armaments all over the globe? How can Christians be agents of reconciliation and hope in today's violent society? What do the beatitudes say about our response to conflict? What are some of the Biblical principles that guide our actions in conflict situations, whether that be in school, among friends, in society, or when facing war?

The ways in which we teach–our pedagogy–also affects whether or not we promote a vision of the Kingdom of God. The Bible does not prescribe specific "correct" teaching methods. It does, however, emphasize that learners must respond to what they learn in a personal way. Ms. Jones may be well organized. Her students may do well on their exams. However, do they learn to understand and take up their calling as agents of reconciliation and peace? Mr. Wong's students learn a great deal about positive interaction and cooperation. However, will they apply such learning to the underlying issues that we face when dealing with human conflict? Mrs. Jensen's students learn to think clearly and evaluate different perspectives. However, do they grasp what it means to apply the Great Commandment to issues of war and peace? These questions are difficult to answer on the basis of the brief descriptions at the beginning of this chapter. What is clear, however, is that teachers can use not only the content but also the teaching and learning strategies to affirm or to detract from promoting a vision of the Kingdom of God. I develop this further in the chapters on teaching and learning.

◆ ACTIVITY 1-6

With two or three others, brainstorm ways in which you could promote a vision for the Kingdom of God for a topic regularly taught in
school. After you have listed all your ideas, come to a consensus
about the three or four that would be most effective. Can these become an integral part of teaching the topic?

The aims of learning and teaching

Schools are for learning. Teaching intends to promote learning, but learning also takes place through experience and individual study. This book deals with the processes of learning and teaching based on a Biblical view of persons and of knowledge.

Learning and teaching must take place in humble dependence on God: "Trust in the Lord with all your heart and lean not on your own understanding" (Pr 3:5). The Christian's starting point is that the fear of the Lord is the fountain of life (Pr 14:27) as well as the beginning of wisdom and knowledge (Pr 1:7; Ps 111:10). Psalm 111 adds that all who follow God's precepts have good under-standing. Conversely, if we allow God to give us understanding, then we will be able to keep His law and obey it with all our heart (Ps 119:34).

Christian learning and teaching aims to discover God's laws and apply them in obedient response to God. That may involve applying the laws of gravity and wind resistance in building a model air-plane. It may mean using the laws of language creatively in composing a story. Students may investigate how God's laws of justice and righteousness apply to economic life, or what God's law of love and faithfulness implies for personal relationships and marriage. The key point is that we recognize that God is the Creator and Sustainer of all of reality and the norms of human life (Pr 3:19-20; Job 38-41).

As the sample Christian school mission statement implied, the overall aim of Christian education is to help and guide students be and become responsible disciples of Jesus Christ. Disciples are followers who grasp the vision of their leader and then apply that vision in their everyday lives. Becoming disciples of Jesus Christ, therefore, involves understanding and committing oneself to Christ and Christ's vision of God's Kingdom. Disciples who are responsible begin to carry out the mandate of the Kingdom in their lives. Among the many other things Christ taught, they begin to live as peacemakers and agents of reconciliation. They love the disadvantaged and those who oppose us. They take joy in practicing moral purity. They eschew love of material possessions and oppose societal structures that exploit. Disciples use their God-given authority to serve others in humility, and maximize their God-given abilities to serve Him and those around us (Ma 5:8, 9, 44; 19:21; 20:1-16, 26-28; 21:12-13; 23:8-12; 25:14-30; 2Co 5:16ff.). In short, disciples learn to walk with God both in their personal lives and in their societal callings.

In today's selfishly individualistic and ethically relativistic society, responsible discipleship is a radical challenge! It takes a life of personal faith in Christ. It calls for a willingness to build Christian relationships in the community. And it needs the ability and disposition to participate in and impact our culture in a Christian way.

◆ ACTIVITY 1-7

Christian schools can advance the overall aim of Christian nurture by implementing four broad aims. For each, I have indicated a number of goals that contribute to the broad aim. Assign a numerical value to each goal from 1 (unimportant) to 10 (essential). At the end, you will use your values to write your own set of aims and goals.

1. To unfold the basis, framework, and implications of a Christian vision of life.

- *To acquire a knowledge of the Bible and its basic themes.*
- *To understand the Christian faith and its implications.*
- *To formulate a Christian worldview as a guide for thought and action.*
- *To understand, experience and exercise Biblical mandates such as the creation mandate, the Great Commission, and the Great Commandment.*
- *To discern the influence of Judeo-Christian morals and values on our cultural heritage.*

- To compare and contrast a Biblical worldview with others in order to understand the motivating ideas and spirit of the times and their effects on cultural formation.
- To realize the vital role of the family and church in the community.
- To know the privileges and responsibilities of belonging to families, schools and communities.

2. To learn about God's world and how humans have responded to God's mandate to take care of the earth.

- To explore the concepts of number and space, the orderly laws governing them, and their use in solving everyday problems.
- To investigate the fundamental concepts, structures and theories of physical and living things, and the impact of science and technology on life in society.
- To understand the interrelations between people and their environment and how to use and enjoy resources prudently.
- To know the practices that constitute a healthy lifestyle.
- To become aware of and experience various forms of aesthetic expression.
- To use language to clarify thought, to develop perception and insight, and to serve God and others through edifying and creative communication.
- To investigate the role of humans in shaping culture, including social, economic, and political structures.
- To explore how Christians can be involved in humanitarian service regardless of ethnic, cultural, social or religious background.
- To examine the essential role of government and law in human affairs, and what it means to be a responsible citizen.
- To examine and clarify basic moral and value precepts and their role in human life.

3. To develop and apply responsibly the concepts, abilities and creative gifts that enable students to contribute positively to God's Kingdom and to society.

- To become proficient in using the concepts, processes and skills of language, science, mathematics, physical movement, and aesthetics.
- To extend analytic thinking skills: reflective reasoning, decision-making skills, evaluating situations and making judgments within a Biblical framework, analyzing and rearranging related ideas, etc.

◆ *To develop sound research skills.*
◆ *To acquire social and emotional skills and attitudes for partici-*
pating responsibly in group situations.
◆ *To unfold special talents and learn to cope with weaknesses.*
◆ *To share knowledge and gifts with others.*

4. *To become committed to Christ and to a Christian way of life,*
   willing to serve God and their neighbors.

◆ *To grow spiritually by appreciating and applying the essentials of*
the Christian faith.
◆ *To live increasingly from a position of heart commitment to God.*
◆ *To grow in a lifestyle of being conformed to the image of Jesus*
Christ, becoming disposed (1) to act on the basis of Biblical prin-
ciples for ethical, social and economic responsibility, and (2)
serve others willingly and unselfishly.
◆ *To understand how sin results in problems such as injustice and*
violence, and to strive for reconciliation with God, self, others
and the world.
◆ *To assume a role as a citizen of God's Kingdom and the nation in*
response to God's creation mandate, the Great Commandment,
and the Great Commission.

Use the above and the numerical values that you assigned to each as
a reference point for revising or making an outline of your own aims
and goals. Make one set that would apply if you taught in a Christian
school, another that would be suitable for a public school. Remember
that by law public schools may not promote any particular religion.
Share and discuss your statements with others.

A Biblical worldview and knowledge

A basic question for Christian educators is, "What is God's way
for today?" In school, students need to encounter the contours of a
Biblical worldview and its relevance for living in today's society in
a deeper way each year. Teachers help students deepen their awareness that the whole world is God's creation. They explore with
them how sin often undermines God's intent for the world.

Teachers also help students recognize, however, that they have a
special task in God's reality made possible through Christ's redemption. Christian teachers need to be honest that Christians often
disagree about the application of Biblical norms, for instance, to

politics and economics. Moreover, they also ensure that their students become familiar with views that differ from Christian ones in order to see truth more clearly. Christians often learn much from persons who are not Christians.

In all this, Scripture gives us many clear directives. It must be our final point of reference. Kindergarten children can already understand that they were created as beings with the special calling to give glory to God in all of life. Primary pupils can see how God ordained families with mothers, fathers and children to be the basic "building blocks" of society. In science they can learn how we must care for God's marvelous creation in a trustworthy way. They explore a Christian vision of life and reality and a biblical lifestyle based on the norms of God's Word.

Schools are academic institutions. Therefore they concern themselves with "knowledge-that" (concepts and cognitive content) and "knowledge-how" (abilities and skills). But we must choose concepts and skills as means to an end, not as ends in themselves. Does our content point to the marvelous deeds and power of the Lord and His grace in Jesus Christ? Does it show how God has created a world for which we may care? Does it help students see how God calls them to service both personally and as part of Christ's Body—in social relationships, in the world of commerce and industry, in political life, in cultural pursuits? Do schools develop students' abilities to the utmost to use, shape, and enjoy God's world?

Ultimately all knowledge, including knowledge of a Biblical worldview, is in vain unless through the Holy Spirit our students accept Christ's grace. Therefore teachers invite students to commit their whole lives—their thoughts, words, and deeds—to Christ as their personal Redeemer and Lord of life. They encourage personal commitment to God and to a Christian way of life.

To do so, schools need to do more than proclaim a Christian vision of life. Christ modeled what He taught and called for meaningful response. He modeled Christian service and humility, for instance, by washing his disciples' feet. He sent out his twelve disciples long before we would have considered them ready. He told the rich young man to sell his possessions and give to the poor if he was truly interested in following Jesus—and lived with few possessions himself. Fostering Biblical dispositions and attitudes requires more than formal teaching. It requires teachers to model a Christian vision of life and students to experience it in all aspects of

the learning situation. Students need to practice values and dispositions in harmony with Biblical guidelines.

Knowledge, in other words, involves much more than intellectual comprehension and analysis. It must result in response and
committed action. Teachers strive to be servant leaders and models.
They help pupils use their unique gifts to complete products that are
personally meaningful. They encourage them to make judgments
and decisions within a Biblical framework. They give them space to
become responsible and learn from failures. They help them show
love for God and neighbor through community-oriented activities
both within the school and outside. Their students not only see but
also experience what it means to walk with God in all their activities.

◆ ACTIVITY 1-8

Schools are academic institutions, according to one paragraph in this
section. However, don't the questions that follow in this paragraph
also apply to the education of children in the home, in the church,
and in some community organizations? If so, can you distinguish
among their respective educational roles? What are the specific
educational tasks of each? Under what circumstances, if any, can
parents adequately attain the tasks usually assigned to the school by
home schooling their children?

Realizing the aims: learning about First Nations people

Many sets of goals exist for both Christian and public schooling. It
is one thing to write an inspiring set of goals. It is quite another,
however, to design and implement a set of learning experiences
likely to attain the goals. Below is an example of a classroom unit
that tries to do so (with thanks to teachers Wilma Hettinga and Judy
Newland).

◆ *Mrs. Neufeld teaches a unit on First Nations (North American
Indian) people to her grade 4 class of mainly Caucasian students. She wants them to appreciate cultures other than their
own. More than that, she wants them to see, in concrete ways,
that visions of life affect ways of life. Her class will explore
characteristics of First Nations culture such as the extended*

family and careful resource stewardship. Her students will also investigate how Indian and white interaction has affected the First Nations way of life, often in detrimental ways. Her pupils will consider their personal and our societal obligations to enable diverse cultures to live responsibly in our world. What does it mean to show Christian justice and compassion? How do all ways of life benefit from repentance and faith?

In the section on the Haida Indians on the Queen Charlotte Islands, Mrs. Neufeld's students explore Haida culture both before and after the arrival of whites. She bases the first activities on her students' experiential knowledge of British Columbia's rain forests: the climate, vegetation, types of animals, the resources the Haidas could use. Each child draws a map and makes a brief illustrated report that contributes to a mural on the Haida rain forest. Next, Mrs. Neufeld has her class study Haida village and family life, the nature and reasons for the potlatch, and Haida religion and legends. The students read, discuss and write stories and poems and legends for their Haida "book." The class builds a model Haida village, simulates an extended family, prepares Haida food, makes some masks and model totem poles, and dramatizes a potlatch. Mrs. Neufeld then charts the changes in Haida culture after the arrival of white persons, including recent efforts to restore Haida culture.

The pupils learn many concepts and develop many abilities in this unit. They learn to appreciate how the Haidas used the many diverse God-given resources to develop a unified way of life. As their insights deepen, they also develop further skills in reading, writing, classifying and drawing inferences, map reading, research, art, and so on. Mrs. Neufeld does not just include an activity because it happens to be interesting. Rather, each contributes something to her overall goal of understanding how beliefs structure a way of life. Some activities are highly structured and teacher-centered. Others allow for a great deal of latitude and personal response in creating unique products. Still others require students to plan and work together as a whole class or in small groups.

Mrs. Neufeld carefully leads the activities in this section to a concluding one: the development of a large chart contrasting the Western materialistic way of life with the Haida one. The students suggest competition for the first column, cooperation for the second. Becoming rich is contrasted with sharing, as is the nuclear family with the extended one. Soon, however, the students suggest that a third column needs to be added: a Christian way of life. What does a Christian lifestyle entail? After completing the chart, Mrs. Neufeld discusses how the Haidas recognized some important values that God put into the creation order but that they missed the essential knowledge of Christ as Savior and Lord. She also discusses how people in white communities, although they may have a Christian background, often show little love for God and neighbor.

Mrs. Neufeld does more. The Haidas, she feels, are still too much of a "foreign" culture. None of her students have visited the Queen Charlotte Islands or have met Haidas personally. The next part of her unit, therefore, is the study of a local Indian band. She stresses how white culture has influenced the band: the fur trade, the establishments of reserves, outbreak of diseases such as smallpox, the influence of missionaries, and schooling for First Nations children. Her students pretend to be among the first white people having contact with the band, and they discuss what things they would do differently.

Mrs. Neufeld then takes her class to visit the reserve. The students have prepared questions for the chief. What type of work are your people doing? What are some of the projects your band has initiated? What are your schools like? What changes would you like to see in your community? How would you like your people to be different from white people?

After the students write a report on their visit, Mrs. Neufeld concludes the unit by asking the students' reaction to two quotes by First Nations people: "We don't just want to hear about the religion of whites; we want to see them live it first"; and "The white person speaks with a forked tongue." She discusses why many First Nations people feel this way, and asks the students whether this applies to them personally.

◆ ACTIVITY 1-9

Discuss in what ways Mrs. Neufeld has met this chapter's aims of schooling. Are there any ways in which she falls short? Then look at the personal set of aims that you are developing. How would you change Mrs. Neufeld's unit in order to attain your aims?

Schools as social institutions

Schools are educational institutions that, in the first place, focus on attaining educational aims. Some activities are better done by families or other agencies. Schools need to avoid spreading themselves so thin that they fail to accomplish their educational goals. Teachers and parents should cooperate but should recognize their respective, distinct tasks in nurturing children. Schools educate students by planning and implementing structured learning activities.

Nevertheless, society does implicitly assign roles other than strictly academic ones to schools. Schools are prime agencies of socialization. For at least twelve years, students spend one quarter of their waking hours in schools. There, they learn to interact with others according to certain behavior standards and patterns. Students perceive schools to be important because of friendships and social activity. Parents know intuitively that schools have a big impact on their children's socialization.

Therefore, schools attempt to be supportive learning communities. They help all students to contribute and feel accepted. They appreciate them for their unique gifts and contributions. Students learn to cooperate, not just to compete for the sake of "beating" someone else. A balance of individual, small group and large group activities help students use their talents to contribute to the community in different ways. Students learn to serve each other. They may, for instance, be engaged in peer tutoring or planning projects and assemblies. (See chapters 4 and 9 for more detail.)

Effective schools–Christian or public–are ones where the school board and its committees, the principal and teachers, and parents and students share and cooperate to implement a common vision. Whatever their organizational structures, effective schools maintain close contact between teachers and parents. They involve parents as volunteers. They work collaboratively to establish new policies and programs. Schools need such a setting if they are to attain their goals.

Within a few months of opening, a public school in my neighborhood had a reputation of being an excellent school. My neighbors soon tried to transfer their children into the school. How had this come about? First, the principal had been able to choose a team of teachers with similar views on education, willing to work together in a united and positive way. Next, he involved parents on advisory committees to develop policies and recommend programs. He held a number of public meetings where he solicited input on how the school could serve the community. He also required the teachers to hand in unit plans for every topic—and discussed those plans with them before being taught. His leadership was servant leadership. He had clear goals for the school, but involved the teachers, parents and students in ways that made a difference in how the school implemented its program. He served the community by providing excellence for the type of schooling that they had jointly planned.

◆ ACTIVITY 1-10

A current trend in classrooms involves implementing computer-related technologies. At the same time, many students have dysfunctional backgrounds and do not function well in social settings. Some educators conclude that schools should more and more become agencies of socialization, with the learning of "basics" being left to computer-assisted instruction. Would this be desirable? Why or why not?

Christian schools and their communities

Christian schools are organized in different ways. Some are operated by trans-denominational organizations of parents. With this structure, parents themselves make key decisions through an elected board and an appointed education committee. The parents are directly involved with the educational environment of their children. However, with this structure it may be difficult to maintain a clear sense of direction, despite well-defined statements of mission and purpose. Some schools organized in this way hold compulsory orientation meetings for new parents before they can become involved in governing the school.

Many Christian schools are ministries of particular churches. Such schools often have a clear theological basis and educational direction. However, tensions may arise between the church and school administrations, especially about ultimate responsibility and finances. Further, some church members may wrongly assume that the Christian school is an extension of the church's educational program. While Biblical in focus, the school's educational scope is much broader than that of the church. The school plunges students into the study of all aspects of God's world.

Other Christian school boards have self-perpetuating governing boards. These maintain a clear direction but limit the role and involvement of parents in governing the school. Parents can exercise their responsibility by choosing the particular school for their children, but they do not have the final say in setting school policies.

The Bible does not specify a particular form of organization for Christian schools. However, it does indicate that parents have the primary responsibility for their children's education. Therefore, any organizational structure should allow for meaningful parental input into school policies and practices.

In my experience, Christian schools usually attract all but the highest and lowest social classes, with mean family incomes close to their public school counterparts. Family life is somewhat more stable than in society in general. However, the prevailing mindset of society also influences Christians. Individualism and hedonism also affect Christian school students, and Christian schools will be far from perfect communities. Also, some parents send children to Christian schools because they have not done well in other schools. Nevertheless, on the whole Christian schools have a relatively united and supportive parent community.

This milieu helps Christian schools focus on their educational goals. There is a danger, however, that such schools become hot-house shelters for the middle class. This is especially true since Christians in the western world all too often are at ease with today's materialism. Therefore, schools may need to plan socialization experiences that help students relate to the poor and underprivileged in society in the way Christ commands. They must also help students reject the values and patterns of secular culture. To what extent Christian schools prepare their students to raise and be signposts for the coming of God's Kingdom remains an open question. There is no question, however, that God calls them to do so.

◆ ACTIVITY 1-11

Find out how parents in the schools in your community are involved in the schools. What roles do parents take on in Christian schools operated by parent organizations? In schools operated by churches, are the parents involved in meaningful ways? Do public schools make use of parent advisory councils? Do those councils play an important part in setting school aims and policies?

Parents, as children's primary caregivers, have the responsibility and the right to choose where and how they are schooled (until students reach a certain age of discretion). Schooling, however, is a shared commitment. Teachers make many professional judgments. Society legitimately expects schools to empower students to function effectively in their communities. Governments set appropriate basic standards, and enable parents to make educational choices for their children. Describe and give examples of how each of these stakeholders affects schooling. How could each overstep their roles and infringe on the responsibilities of other stakeholders?

Public schools and their communities

In most jurisdictions citizens elect school board members to operate public schools. While the powers of such school boards vary considerably, there has been a trend to involve parents more meaningfully in local schools. Often, Parent Advisory Councils advise the principal and staff on school policies and programs.

Public schools serve all sectors of the community. Most often they serve a local geographical community. However, publicly-funded special and charter schools that implement particular programs also exist. My local community has schools emphasizing the fine arts and immersion in French and Japanese, for instance. The local neighborhood school often serves a fairly homogeneous socioeconomic group, but the values and beliefs of parents usually differ considerably. The strength of such a school is also its weakness. It helps people of many different religious and ethnic backgrounds learn from and about each other. However, this diversity also makes is difficult to establish and implement a common vision that goes beyond educational platitudes.

By law public schools may not favor any particular religion or worldview. At the same time, it is impossible for education to be neutral. Education always advances certain values. The question for public schools therefore becomes, "Which values do schools promote?" Answers to this question will continue to be debated in the future. Even teachers who studiously try to avoid teaching values cannot escape doing so. First, they then teach the value that all persons are autonomous moral agents, free to choose their own values. Second, by implication they often teach that the only universal absolute is that there are no universal absolutes. In practice, of course, almost all schools teach commonly-held values such as honesty, respect, and equality under the law. A democratic society could not function effectively for long without its citizens holding such values.

On the one hand, it is inappropriate for public schools to promote a Biblical vision of the Kingdom of God. The aims under #4 ("To become committed to Christ and to a Christian way of life") are not suitable for public education. On the other hand, many of this chapter's aims for Christian schools also pertain to public ones. With a few minor revisions, that is true for the goals listed for #2 and #3 on pages 11-12. You can, for instance, choose content and teach it in such a way that students marvel at reality and how it functions. You help them to live responsibly using their gifts within a framework of generally accepted values. You may want to re-read the section on Mrs. Neufeld's unit on First Nations to see how a responsible approach would not differ all that much in a public school setting.

For the goals listed under #1, it is apt for public school students to discern the influence of Judeo-Christian morals and values on our cultural heritage, as long as other influential values and morals are not neglected. Here teachers can discuss how basic values such as integrity and compassion pervade almost all cultures. You can also ask students to compare different worldviews embedded in literary works and in social and political issues. You can point out and discuss the religious roots of cultures and the religious motives that drive people. You can emphasize that everyone holds to personal beliefs and values, whether or not they are religiously-based.

When I taught in a public high school, some of my most vigorous discussions took place with grade 10's about the meaning and purpose of life. While I was careful to discuss different points of view, I did not hide my own basic beliefs and motives. In fact, the grade 10's soon asked me, "What makes you tick?" I remember a view, I did not hide my own basic beliefs and motives. In fact, the grade 10's soon asked me, "What makes you tick?" I remember a number of parents thanking me for being more than just a mathematics teacher for their adolescents. While I received such encouragement, at the same time the school administration and structure did not allow me to do all that I felt would benefit my students.

Western culture is rooted in Christianity. It is important that students, whether of Christian background or not, understand those roots and their implications. Moreover, a Christian voice has as much of a right to be heard in the public sphere as any other voice. In our increasingly pluralistic society, it is more difficult than before, however, to give voice to Christian beliefs and values without appearing to favor this worldview over other ones. How this can be done will no doubt continue to be the focus of much discussion and debate–as well as possible court action.

◆ ACTIVITY 1-12

Christian schools have been accused of indoctrinating rather than education students. How does indoctrination differ from education? Is there some truth to this charge? Is it possible to educate without indoctrinating at the same time? In what ways might public schools indoctrinate students? How can schools avoid the negative aspects of indoctrination?

Choose an issue that is currently controversial. Discuss how you would deal with the issue in your classroom. Would you treat it differently in a public school than a Christian school classroom? Why or why not?

Reviewing the main points

1. *The three main agencies of Christian nurture and education have been the home, the school and the church.* However, other important influences today include the media and technology. While the focus of schools is learning in a structured academic setting, schools also serve other functions such as the socialization of children.

2. *The overall aim of Christian schools is to help students become citizens of the Kingdom of God, responsive disciples of Jesus Christ.* This includes helping them to develop and use their unique gifts for the service of others, to reach out to others with the call of the Gospel, and to live the fruit of love, service and truth. While Christian schools are desirable in a secular age, God also calls Christian teachers to be "salt and light" in public schools.

3. *Education is a shared responsibility.* Parents are the primary caregivers of children and, as such, have the responsibility and right to determine the type of school their children attend. Teachers, society at large, and governments also have responsibilities, however.

4. *Schools are, in the first place, academic institutions that help students learn about God's world and how they can respond with concepts, abilities and creative gifts to serve God and their fellow human beings.* At the same time, schools as *communities* of learning need to consider how they impact the socialization of students.

REFERENCES

Groome, T. 1980. *Christian religious education.* San Francisco: Harper and Row.

Postman, N. 1993. *Technopoly.* New York: Vintage.

Ridderbos, H. 1962. *The coming of the Kingdom.* Phillipsburg, NJ: Presbyterian & Reformed.

Stronks, G. & Blomberg, D. (eds.). 1993. *A vision with a task.* Grand Rapids: Baker.

Chapter 2

A FRAMEWORK FOR TEACHING CHRISTIANLY

*M*s. *Spark thinks of herself as an artist. For her, teaching is like painting a picture or directing an orchestra. "Students are not like machines that you can program," she says. "Rather, I use artistry and drama and surprise. I plan my lessons carefully so that, as much as possible, a sense of excitement permeates my students' learning. I want them to be motivated to explore, to imagine, to be creative. At least once a day, I try to do something special, something that brings out the aesthetic side of teaching. I want my students to appreciate the beauty around them, not only the physical beauty but also how we as people can structure situations creatively."*

During a science unit on weather and climate, Ms. Spark's room becomes a symphony of colorful student-made posters and displays. Ms. Spark shows video clips of tornadoes, blizzards, and thunderstorms. The students act out how different types of weather affect people, locally and in different parts of the world. In their notebooks they sketch the types of clouds that they observe during the first two weeks of the unit. The students read and write stories in which severe weather plays an important part. One day, the class imagines that the classroom is an igloo in the far north; another, that it is an island in the tropical Pacific Ocean. At the end of the unit, the students apply what they have learned in producing videotaped weather forecasts. Ms. Sparks looks at teaching as an art.

Ms. Sharp, by contrast, tries to be a master technician. She structures her lessons very carefully, outlining specific learning outcomes beforehand. In class, she proceeds at a brisk pace but in small steps. She gives detailed instructions and explanations. To ensure that her pupils grasp the material, she gives many examples, reviews concepts constantly, and asks a large number of specific questions. Ms. Sharp gives frequent small seat-work assignments that she monitors conscientiously. She arranges the work so that students have an initial success rate of at least 80% on such assignments, and 90% on follow-up ones.

In her weather and climate unit, Ms. Sharp first teaches well-structured lessons on the layers and composition of the atmosphere, the effects of the sun and the water cycle, and the motions of the earth's air and water currents. She then instructs students on the factors influencing weather, cloud types, weather fronts, and explains how weather is predicted. The students make careful notes. She frequently asks them to read short passages and answer questions both orally and in writing. Using her laptop computer, Ms. Sharp carefully selects and projects CD-ROM images that clarify and expand the points she wants students to know. She gives a quiz every third or fourth day, both to keep her students on their toes and to give her feedback on the quality of her teaching. Students who get less than 80% on a quiz must take another one the next day. Ms. Sharp considers teaching to be a science.

Mr. Helps uses yet a different approach. Before he starts the unit on weather, he sets up six learning centers in his room. The centers allow students to explore various topics related to weather. There are many optional activities at each center. On the first day, he asks his students what they know about weather and climate, and what they would like to learn. The students classify this information and display it on big charts. Mr. Helps then describes how some of what they would like to learn re-lates to learning center activities, and he suggests other possi-ble activities. He tells his students that they must keep a log of their daily and weekly goals, as well as of the work they do each day. He will meet with each student at least once a week to discuss these goals and their portfolio of products. Mr. Helps considers teaching to be a process of facilitating learning.

◆ ACTIVITY 2-1

Ms. Spark, Ms. Sharp, and Mr. Helps think of themselves, respectively, as teacher-artist, teacher-technician, and teacher-
facilitator. These are three of eight metaphors discussed in this
chapter. The other metaphors view teachers as story tellers,
craftspersons, stewards, priests, and guides. Before continuing, jot
down some classroom strategies for teachers who uphold each
metaphor. Can you suggest some strengths and weaknesses for each
metaphor? If possible, do this with two or three other persons.

The teacher as artist and as technician

We can define teaching as the deliberate attempt to bring about
learning. Such a definition is rather sterile, however. Indeed, the
metaphors used to think about teaching affect practice more than
definitions. Sometimes teachers describe and use such metaphors
explicitly. More often, they uphold them tacitly. Metaphors reveal
valuable insights about teaching. However, it is difficult for a
metaphor to capture the full complexity and richness of God's
creation. They may be one-sided or limited in scope. Also, they are
rooted in specific worldviews.

Two common but very different metaphors see *the teacher as an
artist* and *the teacher as a scientist* or *technician*. Artist teachers
bring out the importance of creative teaching strategies and student
response. They do not treat students as objects to be processed in
assembly-line fashion. Instead, their teaching benefits from artistry
and spontaneity. They help students use content and abilities in
original and inventive ways (Highet 1950; Rubin 1985).

The excitement generated by original and well-crafted strategies
does enhance learning. Teaching, however, is more than an art. An
important focus in teaching is the understanding, insight and wisdom we want students to acquire. The apostle Paul was known for
his long sermons and difficult writings. Yet the content of his
message was so powerful that he still influences Christians today.
Looking at teaching just as an art can make us lose sight of the goal
of enculturating students to their heritage.

Teacher-technicians, on the other hand, emphasize efficiency
and precision learning. They use a structured approach to teach
precise concepts and abilities. They also apply specific steps to

prevent or correct classroom management problems. Examples include Rosenshine's seven steps of direct instruction and Bloom's mastery learning. These prescribe well-defined goals, structured skill instruction, high expectations for student achievement, and frequent positive reinforcement (Hunter 1984; Rosenshine & Stevens 1986).

However, viewing the teacher as a technician falsely assumes that prediction and complete control of human behavior are desirable and possible. It fails to recognize that students and teachers bring their own personality and background to learning situations. Teachers and students both are active agents. They do not react to stimuli in the same way. Their motives and personality affect learning in complex ways. Further, persons favoring this metaphor often focus on the means of attaining sequential, measurable learning outcomes. As they do so, they often neglect overall long-term aims as well as the environment within which learning takes place. Even for learning specific skills and concepts, long-term benefits of scientific instruction are uncertain.

The teacher as facilitator

Another common metaphor that today pervades the thinking and practice of many is teaching as *facilitating*. The teacher's main role is to *facilitate* learning. In other words, teachers provide the right environment and motivation for learning. They pose problems and encourage students to set personal goals, often choosing their own activities. The aim is that students create their own understandings and interpretations. Teachers may ask questions about whether work is coherent and useful, but their primary focus is to enable students to generate and explore concepts and theories, and to resolve discrepancies. Many who favor this metaphor consider themselves *constructivists*. That is, they believe that students do not discover knowledge but that they *construct* it, either individually or through social interaction. Learning must help students create their own world of meaning. We *make* the world rather than mirror it.

Again, there are positive aspects to this metaphor. In the long run, learning will attain the goals of Chapter 1 only if teachers involve students in their learning in a meaningful way and encourage them to respond personally. Teachers who see themselves as facilitators recognize that imparting information for regurgitation on tests is an unacceptably narrow approach to teaching. They see the need for students to reflect on important issues, both personally and in group situations. They stimulate curiosity and wonder. They give students a serious voice in their learning. There is no doubt that a key role of teachers is to facilitate learning.

Yet this metaphor, too, falls short. Teachers must do more than facilitate. Jesus facilitated learning in a number of ways. He asked pointed questions, often in response to questions his listeners asked. He told stories whose meaning became clear only after personal reflection. He led an unusual lifestyle that led people to consider important issues. But He did much more than that. He gave guidelines for everyday living in the Sermon on the Mount. He worked closely with a small band of disciples, explaining what the Kingdom of God was all about. He sent them out with detailed and clear instructions in response to what He had taught. He condemned the Pharisees for their legalism and hypocrisy.

In other words, Jesus did more than facilitate. He also clearly enunciated a way of life, and called people to follow that way of life. Similarly, God calls teachers to make clear that there are universal God-given values that uphold our personal lives and those of society, and that God has given us an orderly world. Of course, we develop personal interpretations. But certain of those interpretations are more valid than others because they are closer to God's laws and intentions for His creation. Those laws include both the physical laws of nature and the precepts He has established for human life (Psalm 19). Teachers, therefore, are much more than facilitators. They walk with God in their classrooms. They are guides who share insights and stimulate students to use their gifts. Such guidance enables them to serve God in responsive and responsible ways.

The teacher as story teller

Seeing teachers as artists, technicians, and facilitators are three common metaphors. They are not the only ones, however. Another one worth considering is teaching as *story telling*. Kieran Egan (1986) promotes this metaphor, particularly for teaching at the elementary grades. Piaget, Egan says, looked too narrowly at rational cognitive skills for his theories to be useful for classroom application. Children understand profoundly abstract concepts very early, Egan points out, as long as we present them in concrete story settings. That is especially true for those which can be expressed in terms of binary opposites such as good and evil or courage and fear. Therefore we should set up a sense of conflict or dramatic tension at the start of *any* unit or set of lessons, especially at the primary level.

Egan continues that teachers should design classroom units to tell a "story." The unit would end with the resolution of the tension between the two opposites. A unit on nutrition, for instance, might focus on scarcity versus plenty. It might trace how people have succeeded but also failed at providing adequate and healthy diets. Throughout the main "story" of the unit, shorter stories contributing to the theme could be told or read. John Bolt (1993) develops this concept more specifically for Christian schools in that the latter must pass on our Christian and cultural "story" so that students appropriate their heritage and vision.

It is true that children can deal meaningfully with abstract concepts and themes if teachers present them in a specific story context. Children benefit from considering the underlying themes of Biblical and other stories, even if not on a purely analytical level. They can consider story themes in the context of human intentions and emotions, often in spontaneous, creative ways. Yet to cast all learning into a story telling mode can become one-sided and artificial. Jesus saw the power and value of stories and parables in His teaching. However, He also taught through modeling, demonstration and direct instruction. This metaphor, like the previous, contains some useful insights but fails to give a complete view of teaching.

The teacher as craftsperson

Teachers are craftspersons insofar as they use reflective, diligent and skillful approaches in their teaching (Tom 1984). Some persons have more of a natural bent for teaching than others. Yet all prospective teachers benefit from learning various teaching strategies and how to structure the classroom. They do not learn them simply by listening and reformulating, however. Rather, as for any craft, they must practice them in a real classroom setting.

Teachers who become master craftspersons are ones who continue to do so diligently, reflectively, and perceptively. They systematically analyze and reflect on their teaching and its effects, constantly learning from practice. They use this to make specific decisions about their day-to-day teaching. They keep in mind their goals as they teach, but do not just unthinkingly follow the steps suggested in a teachers' guide. Gradually, they develop a versatile repertoire of teaching approaches. They show their mastery by using some approaches intuitively, but always continue to look for ways to improve their expertise and proficiency. They use a conscientiously deliberative approach to teaching. They are courageously self-critical as they react to what they perceive. They revise their teaching accordingly. This metaphor includes but goes beyond another common one: the teacher as a reflective practitioner.

Effective teachers hone teaching as a craft. But being a craftsperson is not enough. Carpenters can be craftspersons by skillfully building plans that someone else designed. The moral and religious aspect of their trade is limited to doing an honest job well. In teaching, however, we set out a direction and thus influence the lives of students. We affect the way they view life and act on what they hold to be important. We help forge their personalities. We set the stage for interaction and relationships in the classroom. We decide not only what content but also how students will learn it. We do all this on the basis of our own explicit and implicit beliefs that frame our worldview and our preferred classroom approaches. Teaching has strong moral and religious components that go well beyond it being just a craft.

Tom (1984) therefore develops the metaphor that teaching is a *moral* craft. I believe we should one step further. If we define religion in its broad sense as a system of ardently held beliefs that guide practice, then teaching can be said to be a religiously based act. The Bible itself makes clear that teaching is a religious act. Scripture usually discusses the concept of teaching in one of two contexts. First, teaching must lead to walking in the paths of the Lord or the "way you should go" (Dt 11:19; 1Sa 12:23; Ps 32:8). Secondly, teaching must point to the marvelous deeds of the Lord (Ps 71:17; 78:4; and the "teaching psalms" 104-106). In both cases we teach the law of the Lord, His law of life. That law includes both the wonderful physical, life-sustaining laws embodied in God's physical creation (Ps 19:1-4), and His laws that shed light on endeavors involving human relationships (Ps 19:7-11). Consequently, if teaching is a craft, it is a *religious* craft.

◆ ACTIVITY 2-2

Discuss the classroom implications of using the metaphor "teaching as a religious craft." To what extent do you think that this metaphor contains aspects of each of the other metaphors discussed thus far?

The teacher as steward

The next three metaphors differ from the previous ones. The ones up to this point are not ones directly mandated by Scripture, although they do not necessarily contradict Scripture. But the next three metaphors are Biblical injunctions for Christians in general, and therefore also for Christian teachers. None of the metaphors is complete in itself; each, however, describes an important dimension of what it means to teach Christianly. The three I will discuss, giving some implications that I believe stem from the Bible, are the teacher as steward, the teacher as priest, and the teacher as guide or shepherd. As an extension of the section on the teacher as priest, I also discuss the tone of teaching.

Jonathan Parker (1995) develops the metaphor of the teacher as steward. His starting point is the Biblical parable of the talents (Mt 25:14-30). This parable "portrays stewards as people who are assigned responsibility for the growth and development of someone else's assets" (179). He then describes how teachers are stewards of knowledge, of pupil characteristics, of the school environment, and of instruction.

All four of these components are necessary for good teaching; none is sufficient in and by itself. Good teachers have broad general knowledge, knowledge of their specialties, and professional knowledge. They also must honor and be able to work effectively with students with a broad spectrum of characteristics. Being stewards of the environment includes being able to provide positive classroom structures and discipline, and work well with colleagues and parents in fostering affirming surroundings for learning. Stewardship of instruction involves managing strategies and activities to bring about optimal learning.

Jesus himself compared teachers of the law (and all Christian teachers teach God's laws!) to householders or stewards who bring both old and new treasures out of their storeroom (Mt 13:52). Jesus' parables made clear that teachers have "talents" entrusted to them for use in serving their students. As the apostle Peter put it, "All should use whatever gifts they have received to serve others, faithfully administering God's grace in its various forms" (1Pe 4:10). While Jesus thus calls teachers to be stewards, not all stewards are teachers. As such, stewardship itself is a necessary facet of teaching but it does not encompass the totality of teaching.

The teacher as priest

That teaching has a religious basis and focus becomes clear when we recognize that it is a calling or ministry with the purpose of preparing students for works of service (Eph 4:12, 1). As teachers, we work at this calling with all our heart, as working for the Lord, not just for our school board or even for our students (Col 3:23). We are chosen to be a royal, holy priesthood that declares God's praises (1Pe 2:9). We exercise godly authority "worthy of our calling" only to the extent, however, that we possess and continue to deepen our pedagogical insight. Such insight grows as a result of our study of Scripture, reading about and discussing educational issues, and, especially, teaching in perceptive and reflective ways.

1 Peter 2:9 makes clear that God calls teachers, like all believers, to be *priests*. As such, we foster a loving and caring learning community in our classrooms. We accept all students for whom they are (not that we always condone what they do!). Prayerfully, we try to heal broken relationships. Our own repentance and surrender to Christ enable us to intercede in broken situations. We listen carefully to the students involved and confront them in order to bring about healing. We ourselves and our students may face periods of tension and frustration before God grants victory over sin. We help students develop specific skills to deal with frustration and conflict. Sometimes we may have to confess our own mistakes to the class, asking forgiveness and forgiving those who have offended us. As priests, we are ambassadors of Christ. We experience and demonstrate His reconciling love (Steensma 1971).

Note that Peter speaks of a *royal* priesthood. Sovereigns in Scripture were to rule wisely in justice, fairness and righteousness (Pr 29:14; Jer 23:5; and Isa 9:7). They were to administer or manage affairs so that they served people unselfishly. Moreover, they were to "testify to the truth" (Jn 18:37). In the classroom, you therefore determine and implement structures that help students perform their tasks in loving, just and righteous ways (see chpt. 3).

Another important "royal" task of teachers is to plan a curriculum that "testifies to the truth" and "declares the praises of God." We choose topics that help students grow in their understanding of God's world and their place in it. Does the material help students to be "hearers and doers" of the Word in their situation? Do they experience the relationship of concepts and skills to real situations? Are the interpretations balanced and fair? Do the methods contribute to students' understanding and personhood? Chapters 5 and 6 discuss how you can exercise such responsibilities.

Finally, Peter adds that our priesthood is a *holy* one (1Pe 2:5). God calls His people to be holy, separated from the evils of the world. Yet God places teachers and students in the middle of life, to be agents of healing in a broken world. We encourage our pupils to commit their hearts to the Lord. We model Biblical piety. We give evidence in our own lives of wanting to listen to the Word of God, and of taking our concerns to our Father. We bring students into frequent contact with the Bible and encourage them to search the Scriptures and apply them to everyday situations. We show how God concerns Himself with the details of daily living. We deal with our pupils in a Christ-like attitude of love, and we expect them to reciprocate. In these ways, we sow the seeds for holy living. We may then depend on the Holy Spirit to give the increase and lead students into a holy life.

◆ ACTIVITY 2-3

The metaphor of the teacher as priest is an unusual one. In what ways is it a powerful one? In what ways does it fall short? Read 1 Peter 1 and 2. How is the concept "royal priesthood" relevant when thinking about teaching? Give some specific examples.

The tone of teaching

It is clear from the last section that being a teacher-priest does not involve being in charge of religious rituals like Old Testament priests. What it refers to is that we represent God to our students, model a holy lifestyle, intercede for them with God, and prevent and heal broken situations. All this relates to the tone for teaching that as teachers we set and maintain in our classrooms.

♦ *I vividly remember my first elementary school experience. Because my reading and arithmetic skills were already at the grade 2 level in my kindergarten year, I was placed directly into Miss Sweet's grade 2 class. Miss Sweet disapproved. When my mother brought me to school the first words I hear her say were, "Boys with big heads like that can never learn well." I sensed she was out to prove her point.*

On the very first day she forced me to switch from left-handed to right-handed writing. I aroused and feared her wrath when my lack of right-hand coordination resulted in writing she considered to be inexcusably poor. I even committed the unpardonable sin of somehow producing a large, smudged inkblot on my paper. My dislike for Miss Sweet never lessened. We remained antagonists throughout the year. I found it ironic (without knowing the word!) that her name was "Sweet." I looked out the window at times, fervently hoping that I would see Jesus return on the clouds right there and then. Generally, I was a good student. For pupils with less ability Miss Sweet's class must have been even more of a sour experience–even though, today, I have no doubt that Miss Sweet meant well.

♦ *I also have vivid memories of my grade 6 teacher, Miss Milligan. As a recent immigrant boy who knew no English, I was confronted for the first time in my life with school work that I couldn't do. On a spelling test three or four weeks into the year, I cheated. Miss Milligan saw me. She said nothing, but at recess time, on my way out, called me and asked whether I had anything to say. I tried to explain things away, in broken English. It didn't work; it wouldn't have worked in any language. I just saw her sad but penetrating gray eyes look into mine, not accusingly, but deeply disappointed. I sensed I had hurt Miss Milligan profoundly. She had loved me, encouraged me, challenged me, supported me–and I had let her down. The silence between us spoke volumes. I had failed much more miserably than if I had just done poorly on a spelling test. After a while she just asked, "It won't happen again, will it?" I shook my head, fighting back tears. Miss Milligan had gained a student who set out to prove that he wouldn't let her down again.*

Each classroom has a mood, a certain atmosphere that sets the stage for learning. A good tone is fragile, subtle, yet all-important. The mood of classrooms is set by how we are present and interact with our pupils, and how they in turn are present and interact with us and each other (Van Manen 1986). Miss Sweet projected to her children that she wanted to process them uniformly, as objects, with as little bother to herself as possible. Woe to those who didn't fit her predetermined mold! The tone of Miss Milligan's class, on the other hand, was one of respect and compassion. Her pupils felt secure and wanted to work together on learning, while being motivated individually to strive for excellence.

Perhaps Miss Sweet's explanations were clearer than Miss Milligan's. Perhaps her students even did better on standardized tests of basic skills. But Miss Milligan's pupils learned a great deal more about living as children of light (Eph 4). They not only gained intellectual knowledge but also stretched their creative and social gifts. They became excited rather than fearful about learning. They experienced what it meant to live as a Christian community. Both Miss Sweet and Miss Milligan were Christians. Sad to say, Miss Sweet taught in a Christian school; Miss Milligan, in a public one.

The atmosphere of a classroom can easily become alien, threatening, tension-filled. As teachers we may not understand what motivates students. Our failure to get to know them personally may create misunderstanding or apathy. Without intending to do so or even realizing it, we may be impersonal, abrupt, or unnecessarily sharp with our students. Our students, in turn, become fearful or resentful. As teachers we can be too demanding—or not demanding enough. If too demanding, frustration or resignation sets in. Students may develop a dislike for us that reveals itself in behavior problems and friction. If not demanding enough, students express boredom in idle chatter, mischief and noise. We need to take stock frequently and make adjustments when we realize that we have inappropriate expectations.

In many classrooms teachers set a tone that encourages acceptance and security. Here as teachers we understand our students and deal with them as persons with their own feelings, beliefs, interests and goals. We then recognize that we teach for the sake of our students. We try to understand our pupils' motives, especially when things go wrong. We try to see how things appear through our pupils' eyes. We listen and respond. We receive before we send messages. We communicate with our pupils at their level. We establish trust by allowing pupils to express their thoughts and feelings. We regularly give students personal attention and recognition. We allow students to fail when they meet new challenges, and to learn from failure. We don't expect pupils to do things for which they don't have the prerequisite skills. We encourage all positive efforts.

Of course, sin affects all classrooms. Sometimes we have a class where no matter how much we try to set a positive tone our pupils undermine our best efforts. They may always insist on having their way. They may refuse to abide by basic classroom rules involving respect and responsibility. Fostering a positive tone can be a year-long effort. It may require immense patience, steadfastness, and stamina. Yet even under arduous circumstances we have the responsibility to set and continually re-set the tone. We also hold students responsible and accountable for following our leading. Our goal is to foster, as much as possible, a mutually supportive attitude. That is essential for a healthy emotional classroom tone.

As teacher-priests, we demonstrate compassion and forgiveness. At the same time, we set a tone that directs and re-directs them and ourselves into walking in God's way of truth and uprightness.

◆ ACTIVITY 2-4

List four or five ingredients that you consider important for a tone that encourages meaningful classroom learning. Compare your list with that of several other persons. How do your personal beliefs about schooling and your own personality influence your list?

◆ ACTIVITY 2-5

Give examples of cases where teachers demand too much or too little of their students. Discuss the results of such situations for the tone of the classroom and the effectiveness of learning. How can teachers set high but realistic expectations?

The teacher as guide

Christian teachers are knowledgeable stewards of God's gifts within themselves and of those of the students God entrusts to them. They are loving priests who bring encouragement and compassion to their classrooms. Yet, we all know persons who have these characteristics and who serve the Christian community in notable ways, but who cannot teach students effectively. Teaching also requires diverse competencies as well as a sense of direction and purpose that enable a person to be an effective *guide*.

God calls Christian teachers to guide young persons into the knowledge and discernment that leads to service for God and fellow human beings. It is in Christ, Paul says, that all the treasures of wisdom and knowledge are hidden. He adds that we must shun hollow and deceptive philosophies based on human tradition (Col 2:3-8). Instead, "let the Word of Christ dwell in you richly as you teach and admonish" (Col 3:16). That is the basis of our guidance as we walk with God in the classroom.

The Bible calls Jesus our great Shepherd (Heb 13:20). A shepherd guides his sheep, using his rod and staff to nudge them in the right direction. The intent of such guidance was that the sheep would go in the direction where they would have food and be safe from danger. In other words, they would be able to fulfill their intended role. Today, just like the Spirit of Truth guides us into all truth (Jn 16:13), God calls teachers to guide their students in the way of wisdom (Pr 4:11). We are shepherds: pathfinders, mentors, coaches, and counselors. We guide students to develop their gifts and take on life's calling in an ever deeper and fuller way. We guide them into becoming competent, discerning, responsive disciples. Such guidance requires unfolding content and structuring our classrooms in such a way that we enable students to take on their life's calling. [This section is a modification of John Van Dyk's model of teaching as guiding, unfolding and enabling (1986-87).]

To guide students into paths of wisdom requires much more than disclosing content. As teachers we need to provide classroom structures that let students experience the meaning of living out of a Biblical worldview. We permeate classroom structures with righteousness, justice, compassion and respect. Without this, teaching reaches the minds but not the hearts of students. Then it is relatively ineffective in guiding students to become persons who understand and do the will of the Lord. Teachers must set high but realistic expectations. Their strategies must consider the diverse learning styles and modes of knowing, and treat each individual as an image of God. Chapters 3 and 4 suggest how teachers may implement a pedagogically and Biblically responsible framework as they structure their classrooms.

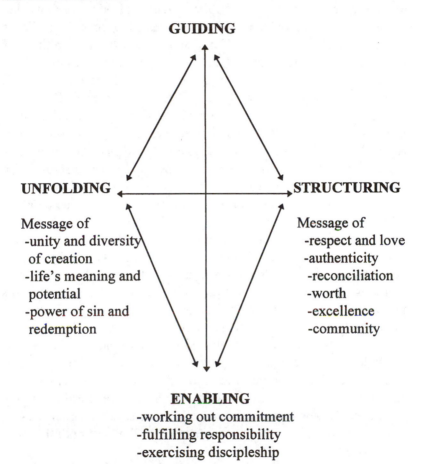

GUIDING

UNFOLDING   **STRUCTURING**

Message of
 -unity and diversity
  of creation
 -life's meaning and
  potential
 -power of sin and
  redemption

Message of
 -respect and love
 -authenticity
 -reconciliation
 -worth
 -excellence
 -community

ENABLING
-working out commitment
-fulfilling responsibility
-exercising discipleship

FIG. 2.1 COMPONENTS OF CHRISTIAN TEACHING

Failing to structure a classroom on such Biblical guidelines for human interaction has been the downfall of many teachers. Teachers may teach content from a Biblical perspective. They thwart their intents, however, by not wanting or by not being able to create Christian learning communities in their classrooms. Consequently, the students' intellectual knowledge of Christian principles may have little effect on their personal lives. In some cases, students have become bitter about their school experience because of a teacher's inability to provide a stable structure that encourages learning.

Effective guidance also calls teachers to *unfold* the basis, contours and implications of a Biblical vision of life. As Christian teachers we are prophets in that our teaching proclaims God's handiwork in creation, the effects of sin, and the possibilities of reconciliation and restoration (Lk 1:76-79). This requires us to have a thorough knowledge of what we teach, the ability to interpret such knowledge authentically, and the gift to communicate effectively. Presentations should be well prepared. They should relate new information to students' experience, emphasize key points, and regularly monitor understanding. They should also be given in a friendly and enthusiastic manner. Presentations are useful when students need an organized overview or interpretation of a topic that is not available in suitable form in other sources such as textbooks.

Unfolding requires more than just telling or lecturing, however. We use a variety of strategies to unfold knowledge. We use incisive questioning and case studies for classroom discussions that stimulate higher order thinking about topics and issues. We use brainstorming activities, field trips, and simulations. We give students perplexing problems to solve. We ask them to pose problems for other students to solve. We have pupils unfold and reformulate knowledge themselves through independent reading and study, through interactive computer programs, and by working on activities and projects. Sometimes students become "unfolders" by tutoring a peer or a small group in a collaborative learning setting, by a class presentation, or by role play. What is important here is that we use a variety of unfolding strategies that suit both the topic and class dynamics.

Unfolding deepens students' insight into God's world and their place in it. It leads them to take delight in God's creation as well as feel hurt by the effects of sinfulness. As such, unfolding demands far more than the imparting of factual information. Pupils must evaluate concepts, theories and issues. They must think critically about them, solve problems, and consciously develop related value systems.

An obstacle that we as Christian teacher-guides must overcome is the pervasive influence of our secular society on ourselves and on our pupils. God calls us to help students develop the insights, abilities and dispositions necessary to serve God in all aspects of their lives in society. But Jesus also warns of the grave risk of leading children astray (Mt 18:2-6). Teaching is a responsible and rewarding profession, but, as James points out, also a potentially dangerous one (Jas 3:1). We must guide in the truth. That means we must search out the will of God for our content and how we go about teaching it.

Let me give some examples. When our unfolding teaches that applying the scientific method or using the most up-to-date technology can solve humankind's problems, then we are leading our students astray. That is also true when we fail to counter the superficial humanism or the self-centered ethical relativism of resources. When our classroom structure does not set out clear expectations, or we do not enforce rules lovingly but firmly, we hinder students from living as disciples. That is also the case when we plan only one type of learning activity in a subject, day after day. Then we fail to adequately nurture the abilities of pupils with learning styles unsuited for that type of learning. As Christian teachers we constantly consider how our unfolding and our classroom structures can foster discipleship.

Teachers guide their students in order to *enable* them to use their gifts in service to God and their fellow creatures. Enabling is a natural consequence of effective structuring and unfolding and overlaps with them. It embraces exercising abilities and developing dispositions on the basis of Scriptural norms and principles. It starts in kindergarten when, for instance, children learn certain prereading and coordination skills. But enabling goes far beyond such basic skills. We also enable kindergartners by helping them relate to each other in positive ways and learn to deal with interpersonal problems themselves. We enable students when they learn to solve mathematics problems as a tool to enrich their lives. We enable them when they learn to apply research and investigation skills in new situations and when they learn to produce poems, stories, videotapes and art works. We enable them when they learn to think through problems that they face at home, in school, or in the marketplace. We also enable them when they learn to exercise communication and cooperation skills that contribute positively to human relations. Further, we enable them when they learn to apply God's laws for morality, for family and social interaction, for leisure, and for economic life.

All four components of teaching (guiding, structuring, unfolding and enabling) are closely intertwined. Any one of them affects the others. Our structuring and unfolding must lead to enabling our students. In turn, the degree and scope of their enabling affect our further structuring and unfolding. Throughout, we push pupils toward becoming responsible themselves for their own enabling. Gradually but consistently we attempt to diminish our own structuring and unfolding and encourage students to take charge of their own enabling. Our intent as teacher-guides is that eventually our pupils can function responsibly independent of our guidance.

◆ ACTIVITY 2-6

Make a chart with four columns headed guiding, structuring, unfolding, and enabling. Then divide the chart horizontally into two parts. In the top half, give examples for all four aspects that would advance your aims of schooling. In the bottom half, give examples that would hinder your aims. From this, can you draw any general conclusions about effective teaching?

An example of the teacher as steward, priest and guide

◆ *Let's look in on the unit on work that starts off Mr. Reid's grade 10 Career and Personal Planning course (based on Fritschy & Reedyk 1985). Two Bible texts above his chalkboard set out the theme: "If anyone serves, do it with the strength God provides, so that in all things God may be praised in Jesus Christ," and "Whatever you do, work at it with all your heart, as working for the Lord and not for humans" (1Pe 4:11; Col 3:23). Mr. Reid's unit emphasizes that while sin often distorts the meaning and results of work, through the regenerating power of the Holy Spirit human work can be a calling in the service of God. Specifically, he wants his students to become aware of and experience Christ-like attitudes toward work. Work, Mr. Reid believes, can be joyful fulfillment rather than just a means for personal gain and glory. He also intends that his students begin to think about how to choose a vocation in which they can work "unto the Lord."*

Mr. Reid starts the unit by eliciting students' conceptions of work. On an overhead transparency he presents a list of everyday activities. He asks students to distinguish between leisure and work activities. He asks his students, How can both be enjoyable as well as emotionally demanding? How can both be done in service to God and our neighbors? Is all time God's time? Next, he presents a time line of historical highlights. This leads the students to discover how work and jobs have changed throughout history, and are still changing today. The students then research and write short compositions about one occupation gleaned from the past and one contemporary one. Mr. Reid structures this by having available lists of occupations from which they choose. He has students make a list of points that can be included in the compositions. Later, students share their compositions in small groups.

Mr. Reid chooses two or three of the compositions as a starting point for analyzing how technology is changing the workplace. The students complete a large chart indicating past and possible future technological changes in factories, offices, service industries, medicine, agriculture, and resource industries. Mr. Reid does the first with the whole class, discussing both beneficial and undesirable changes. Small groups complete the others and then present them to the whole class.

Next, Mr. Reid asks the students to read a number of case studies, "The Work of Our Hands." He has the students arrange the desks in a U-shape so they can see each other as they debate pointed questions about the cases. Mr. Reid then gives a presentation and discusses the meaning of work with the class. To what extent may we choose an occupation because the pay or the working conditions are good? Do we take into account how we can use and develop our gifts in various occupations? In what ways can we serve (or fail to serve) God as a missionary? A carpenter? A dietitian? A lawyer? Why is assembly line work often a deadening experience? Should the ultimate goal of business be to make a profit or to provide a useful service? For homework, Mr. Reid has the students look up twenty Bible passages, asking them to reflect on how their content should affect our attitude to work.

The students have kept a daily time-chart journal since the beginning of the unit. They now discuss these in terms of the amount of time they spend on "work," including school work, chores at home, and part-time work opportunities. What motivates students to take them? What problems have they faced? What about pay and its relationship to responsibility? What is the place of management and unions in the workplace?

Mr. Reid lets the students react to his view that all persons, including teenagers, have gifts. Therefore they also have the responsibility to contribute "work" at home, in school, in church, and in the community. He asks students to complete a chart of their abilities and how they could use them in various settings, as well as an interest inventory. The students use these to plan their community service projects. These form an integral part of the unit. All students must complete a certain number of hours of volunteer work in day-care centers or senior citizens' homes, local businesses, and so on. Mr. Reid plans these to capitalize on students' abilities and interests as much as possible. At the end of their service project, the students write a short report about their experiences. They include a description of what it is like to work in that setting.

Mr. Reid then has three concluding activities. First, his students plan the annual career day for the school. Mr. Reid also recognizes that many students worry about their future. They worry that there do not seem to be enough jobs to go around, especially for young adults. He therefore brings in a person from the local employment office to discuss the changing nature of jobs. The class investigates the need for taking personal initiative. It considers the problem of under- and unemployment as it affects young people. Finally, he asks the students to sum up the themes of the unit by dramatizing, in small groups, an imaginary discussion about work ten years from now.

◆ ACTIVITY 2-7

List ways in which Mr. Reid guides, structures, unfolds, and enables. Can you suggest ways to improve this unit? In some school teachers are reluctant to teach such a unit since it is not sufficiently "academic." Do you agree? Why or why not? How does this unit help

prepare students for the workplace? How would you change the unit
if it were taught in a public school?

Teaching responsively and responsibly

As you probably concluded from the last section, Mr. Reid's
teaching is creative and yet carefully structured. He looks for
innovative ways to present his lessons. He also applies some research findings on maintaining time-on-task and setting high expectations. He designs his learning activities to attain certain goals
as well as to facilitate learning. He uses narratives about how work
developed and how work today can be meaningful or deadly, but
this is only a small part of his unit. His careful organization
throughout the unit and his outstanding questioning skills when
leading the case study discussion show that he is an expert teacher-
craftsperson who reflects constantly on effective teaching strategies. Mr. Reid realizes that he does not always succeed in reaching
all his students. Sometimes his lessons fall flat. But he tries to be
perceptive and considers how the next time he may improve such
situations, even while he recognizes that some factors are beyond
his control.

But Mr. Reid is much more than a teacher-artist, a teacher-
technician, a facilitator, a story teller, or even a craftsperson. He is
also a steward. He faithfully administers the content he believes to
be important, the gifts he wants students to develop, and the classroom environment so students can work and learn in a positive
learning environment. Further, he is a priest in the sense of encouraging and supporting his students to develop their various gifts.
More than half of them work part-time outside school hours. He
therefore also tries to help them contribute positively to their work
environment and overcome problems they may face in their part-
time jobs. He becomes a personnel mentor to some of his students.

Above all, Mr. Reid is a *guide*. Throughout the unit, he models a
Christian approach to his own work. He plans conscientiously,
making sure that his units have a clear Christian focus. He takes joy
in his teaching, and show genuine interest in the views and progress
of each of his students. For each class, he structures learning
through varied learning activities that will meet his goals and
stimulate student thought and learning. He keeps in mind his main
themes as he guides class and group discussions as well as individ-

ual work. He does not just "deposit" information in students' minds, but designs his class and home assignments to enable his students to internalize concepts and apply them in personally meaningful ways.

For Mr. Reid, teaching is a rewarding calling in and through which he serves his Lord. He sees his task in the context of helping his students become responsive disciples of Jesus Christ. He leads students to the truth, but avoids forcing them into accepting it. He gives direction, but does not put his students into a straitjacket. He knows he cannot *insist* on commitment. That, after all, is the work of the Holy Spirit. He guides response but allows his students to discuss conflicting views and forge their own responses. He determines an instructional and disciplinary framework within which his students have to make choices and gradually take on more responsibility. He regularly lets them choose among alternative assignments. He gives them responsible tasks in the classroom and the school (such as planning the school's career day).

Mr. Reid also holds his students accountable for their choices and tasks. Generally, they react well to being given such responsibilities, although sometimes they fail. For the few who show that they cannot be responsible, Mr. Reid lays down strict guidelines and enforces them firmly and consistently. In all these ways, Mr. Reid guides his students into responsive discipleship.

◆ ACTIVITY 2-8

Read over your personal statement of aims for schooling. In view of those aims and what you have read in this chapter, are there any one or two metaphors that would guide your teaching? Are there metaphors of teaching not discussed in this chapter that are also relevant for teaching? With several persons, act out a skit of a classroom situation that demonstrates your preferred metaphor(s).

Personal characteristics of Christian teachers

We cannot guide pupils in the truth in authentic and effective ways unless we possess certain personal characteristics. We must, in the first place, be committed personally to Jesus Christ. Being new creatures in Christ changes our perspective and our purpose.

Jesus saved us from sin so that we would consecrate ourselves to serve God and our students in and through our teaching. We see our authority as servant authority. We seek His guidance for our guiding. Our personal commitment to Jesus Christ is the basis for teaching our students to walk in God's ways and delight in His faithfulness. Modeling a Christian way of life is effective only if we are committed to it ourselves and show this in our dealings with our students.

Our commitment to Jesus Christ leads us to being Spirit-filled. Becoming Spirit-filled can take place momentarily, as with Paul, or be a gradual process that takes place through prayer, searching the Scriptures, worship, and service. Whatever way God uses, the Holy Spirit produces in our lives, both outside and inside our classrooms, the qualities that Scripture calls the fruit of the Spirit: love, joy, peace, patience, kindness, goodness, self-control and truthfulness (Gal 5:22-23; Jn 14:16-17). The Spirit empowers us to teach with wisdom and responsibility.

Note that *love* is mentioned first. Love is the undergirding characteristic that all teachers must possess. Biblical love is not wishy-washy sentimentality. Rather, it seeks to understand students and what is best for them. That calls for empathy and patience, but also for firm action. True love is compassionate but demands obedience. We try to see situations through the eyes of our students, discovering their motives. We see students not just as objects to be instructed, but as unique images of God with their own characteristics, abilities, shortcomings, and pedagogical and emotional needs. Such insight helps us guide them "in the paths they should go."

We use loving nurture, for instance, when we patiently help students write with a pen or when we teach them to patiently wait their turn when they want to our attention or to work at a particular learning center. We fail to love, however, when we punish a student who still lacks the fine motor coordination needed for skillful handwriting. Similarly, it is not love when we value students for superficially conforming with the "rules" when their behavior does not reflect a genuine attitude and disposition. Loving nurture, at the same time, involves calling students to commit themselves to definite responsibilities–and enforcing consequences when they do not live up to such responsibilities.

Christian teachers also *model* Christian love and the fruit of the Spirit. Pupils preach as their role models preach but act as they act (Wolterstorff 1980, p. 57). Teachers have formative influence on their pupils, especially by being role models. Sometimes I ask university students which teachers they admired most and why. They usually point to the ones who affected them personally. That includes those who cared for their students, those who inspired through their love of people and learning, those who were fair, those who went out of their way to be helpful. Such personal characteristics yield more long-term effects than the content taught. Research shows that people tend to adopt the beliefs and values of a community where they find love and acceptance (Wolterstorff 1980, p. 60). Students may experience countermodels, for instance, of selfishness and violence in other parts of their lives and on television. Yet, by God's grace, schools and teachers may still have positive effects by modeling the fruit of the Spirit. That takes place, however, only when love sustains the practices of the school.

We all fall short as teachers, also in our personal characteristics. We need not hide that from our students. They need to see in us, however, that we humbly and prayerfully let Christ's Spirit rule our lives as we make daily decisions while we teach.

◆ ACTIVITY 2-9

Make a list of personal characteristics that enable a teacher to "walk with God in the classroom." Which of these are essential? desirable? Which personal characteristics can undermine a teacher's effectiveness? Now reflect on how your personal characteristics may influence your teaching both positively and negatively. How can you work at building on your strengths and overcoming your weaknesses?

Ethical concerns in teaching

◆ ACTIVITY 2-10

◆   *Alan had good academic ability except for one thing: he could
not spell. His father, a respected and well-educated community
leader, had a similar disability. In fact, the family would regularly get up early in the morning to practice spelling. But it was
to no avail. As a result, Alan averaged thirty-five percent on his
French tests no matter how much effort he put forth. At the
end of grade 12, he did very well in all subjects where spelling
did not count as part of the final assessment, but he failed his
French final exam.*

*For Alan, grade 12 French was a requirement for university
entrance. With French, he would be accepted. Without it, he
would be rejected. Explaining his situation, the school counselor
found out, made no difference.*

*The teachers were divided about what to do. "Let's give Alan
the 50% minimum pass mark that he needs to get into university," some said. "He'll do well in the science program he wants
to take, and will never again take another language. The 50% will
indicate, particularly when compared to his other grades, that
he is weak in that subject." But other teachers argued, "No, our
grades mean something. The integrity of our school is at stake.
Alan failed the course. Granting him a pass would not be honest.
Besides, how could we justify this decision to parents of children who did better than Alan but were given a failing grade?
We feel badly for Alan. Universities have a reason to demand
success in a foreign language, however. We're not being up front
by acting as if he passed the course."*

What side would you have taken? What is the ethically proper
decision to take? Do you become an ethical relativist when you pass
Alan? Do you put yourself into a position where other parents who
find out might accuse you of favoritism? Are there any legal ramifi-
cations? If you fail Alan, however, are you denying him an education
that would benefit not only him but also society? Shouldn't you take
into consideration the special effort he put forth? Shouldn't you be
somewhat flexible in your evaluation approaches?

In Alan's case, the teachers eventually reached a consensus to
grant him the pass he needed. Today, Alan is a successful profes-

sional who applies his Christian beliefs in his work. As a result, the teachers probably feel justified in the decision they made. However, does the end justify the means? Whether or not Alan did well is not the point, others would argue. But should Alan's potential have influenced the decision? Indeed, is it possible to evaluate potential fairly? How do we make difficult educational decisions that reflect our calling as stewards, priests and guides?

Alan's situation was a real one. It had both ethical and legal implications. Teachers regularly need to make decisions where the norm such as fairness or honesty is clear, but where the application of the norm poses a dilemma. "Love God above all and your neighbor as yourself," said Jesus Christ. That norm, as well as others in Scripture, is easy to understand. However, it is not always as clear how to apply such principles to specific cases.

Many ethical norms to guide teachers are obvious ones. We expect teachers to treat students with respect and dignity. They should unfold knowledge in up-to-date, representative, honest, and appropriate ways. They structure their classes to optimize learning for as many students as possible. They deal with sensitive and controversial issues in open, honest and positive ways. They avoid discriminating against or exploiting students, or putting themselves in positions of actual or perceived favoritism. They treat information about students confidentially, releasing it only for legitimate academic or legal reasons, or with the students' consent. They work cooperatively with colleagues in the interest of fostering student development. They assess students fairly and openly, based on our stated goals. They respect the mission and goals of our school and uphold generally accepted community moral standards. They uphold their colleagues' reputation and go to them directly with any concerns or criticism. If that does not resolve the dispute, they involve the principal (B.C. Teachers' Federation 1996; Murray et al. 1996).

Let's look at two of these principles more closely. First, *they unfold subject matter in a truthful and fair way.* Damon (1993, p. 143) points out that "truth shading" is a common problem, sometimes with the best intentions. A teacher may exaggerate the risks of smoking and drinking in order to keep students from starting such habits. She may gloss over the faults of a historic figure that she admires. Another may downplay the cruelty that occurred between aboriginal tribes because of sensitivity to current political correctness. Both evolutionists and creationists have been known to present one-sided evidence to promote their own point of view. Some teachers emphasize only one side of political or social issues, sometimes deliberately or, at other times, because textbooks are unbalanced. Many textbooks, for instance, neglect the place of religious motifs and motives in the past and present.

Such shading of truth is dishonest. It will also immediately or eventually undermine the trust relation between teachers and students. And a relationship of trust is essential for students to accept their teacher's guidance. Furthermore, dishonest communication will undermine some of the aims in Chapter 1.

Of course, no teacher is objective. All of us have certain explicit and implicit worldview beliefs. But that does not mean that we cannot present content and issues fairly. Fair presentations provide a base for meaningful and engaging dialogues. Students may express their own beliefs, feelings and views (even if we disagree with them). We ask them to consider and weigh evidence. They analyze and advance arguments. They apply the basic principles in which they believe to the situation. But we may then also give our own view, with reasons, in ways that pupils can understand. In this way we engage pupils with respect for their views while they learn to respect our own sincerely held ones (Damon 1993, p. 147).

A second principle is that *teachers may not play favorites or discriminate against individuals or groups of students*. Research shows that unless teachers consciously analyze their own actions, they may not always recognize their own favoritism. They may, for instance, make implicit assumptions when they select students for reading or other ability groups. Also, remember that you may not use your relationships with students for private advantage. Most upsetting here are cases of sexual or emotional abuse. However, it is also unacceptable for teachers to offer goods or services to their pupils for personal profit. Similarly, I remember a case where as a principal I had to turn down the offer of a free encyclopedia. The condition was that I had to endorse the purchase of the encyclopedia to parents of my students. Always treat each and every one of your students equally and fairly, no matter what their circumstances or background. Ensure that your position of authority does not lead you to take advantage of any of them. Here we need to take to heart the warnings of Jesus and James (Lk 17:1-4; Jas 3:1-2).

◆ ACTIVITY 2-11

Discuss what course of action you would take in each case.

* *You invite a politician to speak to your class about her views on a bill on gay rights that will be debated shortly. Several parents object when they hear about it. They claim that the member will just spread "left wing propaganda." If you don't withdraw the invitation, they say, "We will make life difficult for you."*

* *You have recommended that Kevin stay in kindergarten one more year. He is younger than most children in the class. Late in May, he knows only five or six letters of the alphabet, and does not recognize all numbers up to 10. You feel that an extra year will help him develop to the point where he will not be frustrated by grade 1 work. His parents, however, have obtained research reports that show that retention usually does not help children. They want Kevin to move to grade 1 with the others. You arrange a three-way meeting with your principal. If the parents continue to insist, what recommendation would you make? Why?*

* *As a Christian pacifist, you teach a unit on war and peace that emphasizes the horror of war. You hope that your own point of view will influence your students. Several parents, however, go to your principal demanding that the unit be dropped from the curriculum since it "distorts" the issues. Your principal comes to you stating only a few parents share your personal views. Therefore he thinks it would be wise to revise your course. What is your response?*

* *Juan comes to see you about receiving a C+ final grade. He complains that Rick received the same or slightly lower marks on his assignments and yet received a B-. You know that he is right. You gave Rick a B- because usually he struggles to get even a C and you wanted to reward the exceptional effort he put into the course. Juan also says that you must be racist since you did nothing about a racial slur against him some months ago. What do you tell Juan? If his parents go to the principal to complain, how do you deal with the situation?*

Legal concerns in teaching

Upholding high ethical standards and following legal requirements are both necessary in your role as teacher-priest and teacher-guide. Ethical and legal issues often overlap, of course. When we disclose information about a student to unauthorized persons, we are breaking both legal and ethical guidelines. Here we may face difficult decisions. If students ask to speak to us in confidence, point out to them that we have a legal duty to pass on information in cases of suspected sexual abuse or criminal activity.

As teachers we stand *in loco parentis* and are therefore responsible for our students' safety and health. Guard against hazards and provide proper supervision before, during and after school hours (unless the school uses other persons for such duties). Do not administer any drugs, including headache tablets, except with written permission from the parents and a doctor. You may administer necessary first aid, but should have students see a doctor or a nurse if there is any doubt about diagnosis or treatment.

For all activities involving potential danger, courts expect you to teach and enforce specific safety procedures (for instance, the wearing of safety goggles during science experiments). Always be present in situations where accidents may happen: the gymnasium; science, industrial arts, and home economics rooms; and the playground. In one court case a kindergarten teacher and her school were held negligent when an accident resulted from a child wandering out of the room into the street while the teacher had gone to the washroom to bandage another child who had cut himself (Giles & Proudfoot 1984, pp. 114, 118).

Social activities are an important and exciting part of the educational program. They promote different kinds of learning and build personal relations. For these activities, take special precautions to minimize risks. Field trips require prior approval from board, principal and parents. Written consent slips from parents indicate that parents recognize and accept normal risks involved in such activities, and know the purpose and educational value of the trip. Signing such slips, however, cannot and does not prevent legal action resulting from teachers not taking due care.

As a Christian teacher, be sensitive to legal regulations. Honor your students' legal rights. Find out what they are if you are unsure. In Canada students suspected of criminal activity must be told, for instance, that they may refuse to answer any questions except their identity and that of their parents, and that information obtained from them during an interview may be held against them. Similarly, know the copyright regulations in your jurisdiction. School choirs are usually disqualified in competitions when they use photocopied music. There are restrictions on how much you may copy from a book or magazine or tape from television broadcasts for class use.

In all your teaching activities, the overriding principle must be to act justly, love mercy, and walk humbly with God (Mic 6:8). Be aboveboard with students and parents. Be evenhanded and fair. Supervise and discipline much like a wise and careful parent would. Finally, be willing to apologize if you mishandled a situation, as we all do from time to time.

◆ ACTIVITY 2-12

Discuss what course of action you would take in each case.

◆ *Bill Jones, a senior colleague, teaches physical education to your class while you teach music to his. Your students tell you that often he leaves them in the gymnasium by themselves for five or ten minutes. You mention to him that for safety reasons you don't like this. He shrugs his shoulders and says that he needs a coffee "fix" once in a while because of his heavy teaching load. What do you do?*

◆ *You have planned a simulation game dealing with world poverty. This year the copyrighted worksheets for the game were not available from the supplier. You wrote the publisher for permission to copy the old ones, but received no answer. The game proved very popular and worthwhile in the past, but you can't do it without each student having a copy of the worksheets. What do you do?*

Teaching in a public school

Is it possible to teach Christianly in a public school? Obviously, it is easier to do so in a Christian school with its expectations that you do so and where you have the support of parents and fellow teachers. Public schools enroll children of parents of all faiths, including agnostics and atheists. The law is clear that teachers may not use their privileged position to proselytize or promote particular beliefs.

If you have chosen to teach in a public school, your task will be more difficult. On the one hand, you earn more money and have more educational support services available than in a Christian school. On the other hand, however, some of your colleagues, parents and students may be skeptical of your Christian beliefs. There will be those who are antagonistic toward evangelical Christianity. There will be those who object to traditional carols being sung in a Christmas (or Winter Festival) program. You may disagree with curriculum materials you must teach. You may be frustrated by the confrontational attitude of your teachers' union. You may balk at how your school board tries to save money at the expense of meeting the needs of exceptional students. You may feel confined in that you may not openly express in your classroom what is most dear to you in life.

Nevertheless, if you look back over this chapter, you will see that you can implement most of the suggested approaches. You are still a guide who enables students as you unfold content and provide structures that enhance learning. You set the tone of the classroom on the basis of your personal beliefs about the nature of human life in community. You are even a priest in that you model a Biblical lifestyle and show respect and compassion toward your students. You can teach Mr. Reid's unit on work with just a few revisions. Instead of Bible texts, you might use a quote such as the one by Maya Angelou, "Work is something made greater by ourselves and in turn makes us greater" and contrast that with "It is not real work unless you would rather be doing something else" (J.M. Barrie). Books of quotations (now available on CD-ROM) provide a good basis for students exploring different attitudes about work, and developing their own points of view.

In short, also in a public school classroom you can go beyond being a teacher-artist or a teacher-technician. There too you can gradually develop a repertoire of approaches that enable you to teach responsibly and for responsibility.

Reviewing the main points

1. *Metaphors of teaching are rooted in worldviews.* Teaching using a metaphor, either explicitly or implicitly, influences classroom practice. Teachers may see themselves as artists, technicians, facilitators, story tellers, religious craftspersons, stewards, priests, guides–or as a combination of these or others. Most metaphors grasp some kernel(s) of truth about teaching, but many are one-sided or limited in scope.

2. *The tone of teaching has much impact on learning,* and teachers should model and foster a commitment to a positive tone while maintaining high but realistic expectations.

3. If we think of the teacher as a shepherd or guide, *teaching has four interrelated dimensions: guiding, unfolding, structuring, and enabling.*

4. *Teachers should prepare themselves to deal with ethical and legal dilemmas* that inevitably arise in schooling. They should always have the best interest of their students at heart in dealing with such issues.

REFERENCES

Bolt, J. 1993. *The Christian story and the Christian school.* Grand Rapids: Christian Schools International.

British Columbia Teachers' Federation. 1996. *Members' guide to the BCTF 1996-97.* Vancouver.

Damon, W. 1993. Teaching as a moral craft and developmental expedition. In Oser, F., A. Dick and J. Patry (Eds.), *Effective and responsible teaching: The new synthesis.* San Francisco: Jossey-Bass.

Egan, K. 1986. *Teaching as story telling.* London, ON: Althouse.

Fritschy, H. & Reedyk, P. 1985. Work. A teacher resource unit in the *Look around!* series. Langley, BC: Society of Christian Schools in British Columbia.

Highet, G. 1950. *The art of teaching.* New York: Random House.

Hunter, M. 1984. Knowing, teaching and supervising. In P.L. Hosford (Ed.), *Using what we know about teaching*. Alexandria, VA: Association for Supervision and Curriculum Development.

Murray, H. et al. 1996. *Ethical principles in university teaching*. North York, ON: Society for Teaching and Learning in Higher Education.

Parker, J. 1995. Effective stewardship: A model for teacher education programs in Christian liberal arts colleges. In *Faculty Dialogue* 23:177-83.

Rosenshine, B. & Stevens, R. 1986. Teaching functions. In M.C. Wittrock (Ed.), *Handbook of research on teaching*, Third edition. New York: Macmillan.

Rubin, L. 1985. *Artistry in teaching*. New York: Random House.

Steensma, G. 1971. *To those who teach: Keys for decision-making*. Terre Haute, IN: Signal.

Tom, A. 1984. *Teaching as a moral craft*. New York: Longman.

Van Dyk, J. 1986-87. Teaching Christianly: What is it? *Christian Educators' Journal* 26(1, 2, 3 & 4).

Van Manen, M. 1986. *The tone of teaching*. Richmond Hill, ON: Scholastics.

Wolterstorff, N. 1980. *Educating for responsible action*. Grand Rapids: Eerdmans.

Chapter 3

STRUCTURING THE
CLASSROOM FOR LEARNING

M *arilyn Chung and Donna Van Dyke both teach a grade
2 class of about twenty-five pupils. Both consider their
teaching to be a vocation, one to which they give much time
and effort. Both have the best interests of their students at
heart. Both use the curriculum outlines that the school has
developed for the various subject areas. Parents regularly express their satisfaction with both teachers to the principal,
Marsha Hall. Yet, Marsha knows, grade 2 is quite a different
learning experience for each group of pupils.*

*Marilyn Chung's verbal and body language–even her
clothing–sets the tone for her teaching. She projects that
learning is serious business, and that no one is going to waste
time in class. Her organization breathes efficiency. Learning
materials are filed neatly in their designated spots. Classroom
routines are well established. Students know exactly what she
expects of them. The classroom has five rows of five desks
each, with three small tables for carefully planned learning
centers at the back. When Marilyn works with one of her
reading groups, the other students follow the precise instructions on the chalkboard. They know that they may not interrupt the teacher or each other with questions. In all their
work, from reading to art, neatness and accuracy are the
foremost concern. In mathematics, each unit begins with
hands-on material but Marilyn quickly moves on to practice
worksheets. Her class functions as a quiet, efficient machine.*

*Principal Hall knows that students in Marilyn's class
learn the "basics" well. Yet she has some questions. Does*

Marilyn's approach stifle her pupils' creativity and spontaneity? The projects, compositions and art work that are displayed in rather regimented fashion all seem very similar. Also, some pupils seem uptight and even fearful in Marilyn's class. Marsha knows that Marilyn is a loving person, but her perfectionism and urgency to get things done lead her to be unnecessarily sharp with her students, sometimes even when they try their best.

Donna Van Dyke, on the other hand, maintains a warm, loving classroom atmosphere. She greets each child personally at the door each morning. During her opening exercises and devotions children share some of their experiences, practice some mathematics skills informally using the daily calendar, and give input as they discuss the plans for the day. The room displays, put up by the students themselves under Donna's direction, are colorful and vibrant but not very well organized. The reading corner has a large number of books but looks messy. She says nothing when children put down their books almost anywhere as they exchange books for their personalized reading program. While there is some group skill instruction in language arts, Donna puts more emphasis on having a number of individual conferences with children each morning. In mathematics, the pupils usually work in small groups of four, but get moved around for different types of activities. The children enjoy and get excited about their learning. Things get noisy from time to time, forcing Donna to flick the lights as a signal that the children must work more quietly.

When Principal Hall visits Donna's room, she sees a group of enthused students engaged in stimulating learning activities. Yet here too she has questions. Shouldn't Donna put more emphasis on the focused learning of specific skills? The students' printing skills, for instance, are below par. Some activities seem to be done on the spur of the moment just because they are interesting, rather than because they fit the intended learning outcomes. But, Marsha asks herself, can Donna tighten up her structure without losing precisely what makes her a good teacher? Would she continue to have her pupils use their unique abilities in so many creative ways?

Marsha Hall reflects, as she plans follow-up discussions, how she can help both grade 2 teachers. She wants them to use their personal strengths and overcome or at least cope with their weaknesses as they try to structure their classrooms as effective learning communities. Yet she does not want to cast them into a mold that would not fit their personalities.

◆ ACTIVITY 3-1

Identify what you think are the positive and the negative aspects of Marilyn Chung's and Donna Van Dyke's classroom structures. Which of your personal tendencies can you use in teaching to build positive classroom structures? Which may detract from it? Think about how you can suppress the latter or channel them positively.

Classrooms as learning communities

Marsha Hall's school is blessed with two good grade 2 teachers. The learning environments in both classrooms are basically sound even though improvements are possible. Yet, as may be seen from these examples, good classrooms vary a great deal. Teachers are unique by birth and experience. Moreover, they face unique classes. The practice of sound pedagogy has common elements, but the way a particular teacher applies these elements will differ. No two classrooms will ever look or feel quite the same. No two teachers will deal exactly the same way with a similar situation. Teaching is not a mechanical but a personal act. Teachers should use rather than suppress their personalities in carrying out their roles as stewards, priests, and guides. At the same time, as in the case of Marilyn Chung and Donna Van Dyke, they may have to learn to compensate for personal traits that detract from a good learning atmosphere.

The Bible makes clear that God calls us to be a community where we all contribute our special gifts (Ro 12:5-8; 1Co 12:12-30). As a teacher you therefore consciously strive to forge your class-room into a learning *community* where students experience the richness of living in a caring environment. Ideally your classroom is a place where students learn to accept and use their abilities in relation to themselves and others. Here they experience the joys and difficulties of working unitedly toward common goals. These are essential aspects of learning to live and work in the larger community. With technology taking over some of the repetitive tasks of life, it becomes even more important for people to relate well to others.

A classroom that is a learning community works and prays together. When one member fails or suffers, all feel the pain. When one rejoices, all rejoice. As much as possible, all members contribute to the learning success of others. As a teacher you structure your classrooms for meaningful learning. You convey trust and respect. Your enthusiasm, warmth and humor not only motivate your students but show them you want to encourage and support them. You demonstrate that you are trustworthy and committed to helping each student make a special contribution to the class community.

Your students, at the same time, are called to respond to your guidance to the best of their abilities; second best is unacceptable. They must realize that they have responsibilities beyond themselves. Their conduct affects how well others will be able to learn. They have direct obligations with respect to others when they work at collaborative learning tasks.

Another key to a classroom functioning as a community is that the teacher engenders common motives and goals. If you allow students to have significant and successful roles and give them recognition for their work, they will more likely see themselves as your partners. Set and discuss rules together to create a sense of ownership. Ask students what they already know and what they would like to know about a topic in order to allow them meaningful input into unit planning. Require students to set personal learning goals. Discuss how they can or have achieved them. That lets them celebrate their successes and renew their determination to do well. Give each student special responsibilities ranging from setting up equipment to peer tutoring. That makes them realize that they contribute to the fulfillment of the community's goals. Appreciate student work for its merits in terms of their own abilities, not in comparison with that of others. Otherwise, their motives easily become competitive and self-centered, with potential disruptions of positive relationships.

Also, plan academic and social activities with your students that encourage them to interact and cooperate in a variety of settings. The more everyone in the class knows and accepts others and recognizes their special strengths and needs, the more the class works together as a cohesive group. Celebrate cultural differences, diverse learning styles, and strengths in certain modes of knowing and personal characteristics. Emphasize that God made all persons unique in order that they can contribute their gifts and experience and insight to the whole community. Collaborative learning methods as described in the section on grouping for learning help students to respect and learn from each other. If carefully designed, it also improves achievement. God created us to function best as contributing members of His Body, the community of Christ.

◆ ACTIVITY 3-2

Discuss classroom features that affect its atmosphere as a learning community both positively and negatively. Then make a list of ways in which you can engender a positive sense of community in your classroom.

Personal relationships in the classroom

Classrooms cannot function as effective communities of learning unless harmonious relationships exist. Marilyn Chung's efficiency sometimes got in the way of such harmonious relationships. Marilyn's pointed disapproval or censure made some students afraid of her—to the point where it curtailed their learning. But the fact that Donna Van Dyke did not set consistently high standards also affected her relationships with her pupils. They liked her as a person, but intuitively sensed that they could get away with things. To an outside observer the relationships in each classroom did not seem harmful. Nevertheless, they were not as wholesome as they could be.

In a sinful world harmonious relationships are not easy to establish and maintain. Nonetheless, as a teacher you are strategically placed to do so. The types of relationships you nurture and establish have an immense impact on the success of your teaching. As teacher-priests and teacher-guides, listen carefully. Interact sensitively. Show personal interest. Teach enthusiastically. Praise genuinely. Confront sensitively when needed. And forgive freely (Eph 4:32). Treat your students as images of God. Each pair of eyes looking at you represents such an image! That does not mean that you should not be firm. Demand that students treat you and each other with respect and responsibility. Speak the truth in love but also insist on students speaking the truth (Eph 4:15, 25). Firmness, however, needs to go hand-in-hand with fostering an atmosphere of openness, warmth, and care. God gives you authority as a teacher to serve your students and to enable them to be responsive disciples.

Vernon and Louise Jones (1990) give a number of suggestions for building sound relationships. They suggest that you maintain a high ratio of positive to negative statements. Respond as much as possible to positive student behavior. Communicate high expectations of all students. Call on and give feedback to the academically weaker as often and as much as the stronger. Create opportunities for personal discussions about students' activities. Demonstrate personal interest in your students by having lunch with individual · students, joining in playground games and community events, greeting them individually each morning, and so on. Moreover, plan activities that nurture group cohesiveness, especially at the start of the year. This could include organizing and decorating the classroom together as a class, creating special days, asking questions at the end of the day about what they liked and disliked about the day, maintaining a class photo album, and so on.

Confident and authentic communication is an essential ingredient of community. That requires being knowledgeable and prepared. You transmit thoughts, feelings, instructions and concepts calmly, smoothly and clearly. Nervous, overpowering, threatening or disinterested communication through body or verbal language hampers your role in shaping community. Seeing yourself on videotape may be a humbling experience. It may show you, however, that *how* you say things to your students undermines *what* you say. You also insist that students communicate with you and with each other with respect. They must listen as well as speak, and not interrupt others. If they are angry or frustrated, you help them express that in terms of "I feel . . ." instead of loudly accusing others.

As a teacher, you need to be confident and constructively assertive without being aggressive or argumentative. Describe issues and concerns clearly. Maintain eye contact. Be unambiguous in your body language. Let your facial expression reflect what you are saying orally. Respond empathetically to your students. Listen carefully to their perspectives and concerns, paraphrasing their input. Respond so that you invite further discussion rather than cutting it off ("Tell me more," "I'm interested in hearing your ideas about this"). When applicable, work with students to develop future goals or plans for improvement or change (Evertson et al. 1989).

Try to be a *counselor* to your students. That is, work at providing a secure, loving environment in which honest interchange is possible. Pay close attention and remain open to what students say or write. Through active listening (for instance, "Are you saying that . . .?), draw out and clarify students' thinking. Create a climate where students feel free to question, explore, discuss, and reach conclusions. When students express beliefs contrary to Biblical teachings, ask probing, directed questions that help them reassess and guide their views and behavior. Accept that a diversity of views and insights is possible, even within a Biblical framework. Being a counselor is a long-term commitment, for usually you need to mold students' thinking and behavior incrementally over a period of time.

◆ ACTIVITY 3-3

Discuss the implications of teachers being counselors to students. Is it possible for a person to be an effective teacher and yet not be able to establish a "counselor" relationship with students? Why or why not? Teachers are not trained to be professional counselors, of course. When should teachers refer students to professional counselors? Are there any circumstances when teachers should avoid counseling students? What precautions should teachers take to ensure that they remain professional teachers who lend students a listening ear but do not cross the boundaries into unwise or inappropriate involvement?

Disruptions in community

Of course, a classroom never functions as a perfect community. Sin disrupts, and we need to deal with its reality. To build and maintain community, you must establish, teach and enforce positive behavioral norms. Your students need the security of knowing what you expect and will enforce (see the section on expectations and limits later in this chapter). When students cause community relations to break down through word or deed, confront them with the need to repent and heal the resulting brokenness. Ask from time to time whether your own actions weaken a sense of community.

Students sometimes create a tension-filled tone in a class. This affects learning. Deal quickly and openly with momentary flare-ups. Discuss with your students their perceptions of more serious problems. Attempt to draw out the root causes. Develop acceptance and commitment for improvement. Ask how the conflict or problem may be alleviated. Encourage openness, admission of guilt and forgiveness. Hold students accountable for their commitments. Seek the guidance of the Holy Spirit while working toward a solution. When a student becomes a "scapegoat," work with the class for greater acceptance. Sometimes use a "reaction story" that mirrors the existing problem in a slightly different form. By having the pupils discuss and present possible solutions, they may be willing to commit themselves to a parallel solution for the classroom problem.

Occasionally personality clashes do occur between a teacher and a student. When this happens, recognize that the problem exists. Then try to develop an acceptance between yourself and the student. Make a distinction between students and their behavior. Reject inappropriate behavior but *not* the person. Once forgiveness is obtained or given, grudges may not be held. Remember that we do not like all students equally. We may even find it hard to like a particular student. God calls us, however, to accept all in love, to reach out with understanding, and to guide them into discipleship. Prevent communicating negative feelings by tone of voice, posture, verbal responses, grouping students, or informal or formal evaluation.

Walking with God in the classroom means expressing love and concern for all, without exception. Listen to the apostle Paul: "Love is patient, love is kind. It does not envy, it does not boast, it is not proud. It is not rude, it is not self-seeking, it is not easily angered, it keeps no record of wrongs. Love does not delight in evil but rejoices with the truth. It always protects, always trusts, always hopes, always perseveres" (1Co 13:4-7). But remember that love, when necessary, also involves discipline in order to "produce a harvest of righteousness and peace" (Heb 12:11).

◆ ACTIVITY 3-4

If you discuss this chapter with a group, role play some classroom situations and analyze them together:

♦ *communication about an incident between a student and a teacher that harms or fails to advance community*

♦ *a student revealing to a teacher that he or she is a homosexual*

♦ *a teacher dealing with the negative attitude of a class "leader" that has a disruptive effect on a class*

♦ *a teacher discussing class rules at the beginning of a school year*

♦ *a class learning how to resolve personal disputes or conflicts*

♦ *a teacher dealing with a student who has been caught smoking in the washroom three times*

♦ *a class being taught rules for cooperative learning or for using learning centers*

♦ *two teachers teaching the same grade level or subject discussing how they can best arrange their classroom set-up*

Keep notes on how you feel the situations are best handled. Then, after you have read the whole chapter, revisit each situation and discuss whether you would change your approach.

Discipline unto discipleship

The purpose of discipline is to disciple students in the Lord's way. Discipline is an opportunity to redirect students: to strive against sin, to overcome weakness, to build inner peace and righteousness, and to partake in the holiness of God. Through discipline students must realize the grace of God (Heb 12). Discipline may not be harsh retribution. It may not cause bitterness from perceived lack of grace and forgiveness.

School boards give teachers *legal* authority to conduct their classes. Teachers can also rely on *traditional* authority since most parents do communicate their respect for teachers to their students. If the authority of teachers is based solely on formal appointment and tradition, however, teachers can maintain themselves only through authoritarianism. That, in turn, leads to power struggles between students and teachers and breaks down a positive learning milieu. Teachers need to establish their *personal* authority. Personal authority results from the teachers' insight and ability to guide students, to unfold content, to structure classroom learning, and to enable students to develop and exercise their gifts. The proper exercise of these four interrelated aspects will allow teaching to take place in a personally authoritative way (Mk 1:22; Lk 4:32). We use such authority to serve our students, both through encouragement and, when needed, through rebuke (Tit 2:15).

Ultimately, it is God who gives teachers authority to perform their task to guide and enable students. He endorses them in their calling as teachers and gives them the abilities that make it possible for them to establish personal authority. When teachers apply such authority through discipline, they do so not for the sake of exercising power over their students, but to give understanding and wisdom about the way to life (Pr 3:12-13; 6:23). Godly discipline is always administered in love (Pr 13:24b; Rev 3:19).

As a teacher you exercise discipline in at least four ways:

♦ *First and foremost, structure your classroom learning so that pupils can work productively and have a measure of responsibility for their own learning decisions. Pupils who are engaged in well-planned, meaningful activities are less likely to disrupt and more likely to develop self-discipline.*

♦ *Secondly, be a role model for pupils, particularly in showing and demanding respect.*

♦ *Thirdly, establish and enforce rules that encourage obedience to God's laws, especially those relevant for the classroom situation.*

♦ *Fourthly, set and enforce consequences that attempt to refocus pupils' eyes on serving God in all their actions while helping them experience His grace.*

Note that three of these four ways emphasize *preventive* rather than *corrective* discipline.

◆ ACTIVITY 3-5

Discuss how preventive classroom discipline can be effective. Give some situations when corrective discipline becomes necessary.

Setting and maintaining expectations and limits

Most of this chapter up to this point (and much of what follows) could be said to deal with preventive discipline. Good teachers make a point to practice preventive discipline by anticipating problems.

- *When Jessica becomes distracted, walk through the room and stand close to her while continuing to lead the discussion.*

- *When students get restless or attention falters on a hot afternoon, change your planned activities to break the pace.*

- *When Billy is the cause of frequent playground disputes, build a relationship with him on the playground and ask him to do some playground tasks that he likes.*

- *When Kevin and Jason cannot stop talking to each other, change your seating scheme.*

- *When Wanda continually seeks attention, ignore her as much as possible when she craves it in unacceptable ways, but talk to her and help her when she works quietly and conscientiously.*

There is one aspect of preventive discipline that needs further discussion: setting and maintaining expectations and limits. God has created us to function within certain laws and norms (Ps 19:7-11). A prerequisite for effective discipline, therefore, is to set wise limits according to the expectations of the school, the maturity of the students, and the characteristics of the class and teacher. A class adapts surprisingly easily to the different expectations of different teachers. Students read your mood rather accurately and adjust their responses accordingly. In high school, they do so from period to period as they change classes and teachers.

To create an optimal learning situation, indicate your expectations clearly. Monitor and reinforce them. God's law sets general guidelines (for example, to love God and neighbor), but provides freedom for rule differences from class to class. Which regulations you and your class set and agree on is not as important as that you discuss them fully, explain them clearly, teach them regularly, monitor them constantly, and enforce them consistently. You provide fences within which you and your students live and learn and make decisions. The older your students, the farther the fences are pushed out. At the same time, setting unrealistic expectations frustrates students and discipline may become ineffective.

Wise teachers clearly define procedures, expectations, and rules. Instruct your students in them, and then see to it that they are met consistently. Post a set of simple, clear rules such as:

> - *Be loving and helpful*
> - *Respect other people, their property, and their opportunities to learn*
> - *Don't interrupt the teacher or other students when they are speaking*
> - *Obey all school rules.*

This enables you to give reasons for rules and procedures, and to give examples (for instance, skill learning requires a quiet atmosphere where you can concentrate). Such discussions make students more willing to live and learn within the limits. You also need to indicate your expectations clearly for activities that involve moving around and noise (for example, project research, hands-on science activities, art work).

Monitor your students constantly and reflectively. Scan the room and let students know that you are aware of what is happening. Circulate randomly through the class. Move toward off-task students. When helping one student, keep an eye on the rest. Keep the momentum of your class going. Ensure that all students remain busy. When necessary, remind the whole class of your expectations ("I'm still waiting for two people to turn to page 23."). Use positive language (for example, "Remember that to concentrate we need quiet," rather than, "Don't be so noisy."). Recognize and reinforce desired behavior ("I appreciate how quietly you walked to the music room today."). Provide varied and challenging work (Kounin 1970; Cruickshank, Bainer & Metcalf 1995).

Consequences must follow if students overstep the bounds. Most students want the security of knowing that you are committed enough to enforce the limits. They *will* test the limits! One of the most common weaknesses of beginning teachers is that they do not consistently enforce the established framework. For example, if you have a penalty for late assignments, apply it every time unless there has been an unavoidable emergency. If you expect students not to talk to each other while you are working with a group or an individual, insist on it each hour, each day, each week! A basic rule in establishing your personal authority is to be consistent in your expectations for appropriate behavior at all times and for all students. Only unavoidable extenuating circumstances may demand that you make an exception (for example, a medical emergency or an announced special "fun" activity).

Similarly, students should know that presentation and discussion time requires the participation and attention of all. They must be courteous and listen to the speaker(s). They must maintain acceptable habits of participation: do not interrupt other speakers, speak only when recognized, respect the opinions of others, don't put others down, and so on. You can often deal with those who break the rules in unobtrusive ways. You don't recognize students who speak out of turn. You glance at one whose face shows disdain for another opinion. While you require more severe measures only occasionally, you must take some action *every* time a student breaks the established framework. Otherwise the classroom atmosphere gradually deteriorates. Of course, if a rule seems not to be working, you may have to stand back and ask whether the rule is a reasonable and enforceable one. Then discuss with your students how it can be modified to have the intended result.

Above all, as I mentioned before, foster an atmosphere of respect in your classroom. Each person needs to demonstrate respect for the time, space, property, and integrity of all other persons. Help students to make their own decisions and follow through. Make them see that they are responsible, that they have freedom to choose, and that they are accountable for their decisions about their behavior and work (Fennema 1977, pp. 70-71). The key to a respectful and caring learning community is that we hold each other accountable for our actions.

◆ ACTIVITY 3-6

Construct a set of basic classroom rules for a specific grade level. To what extent would you seek student input when discussing these rules at the beginning of the school year?

Teaching dispute and conflict resolution

Because of frequent conflict among students, many schools now teach students how they can deal positively with disputes and conflicts that they experience with other students. Dispute and conflict resolution programs appear to be most effective when a whole school adopts such a program.

Such programs recommend that a number of steps be carefully and regularly taught and practiced:

1. *What is the problem?* First, the students involved discuss and establish exactly what the issue is.

2. *How does it feel?* The students take turns to describe how they feel about the situation. They are not allowed to interrupt each other.

3. *What can be done about it?* The students discuss how they can solve the problem. They brainstorm ideas, and list options for resolving the situation. Each person comes up with possible solutions. At this point they do not criticize each other's solutions.

4. *Which solution is agreeable to both?* All persons must agree with the solution that is chosen.

5. *Did the solution work?* The students evaluate whether the solution worked. If not, they must agree on another option from the ones in #3 and implement it.

6. *Did we apologize?* The student must apologize to each other when appropriate. This is a necessary "cleansing" for all involved–both the victims and the aggressors.

This approach has several advantages. First, students do not look to the teacher as a "referee." That often is troublesome for a teacher. The accuser as often as not is also the aggressor, but that is often impossible to sort out. Second, students learn to solve their own problems in a positive way. If taught thoroughly and practiced, conflicts seldom escalate to the point where the teacher needs to become involved. Third, problems resolve themselves much more easily and quickly, with the students feeling positive about the outcome and the teacher feeling good about seldom needing to become involved. Fourth, students learn to appreciate each other's feelings and concerns–which builds community. Fifth, students become peacemakers, which is something that God also requires of us in Scripture (Ro 12:18; 1Co 7:15; 1Th 5:13).

♦ *Friction had erupted on the playground several days in a row in a kindergarten class. The teacher suggested that the class should solve the problem. The problem, it turned out, was that groups of students had formed "gangs" that did things together for security but excluded other students from their activities. The students' own solution was to do away with "gangs" but, in order to still feel safe and secure on the playground, to have "teams" instead. This worked well for a week or so when the same problems seemed to reoccur. Again, the class discussed their feeling about the situation and concluded that the problem was that even "teams" excluded some pupils. So they made the decision that anyone was able to join or leave a team at any time. They played happily until the end of the year, without any further major problems. They had solved the problem themselves. The teacher's involvement had been limited to suggesting that they should discuss the problem and find a solution.*

A 10-year-old wrote a letter to our local newspaper: "I have a major problem that has to be solved. My problem is when someone annoys me, and calls me names I tell them to be quiet. Then that person will tell our teacher something like I cursed at them. They do this because I am bigger. The teacher always takes their side what should I do?" (*The Vancouver Sun*, June 25, 1996, p. D10). Teachers who consistently teach and use the above conflict resolution approach in their classroom tell me three things. First, this problem would seldom come to their attention, because almost always students would solve it themselves without coming to them. Second, occasionally they may hear about the problem. However, when they then ask students to resolve it using the steps that they know, they almost always find a solution (and I have seen kindergartners do this very successfully). Third, in the very unusual case where a teacher still has to become involved, the use of the six steps will still yield solutions that are more acceptable to both sides than a teacher-imposed "solution." In short, this method prevents most problems from escalating or becoming long-term, nagging ones.

◆ Activity 3-7

Describe a realistic student conflict at the grade level you teach or intend to teach. With one or two other students, demonstrate how students at that level might resolve the conflict using the steps outlined in this section.

Corrective discipline

Despite your careful planning of preventive measures, sin will still cause derailments in classrooms. Students may seek attention, power or even revenge. In such cases you need to administer corrective discipline. Don't become overly discouraged. Rather, use misbehavior as an opportunity for nurture and spiritual growth for students as well as yourself (Ro 5:3-5; Fennema 1977). Corrective procedures should be fair and should be seen to be fair. Corrective action should fit the severity of the misbehavior. Overreaction can make the problem worse. Also, when pupils need to be reprimanded, avoid doing so in a demeaning, belittling, or sarcastic manner that could strip them of the self-worth they are entitled to as God's images (Col 3:21). Quiet and firm action is more effective than anger or threats. Often eye contact, a walk up the aisle, or a quiet gesture are sufficient and take place just between the teacher and student.

If further action needs to be taken, it is usually best to talk to students privately. In your discussion, ask students *what* went wrong (not *why*!). Let them reflect on and analyze how they have affected the learning situation. Continue until the student describes the situation accurately. You might ask older students to write down their perceptions of what happened. Tell students, "I am disappointed that . . . What can we do to ensure that it doesn't happen again?" Gradually try to find, from a consideration of various options, a mutually acceptable course of action to remedy the situation in the future. Get students to commit themselves to the proposed solution. Once they do, hold them fully accountable for their actions. An in-school suspension may have to isolate a student if he or she continues to refuse to cooperate (Glasser 1986).

Note the "*3 C's*" of a Biblical approach to resolving a troublesome discipline problem:

- *First*, confront *the student with an unacceptable situation, privately if possible. Ensure that love and truthfulness guide how the confrontation takes place.*

- *Second, try to bring the student to the point where he or she genuinely* confesses *that there was a problem that needs correction.*

- *Third, after exploring different options to overcome the problem, get the student to* commit *him- or herself to a plan that spells out the student's future expected behavior as well as the consequences should the student fail to uphold the agreement. You may want to ask older students to sign a written agreement for serious breaches of acceptable behavior.*

In short, three useful steps to follow when grave problems arise are *confrontation, confession and commitment* (Fennema 1977, p. 130-35). In all serious cases, of course, make sure that you inform the parents of the situation and solicit their help in resolving the problem.

Punishment is a last resort, especially since often it does not allow you try to rectify the underlying cause of the problem. To solve defiance or unresponsiveness, for instance, you need to get at the motives of the students. Punishment by itself will not give long-lasting results. Punishment is necessary, however, when there is deliberate and repeated flouting of the rules. It should come only after warning, and be used sparingly.

Punish using logical consequences when you can. If students are still noisy after two warnings, remove them to a "time-out" chair where they have to stay until they decide that they will be able to work quietly in the regular setting. If pupils misbehave at a learning center, remove their privilege of working at one for a day or two. If students look at photographs during silent reading time, quietly confiscate them. If students have not done their homework, have them come in at lunch or before or after school to do it. If pupils litter, get them to pick up garbage in the halls or on the playground. The more related the consequence is to the misbehavior, the more effective the punishment will be. On the other hand, giving pupils extra mathematics problems or some other type of subject-related work may lead to resentment of that type of school work. Research shows that assigning schoolwork as punishment affects learning negatively (Brophy & Evertson 1976). Lowering academic grades is not an acceptable punishment unless it is the logical consequence of cheating on an assignment or test.

As much as possible, administer your own punishment. For instance, students should serve detentions that you assign during class with you to indicate your personal disappointment and disapproval of the students' (in)actions. You may even be able to use such occasions to extend personal relationships that in the long run may benefit your learning community. Be firm, but calm and loving! Continue, even while administering punishment, to help students formulate courses of action to prevent future misbehavior.

In administering reprimands or punishment, make sure that you are in full control of yourself. If you feel you are losing your temper, postpone the confrontation. Simply say, "I will deal with you later." If necessary, remove the student from the class, giving specific instructions where to go and what to do. Disciplining in anger often leads to regret. Remind students at appropriate times that it is not your but their actions that caused punishment. They must realize that they are accountable for obeying the boundaries set for them. This is in harmony with the Biblical view that humans are responsible for their own fallen state and behavior.

Where constant breakdown of the learning situation occurs, you may use positive and negative reinforcement with good effect. Such methods, if carefully thought out and administered for relatively short periods of time, may help pupils break self-defeating patterns of behavior. If talking out of turn is a common problem in a grade 7 class, for instance, write the names of students on the board when they do so. For each additional time, put a checkmark behind their name. If they haven't spoken out of turn for a period of time, erase one or two checkmarks (and/or their names). Students with their names still on the board serve a detention, but forgiveness is possible! Do remember that positive reinforcement (such as assertive disciplining through which students earn points) is generally more effective than the negative kind. Also, with all punishment, both teachers and students should recognize its fairness. Note that in using such techniques your goal is to help students toward responsible self-discipline where they no longer need extrinsic reinforcement.

◆ ACTIVITY 3-8

A rural junior high school in Alberta unexpectedly found itself with a group of grade 9 skateboarders who intimidated and bullied other students, including using physical violence. The school's enrollment had jumped from 390 to 540. It faced overcrowded conditions with many inexperienced new teachers. It found itself with little positive student leadership and many more at-risk students. To counter the bullying and violence, the school quickly adopted a zero-tolerance policy. It immediately suspended students involved in any violent act. It suggests the following to schools where bullying or violence becomes a problem:

- *Be proactive in dealing with student violence.* Have a clear policy in place. Notify students, parents, and the community about the policy.

- *Use a multifaceted approach to dealing with student violence.* Zero-tolerance policies are not enough. Teachers need to increase supervision, teach the values of tolerance and respect, increase student ownership, and build interpersonal relationships in the school.

- *Form an advisory program.* Advisory classes, often held at the start of the day, help the school to become a moral community. These classes focus on building relationships, fostering acceptance, and teaching positive values.

- *Be aware of group dynamics.* Students who are reasonable on a one-to-one basis may become dangerous to other students when part of a group. Consider the effects of group behavior.

- *When in the middle of a crisis, take action, don't philosophize.* When faced with unexpected turmoil, swift action is necessary to ensure a safe and secure environment for your students. A crisis situation is not the time to seek to build consensus; it is time for action. (Litke 1996)

Do you agree with the suggestions the school makes for such a situation? Why or why not? Look back over the previous sections of this chapter and jot down some of the guidelines that would apply to a situation such as this. Which other steps might a school might take to deal with bullying or violence in a positive way?

◆ ACTIVITY 3-9

A school's means of corrective discipline is limited. High schools use suspension from classes as a last resort. Yet parents complain that the school does exactly what such students like: they do not have to attend school. Are there alternative means of corrective discipline for serious infractions?

Grouping for learning

During His ministry on earth, Jesus, the Master Teacher, taught large groups, small groups, and individuals. Sometimes He taught hundreds of people at a time. But He explained the parable of the sower to just a small group of close followers. He addressed both the Samaritan woman and Nicodemus on a one-on-one basis. He also sent out his twelve disciples with special tasks in groups of two. The point here is that no one "ideal" group size exists for teaching. Rather, the size of a teaching group depends on the aims and nature of the learning activity, as well as on the characteristics and receptivity of the learners. Teaching a whole class of twenty-five or thirty pupils is effective for some but not for other types of instructional situations. As a teacher you need to reflect on how you can group students effectively for different learning outcomes.

What is more important than specific methods of grouping is that teachers treat students with care and concern, and allow them to exercise the abilities that are part of their personhood. You structure learning to involve tasks and methods that, as much as possible, meet the needs of all of your students. You also encourage them, when appropriate, to make choices about their learning, set personal goals, act on them, and bear a measure of responsibility for their own classroom decisions. In short, whatever methods of grouping used, allow students to exercise their calling as images of

God,   helped and encouraged to make responsible choices and decisions.

Large group instruction is an efficient way to disclose concepts that the whole class should know. Most teachers make extensive use of this mode of teaching–sometimes too much so. Large group instruction is often (but not always) effective for the disclosure phase of learning described in the next chapter. Teacher presentations are appropriate under certain circumstances. Use them when you need to arouse interest in a topic. Use them when you want to choose or organize or interpret material in a way not available in another source. Use them when you want to lead into a discussion that clarifies issues or considers different points of view. To be effective, presentations must be purposeful, clear, brief and to-the-point, engaging, and thought-provoking.

Remember that presentations need follow-up individual or small group activities to ensure that learning takes place. You may need to take small groups or individuals apart to meet particular needs. You may want to give individual students or small groups several options to further reinforce concepts, to examine some specific part of the topic under consideration, or to expand what has already been learned. In this way, you see your pupils as having special gifts that they use in the context of a community of learners.

One way you may maintain personal contact and recognize the needs of individual students is by holding individual conferences. Their purpose is to assess students' progress, for instance, in reading or in a unit in order to guide them in further learning. In reading conferences, teachers discuss the content, ask pupils to read orally from a part they enjoyed, make notes, and share with them which skills they need to learn or reinforce. Keep such conferences short (five or six minutes) and ensure that the rest of the class works quietly. Conferences such as these are much more effective than the traditional "reading groups."

Between class grouping or tracking

One controversial topic with respect to grouping students for learning is between class grouping or tracking. This occurs when students of lower and higher abilities are grouped together in one class. Most research evidence suggests that such tracking does not benefit high school students. Grouping by ability or achievement is particularly harmful for the academic and social development of students with lower level academic abilities. Such students become leaderless, discouraged and even alienated. Teachers lower their expectations, spend less time preparing, do not teach as well, and have more discipline problems with such classes. Further, when placing students in a low track they tend to stay there. Academically weak students achieve less in tracked classes than in small high schools where tracking is not possible because of size. Moreover, most good students do not advance appreciably more when grouped by themselves (Oakes 1985, 1992).

The difficulty that arises is that teachers find it more demanding to teach heterogeneous classes. Their planning is more complex and time-consuming, especially since they need to provide alternative activities and assignments on a regular basis. Their whole-class instruction needs to be complemented with small group and individual tutoring, especially for low- and high-achieving students.

For the sake of student learning, nevertheless, schools would do well not to track students in different ability groups except for highly sequential subjects such as mathematics and foreign languages in senior high school grades. Instead of tracking students according to ability, schools could define a core for each topic in a subject that all students should learn, and develop alternatives at varying levels of difficulty for smaller groups within the class.

Tracking just has too many negative implications. It labels students, often to their detriment both academically and socially. It prevents contact among students of diverse abilities and backgrounds. It also creates antagonism in schools, both between groups of students and between teacher and students. Preparing students for responsible discipleship means that we provide a setting for optimal personal development. Tracking largely affects the learning community negatively. Therefore, as much as possible, we should avoid it.

Collaborative learning

One method of in-class grouping that has become popular since 1985 is collaborative (or cooperative) learning. Collaborative learning can be an effective strategy when used judiciously. When carefully planned, it can improve time-on-task and develop social skills that not only enhance community but that are increasingly important in the workplace. It enhances a sense of mutual responsibility and a sharing of gifts ("all for one; one for all"). It counters self-centered individualism and promotes collaborative servanthood. Collaborative learning, however, is not just "group work." Below are some factors to keep in mind (Cruickshank, Bainer & Metcalf 1995, pp. 209-20; Good & Brophy 1994, pp. 277-95; Slavin 1990).

♦ *Group activities must have a clear purpose.* Students must know the expectations and procedures thoroughly: rules for behavior, standards for the work, where and when to get help. While you work with one group, students from other groups should not interrupt.

♦ *Groups must be heterogeneous* (usually 3-5 students). An important objective is to encourage students to accept diversity in aptitude and background. Also, mixed groups benefit the learning of low-level ability students without holding back high-level ones. Moreover, groups of mixed abilities are more likely to function well together.

♦ *You must train students to work cooperatively.* Show students how to share, listen, and handle conflicts. Specify desired behaviors such as listening carefully, encouraging all to participate, and using personal names). Begin with a series of simple tasks so you can focus on cooperative skills. Teach students how to take on specific assigned roles in the group (for instance, the encourager, the summarizer, the mover, the checker, the gopher, the recorder, the reporter, the noise monitor). To ensure that students stay on task, always circulate. This allows you to monitor student behavior and learning, teach collaborative skills, and provide task assistance.

♦ *You must structure for positive interdependence.* What this means is that students must benefit from working together. Always assign each student a specific role such as those above, on a rotating basis. Each student may have to complete a specific part of a project, or be responsible for a specific required resource.

♦ *You must hold group members accountable for their performance, both as a group and individually.* Collaborative groups might complete a summary of the main points of a topic and receive one grade for this as a group, no matter how much each individual contributes. But the students might take the test on the topic individually, with individual grades assigned.

♦ *You must use collaborative learning selectively.* Students do not have the pedagogical and content background for the active instruction they need for systematic development of key concepts and higher level thinking. That is the role of you as teacher. Also, collaborative learning may not work well in primary grades. Moreover, tasks involving routine practice are better done individually. Effective collaborative learning tasks are those that allow a range of formulation and solution strategies, or ones that benefit from collaborative planning.

Many widely used collaborative learning methods are possible. You may ask groups to work on applications of material that you have just presented. You may have the group put together a project requiring library research. You may ask them to design and produce a mural or skit that sums up a unit. You may use a jigsaw technique by which each student learns about a concept or topic and then has to teach it to her "home group." Depending on the class and subject, when collaborative learning is used 10-20 per cent of the time, it appears that students accept greater responsibility, exercise positive social skills, and academically achieve as well as with other types of teaching strategies.

♦ ACTIVITY 3-10

Choose a unit topic at a specific grade level. Brainstorm and discuss how you could use different types of groupings to enhance learning in community.

Providing for diversity

Jesus during his earthly life made a point of seeking out and ministering to all kinds of people. His chosen small group of twelve disciples were very diverse in personalities and gifts. Jesus also reached out with compassion and restoration, however, to those looked down upon in his Jewish context. These included people of different ethnic and religious backgrounds, perceptually and hearing impaired persons, person unable to function normally in society, and social outcasts. Christ's example makes clear that Christian teachers should not only accept but celebrate diversity in their classrooms.

That does not mean that diversity is easy to deal with. Quite the contrary! We need to provide for students with different levels of aptitudes, different learning styles, and different preferred modes of knowing. This requires careful planning, as described in the next chapter. We also often need to provide for students of different cultural backgrounds. Moreover, we will always have students in our classes who may be called exceptional. That is not to take away from the exceptionality of each of our students. I use the term, however, to describe those who are unusually gifted in one or more ways, or who face special difficulties in school learning.

You teach in a multicultural situation even if one or two students have a background that differs from the majority. If so, find out what essential features of the various cultures differ from your own. Since it is easy to misread or ignore significant verbal and non-verbal cues, learn how to interpret your students' behavior. Remember that students may, at the same time, misread your behavior. Don't take unexpected behavior as an affront, but find out whether it reflects the child's culture. Moreover, cultural background may affect how students learn best:

♦ *Pupils from First Nations Indian people in Canada look down rather than face-to-face as a sign of respect. They seem to benefit especially from collaborative learning strategies.*

♦ *Pupils from the Middle East may view the way women are treated in Saudi Arabia quite positively as a way to strengthen the family. Such pupils are not encouraged to be assertive. They will not speak up when they don't understand something, and therefore as a teacher you must regularly check comprehension.*

♦ *Hispanic students learn best when they have a personal relationship with their teacher and can interact with peers (ASCD Curriculum Update, September 1993).*

Whenever you teach students with a cultural background that differs from your own, talk with students and their families and respect their knowledge and conventions. Relate new content to students' own experiences and background. Plan your curriculum so that you deal with history and literature that is particularly relevant for the cultures represented in your classroom. Discuss how cultural diversity can enrich society as long as we all agree to uphold basic Biblical values such as compassion, justice, and integrity.

Inclusion of exceptional students in regular classrooms has become common in North America. All teachers need to be ready to instruct students with a wide array of physical and mental disabilities, ranging from autism or Down's syndrome to visual or hearing impairment. The benefits for such students include higher expectations and achievement as well as better socialization. Other students in the class learn not only to accept differences, but to enhance the learning community by providing help and support. Teachers gain new skills and insights.

♦ *My spouse Wilma recently had an autistic child in her kindergarten classroom. At the beginning of the year, he regularly fell on the floor limp, refusing to do anything. Wilma treated him with respect and much love, but also immediately set certain behavioral standards, telling him over and over again what she required. After a few days the boy did not want to return to kindergarten. Wilma told his mother not to keep him home, but to bring him even if he stayed only a little while at first. Soon the boy accepted what Wilma expected. In the meantime, Wilma read up on autism and watched some videotapes, following the suggestions that seemed to apply. She used a couple of other pupils who related well to the autistic child to do things with him. Gradually the boy voluntarily participated more and more in regular class activities. At the end of the year, the boy was still autistic, but participated in all class activities without question. On the last day he made a card that said, "Good-bye, Mrs. Van Brummelen, I love you," adding a heart and a happy face—an unusual reaching out to another person for an autistic child. He had learned to function well in a loving but firm environment.*

Situations such as these may be constantly demanding, exhausting, and sometimes frustrating for a teacher. There are downsides to inclusion. With limited financial resources, teachers may have to cope without the resources they need—proper training, one-on-one instructional aides, consulting services, and administrative support. Having an aide may be essential but may also require additional planning time and even, sometimes, additional interpersonal pressures. Large classes with a number of exceptional students may mean that teachers need to spend so much time with the latter that other students do not get enough personal attention. It is also still open to question whether, for instance, hearing-impaired students learn more effectively when they remain in a self-contained classroom, at least for some of the school day.

Despite this, it is important that we include as many students as possible in regular classroom communities so that all learn to live and learn together in a supportive environment. As a teacher, don't hold unrealistic expectations. The point of inclusion is not to bring all students with disabilities up to "average" academic standards. What we aim for is that all students learn to use whatever gifts they have as effectively as possible and relate to others in what for them is a secure environment.

◆ ACTIVITY 3-11

Discuss positive and negative experiences you have had with inclusion of exceptional students in regular classrooms. What are the factors that can make inclusion successful? What are some barriers to success? Under what circumstances might inclusion be detrimental?

Learning centers

Learning centers are places where individual or small groups of students work on reinforcement, enrichment, or other independent learning. They are best set up in corners or along the walls of the room. Sometimes students go to them when finished with other assigned work. Sometimes a period of time is set aside for the whole class to work at learning centers (especially in kindergarten and primary grades). Sometimes students may work at centers on a rotating basis (for instance, at a computer center or a science center when you do not have enough equipment for all students).

To be effective, students must be able to use learning centers independently. Provide simple, clear directions. Let the centers be self-contained. For instance, provide a choice of activities for different learning styles and aptitudes. Design them to give students continuous feedback (such as answers on the back of a card). If you are a beginning teacher, move slowly into using learning centers. You can design different centers that relate to your unit theme, perhaps arranged by subjects. Alternatively, you might sometimes plan five or six centers for a social studies or science unit that groups of students visit in rotation. You need to design a method by which students keep track of which centers they have visited and what they have done.

When possible, relate learning centers to topics being taught. Suppose a grade 4 class is studying map reading skills in social studies and the life of Jesus in Biblical studies. One learning center might ask students to find the locations of places discussed during Bible class, and draw a map of Jesus' travels through Palestine. In another center you might ask the students to draw a map of the school or their house (if this is not done with the class as a whole). In your language arts center, you might have pictures of Israel and students might write stories about what Jesus saw as He traveled. Your mathematics center might have some games that reinforce measurement skills in connection with maps. You might have a student-designed center with interesting old and strange maps that they have brought to school. Indeed, a space for student-brought items is always a useful area, as is a reading corner (I used one advantageously in my secondary mathematics room).

◆ ACTIVITY 3-12

With three or four persons, design one or two suitable learning centers for a unit topic. In what ways and to what extent would you use learning centers in the unit?

Arranging your classroom

The classroom is a workshop for learning, and the physical layout and how you use it will affect learning.

Many different classroom arrangements are possible. Research suggests that a well-organized, attractive classroom leads to more receptive and positive students as well as improved learning. Classrooms should include space for individual, small and large group learning activities. You should be able to see and monitor students at all times. In turn, students should be able to see all instructional presentations and displays without difficulty. Keep careful watch for students with sight or hearing problems. Keep high traffic areas separate and easy to get to. This includes bookshelves and storage areas, pencil sharpener, and your desk (Everson et al. 1989).

Classroom displays–or the lack of them–also influence the learning environment. They direct students' attention to topics under consideration, allow them to exhibit and share their work, and provide an aesthetically pleasing and stimulating learning environment. Your displays should challenge students to further thinking and learning. Let all students share and display their best work efforts with others. It is contrary to the concept of Christian community to display only the work of superior students. Teach your class to respect the contributions of all classmates when these reflect genuine, productive effort. Also, gradually involve students in planning and arranging classroom and hall displays, partly to teach them responsibility and cooperation and partly to teach them the principles of aesthetic display.

Have special areas designated to which students bring completed work during the day. At the elementary level, each student could have a mailbox constructed of milk cartons or large tin cans in which you return work that you have checked and send messages and parent newsletters. Such seemingly minor routines help a class function smoothly and thus prevent friction that might break down community.

◆ ACTIVITY 3-13

Draw a detailed floor plan of a classroom for a specific grade level. Discuss how your plan contributes to the classroom functioning as a learning community?

Arranging time

A schedule or timetable is your guide for your daily instructional program. Timetables help you plan a balanced learning program, but use them flexibly. Most elementary teachers frequently integrate aspects of different subjects and thus combine and move around time blocks. They may alternate units with a social studies and a science focus. There is a natural rhythm to the day (as well as to the school year). Some activities are best done early in the morning. When students return from physical education, a transition activity is needed before effective direct instruction can take place. Many elementary teachers give focused skill instruction in the morning when students are fresh. They also frequently plan some time for reading aloud to the class just after lunch. In secondary schools the timetable is usually set.

In grades 8 and 9 there is an increasing move toward longer blocks of time, with one teacher for humanities and one for mathematics and science. That allows teachers to plan combined units and use time in a flexible way. The longer time blocks, especially when also combined with a homeroom period, help to foster the class into a close-knit learning community. At both the elementary and middle levels avoid the temptation, however, to spend more than the allotted time on subjects you like!

No matter what your official time schedule is, what is most important is to maximize the amount of time that students are actively engaged in learning. This is sometimes called *time-on-task*. Conversely, that means you need to develop efficient routines and procedures that take care of organizational matters and logistics. At the beginning of the year, spend time teaching and reteaching and practicing routines so that later on these will become a matter of habit. Have materials and equipment planned and ready before your day or new activity begins. Begin on time and maintain a brisk pace, keeping all students involved. Plan transitions carefully and make them routine so that you don't have to explain them each time. Use special signals such as a bell or raising your hand to get everyone's attention. Establish clear beginning-of-day and end-of-day routines (Cruickshank, Bainer & Metcalf 1995; Evertson 1989). Keeping the learning momentum going helps students to recognize that schools are communities for *learning*.

◆ ACTIVITY 3-14

Discuss specific ways in which the design of a timetable can advance or detract from learning.

Structuring for discipleship

Schools exist for our students. Therefore we must gear classroom structures to helping them learn. That is not to say that a school must be child-centered. Our teaching should be God-centered. As Christian teachers we let God's revelation in his creation and in his Word provide the framework for education. Our classrooms are teacher-directed. We guide and enable students because we believe that (1) God calls them to live responsibly as his images, and (2) our unfolding of knowledge can lead to truth and purposeful response. Our classrooms, finally, are student-oriented. We design our learning structures so that we encourage and assist our students to take on life's tasks in a faithful, responsive and responsible way.

Reviewing the main points

What are the most important points for you in this chapter? We've "covered" a great deal of territory. If you are to be a reflective teacher-guide and craftsperson, you will benefit from reviewing this chapter and making a list of the points that are most significant for you. Keep your list handy as you teach and revise it from time to time. Remember, as you walk with God in your classroom you want to create an atmosphere and structure that will foster responsive discipleship.

REFERENCES

Brophy, J. & Evertson, C. 1976. *Learning from teaching: A developmental perspective*. Boston: Allyn and Bacon.

Cruickshank, D., Bainer, D., & Metcalf, K. 1995. *The act of teaching*. New York: McGraw-Hill.

Evertson, C. et al. 1989. *Classroom management for elementary teachers*. Second edition. Englewood Cliffs, NJ: Prentice Hall.

Fennema, J. 1977, 1995. *Nurturing children in the Lord: A study guide for teachers on developing a Biblical approach to discipline*. Sioux Center, IA: Dordt College Press.

Glasser, W. 1977. Ten steps to good discipline. *Today's Education* 66:61-63.

Good, T. & Brophy, J. 1994. *Looking in classrooms*. Sixth edition. New York: HarperCollins.

Jones, V. & Jones, L. 1990. *Comprehensive classroom management: Motivating and managing students*. Boston: Allyn and Bacon.

Kounin, J. 1970. *Discipline and group management in classrooms*. New York: Holt, Rinehart & Winston.

Litke, C.D. 1996. When violence came to our rural school. *Educational Leadership* 54(1):77-80.

Oakes, J. 1985. *Keeping track: How schools structure inequality*. New Haven: Yale University Press.

Oakes, J. 1992. Can tracking research inform practice? Technical, normative, and political considerations. *Educational Researcher* 21(4):12-21.

Slavin, R. 1990. *Cooperative learning: Theory, research, and practice*. Englewood Cliffs, NJ: Prentice Hall.

Chapter 4

PLANNING FOR LEARNING

Some years ago my second son Tim saved enough money to buy one of the first available home computers. Both Tim and my older son Glen quickly learned to use and program it. Glen studied each page of the manual, carefully trying out each procedure. Step by step, he learned the intricacies of programming. Today, he still uses his laptop computer daily in a linear fashion for his mathematical research.

Tim, on the other hand, had watched the salesperson demonstrate the basics of the computer. At home, he just tried out what would happen if he struck various keys. He referred to the manual only when he got stuck and couldn't reach the salesperson by phone. He immediately started to program games. Unlike Glen, he did not do so deductively, but had some notions that he clarified, modified, and expanded as he programmed. Because he enjoyed and learned from discussing his work, he quickly obtained a part-time job exhibiting computers, using the colorful demonstration programs he developed. Today, he still uses a computer creatively, mainly to compose musical songs.

No two persons learn in exactly the same way. Also with respect to learning, each person has a gift from God. One has this gift, another that (1Co 7:7). Some persons learn best deductively; others, inductively. Some learn best through visual stimuli; others, through aural-oral ones; still others, through kinesthetic ones. Some persons need to try things out in concrete settings; others reflect abstractly. Some persons learn well through individual study; others prefer the give-and-take of discussions in social settings.

A Christian approach to classroom learning needs to take into account these complex variations. It serves no purpose to decry the fact that some students do not learn well with one approach. Instead, we need to plan learning so that it celebrates the diversity with which God has created us.

This chapter first discusses various views about the nature of human beings and the classroom implications of each. It then considers how experiential background and developmental phases affect classroom learning. It develops a model for planning learning that takes into account the rhythm of learning and the needs of students with diverse learning styles. It also deals with two related topics: motivating for learning, and multiple intelligences. In Chapter 3 we discussed how to design the contours within which meaningful learning takes place. The focus of this chapter is more specifically on meaningful learning itself.

Views of the person and implications for learning

In Chapter 3 we saw how students and teachers can interact positively within a classroom. The chapter implicitly assumed a particular view of human beings. That view is the Biblical one that God created persons in His image. To do justice to a discussion of classroom learning, we need to consider what this means and its implications for learning. First, however, it is useful to sketch the four main ways in which educators have looked at human beings during the last 300 years. This helps us see more clearly the distinctiveness and importance of looking at students as responsive images of God.

Traditionalists in education often look at children as *blank slates* on which adults write knowledge, or as *piggy banks* into which we deposit facts and concepts. Learning becomes, to a large extent, a teacher-centered "pouring in." Teachers present and students memorize. Traditionalists correctly see that learning needs a conceptual base. However, they overlook students' personal responsibility for learning. They also neglect that students learn from experience and investigation, posing and solving problems, interacting with peers, and creating products. Moreover, students respond to teaching in unique ways, both in how they interpret and apply knowledge.

Students are more than blank slates that teachers fill with whatever they desire. They are personalities with their own beliefs, traits, abilities, and capacity to make decisions. All these influence learning. Christian teachers who tacitly regard pupils as half-full piggy banks to be "topped up" may teach their students much information, including specifics about God's creation and His love. But they will fall short in helping them discover, interpret, extend and apply knowledge in loving, responsive, and creative service.

Behaviorists look at human beings as *trainable objects*. They emphasize rigid learning structures. Teaching takes place step-by-step and bit-by-bit. They use frequent stimuli and reinforcements (rewards and punishments) to condition students. Students may learn some basic concepts and skills efficiently. However, this approach reduces education to training and even manipulation.

There are some circumstances where behaviorist methods are desirable. I have known students, particularly in lower grades, who could not function normally in a classroom. They disrupted learning for all. The teacher might use stickers to reward such a child whenever he learned in positive ways. Gradually, however, she weaned her pupils away from rewards. She first asked the child, for instance, to determine himself when he deserved a reward. Later, she gradually gave the reward at longer intervals and then stopped altogether.

Why are behaviorist methods limited in effectiveness? Their mechanistic strategies keep pupils from being choosing, responsive persons. They leave little room for personal responsibility and creativity. They fail to recognize sin and its consequences. They believe the right stimuli can resolve all problems. They also neglect the community context of learning. They assume that learning takes place individually using stimuli-response techniques.

Educators from Pestalozzi to Piaget have viewed young persons as *unfolding plants*. Teachers assist their natural and pre-ordained development as they move through universal stages. They see human life as a unity, a wholeness. Humans, they believe, have some inherent thought structures. As these develop, persons move from one psychosocial, rational, lingual or moral stage to the next.

The stages most commonly applied in education are Piaget's cognitive ones. Piaget held that cognitive intelligence organizes the world around us. Learning, however, involves more than cognition. It also has emotional, social, and creative dimensions. Piaget's stages therefore overemphasize the rational dimension of life at the expense of other, equally important ones. Moreover, his stages are not as inevitable or as fixed as Piaget's followers would have us believe. Unlike plants, humans can make personal choices and decisions about learning and about life. They may revert back to earlier stages from time to time, depending on the situation.

Finally, the progressive John Dewey and educators who call themselves critical theorists consider students to be *primary agents of social change*. They emphasize problem solving and critical thinking. They use inquiry and other strategies that help students transform society. They see schooling as a journey in which the process is as important as the destination. They use learning as a means to improve society. However, they put the child rather than God at the center of the universe. They assume that the innate goodness of students will motivate them to study and learn what is good for them. They hold that inquiry leads to truth. But such truth and values may work only for particular persons in particular circumstances. Their efforts to improve society may shipwreck on a lack of agreement on moral, economic, and social values.

All of these metaphors of the learner contain some kernels of truth. Each says something of value about learning. That is understandable, since all educators deal with the data of God's reality. Sometimes learners benefit from receiving information and concepts in a structured way. Sometimes pupils benefit from a carrot-and-stick behaviorist approach. Sometimes it helps to know that pupils are not at a cognitive level where they are ready to learn abstract algebra. Further, the processes of inquiry and problem solving and critical thinking are important if pupils are to contribute to society.

In short, we can learn something from each metaphor. As we will see, however, none reflects the rich Biblical conception of humans as images of God. None admits that in the end learning is meaningful only when it leads to an understanding of God's call that impels us to responsive discipleship and responsible action.

◆ACTIVITY 4-1

On a large sheet of paper, complete the following chart:

Metaphor of child	Classroom structure	Teaching strategies	Curriculum content
Blank slate			

Trainable object			
Unfolding plant			
Agent of social change			

Then discuss which of these four metaphors (or combinations) you would favor for your own class. Justify your position.

Students as images of God

God created all persons, including teachers and students, in His image and likeness (Ge 1:26, 27; Jas 3:9). Being images of God and reflecting God in our lives is not an option for us. God created us that way. We are images by using our unique freedom and abilities. We honor and reflect God's majesty by ruling over the works of His hands in a responsive way (Ps 8).

Yet the extent to which we exercise our calling to be images of God depends on several factors. Are we wholeheartedly devoted to the one true God? To what degree are we committed to and understand God's creation mandate? The Great Commandment? The Great Commission? (Ge 1:28, 2:15; Mt 22:37-39; Mt. 28:18-20) Living as *obedient* images means that we first of all look up to God as we serve Him and our neighbor. We must depend on God. In God we live, move, and have our being (Ac 17:28).

We may not divide our lives into separate secular and spiritual sectors. God calls us to serve Him in *all* that we do, with undivided hearts. Students are holistic, integral beings whose religious "heart" governs all dimensions of life. Some educational leaders absolutize one or another of these dimensions and equate it with our religious "heart." John Dewey, for instance, made the social dimension the focus of all of life. Or a curriculum may prepare students for contributing mainly to economic life. Still others focus on rationality as that which will "save" humanity. All of these hold a reduced view of what persons really are. More seriously, all posit a secular faith in human abilities that replaces faith in God.

Scripture makes clear that humans have a *religious* and not a social or economic or rational heart. Our religious core governs all dimensions of life: the spiritual, moral, political, economic, social, lingual, rational, aesthetic, emotional, physical, and so on. The heart is the wellspring or source of life (Pr 4:23). Faith in God leads to singleness of heart in all our actions. Obedient faith and action lead, for example, to God's blessing in business and agriculture (Jer 32:38-44). A false religious heart, on the other hand, is a deluded heart without understanding or true knowledge (Isa 44:19-20).

Schools highlight explicit growth in a number of identifiable (though inseparable) dimensions of human life. These include the social, economic and rational aspects of life. But we need to remember two things. First, our religious heart rules all aspects of life. If students do not share our Biblically based commitment, they may well reject our basic approach to ethical or economic issues. Their convictions and attitudes will affect their response to us as teachers.

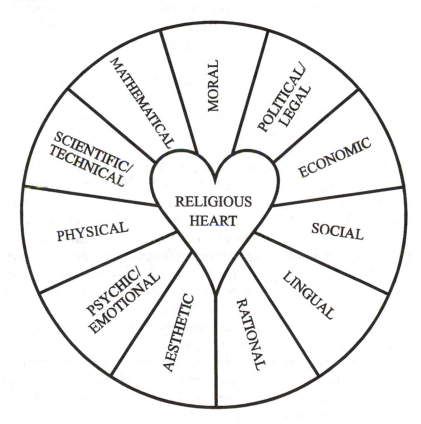

FIG. 4.1 DIMENSIONS OF HUMAN BEINGS

The religious hearts of students–their basic commitments–determine their attitudes and openness to our teaching. Therefore teachers need to take into account the worldviews of their students. Christian schools discuss and call for commitment to a life of discipleship in Jesus Christ. All schools need to teach and demonstrate what basic commitments imply for life in society.

Secondly, even when a school subject focuses only on certain aspects of life, students learn as total, integrated beings. We teach logical thinking, for instance, to students who have brought their whole being to class. Not only their rational ability but also their physical, emotional, social and moral characteristics will affect how well they learn. Similarly, if students' physical or emotional or social needs are not met at home or in their peer group, they will find classroom learning difficult. That is why schools in poor economic areas provide breakfasts. That is also why schools with many students from broken homes start the day with sharing sessions that try to offset the lack of parental love and attention.

All dimensions of students' lives are interrelated. All affect each other. An incident on the playground, the loss of a prized possession, the scoring of a goal in a soccer game, a forthcoming visit by a grandmother–all affect learning. While such events are often beyond our control, we can be sensitively alert to them and to how they affect learning in our classrooms.

Being images of God also means that students are responsible and accountable for their actions. God has established norms and guidelines for our lives. There are rights and wrongs. Absolutes do exist. The Word of God stands forever (Isa 40:8). This is a source of comfort and security for both students and teachers. At the same time, as His images, God holds us accountable for living according to His norms. Starting with Adam and Eve, God allowed persons freedom to choose. Students can make decisions. They can choose to obey or disobey. They can decide how to respond to God's calling. Students need to experience being responsible and accountable for their actions. This means, as much as possible, that we give them responsibility and hold them accountable for their own learning. We use our God-given authority to enable students to become ever more responsible themselves. Kindergartners already can learn to keep checklists of center work they have done, and to solve conflicts with other students.

Students, like teachers, will fall short, even when they have turned their lives to Jesus in trust and service. They are sinners in need of redemption and daily renewal (Ro 3:23-24). That students are sinners does not mean, however, that they are corrupt and can do no good. Rather, it means that they will fail from time to time even when they try to make good decisions or take correct action. Their conduct, effort, and relationships with others will not always reflect a Biblical lifestyle. Therefore students need guidance, supervision, and discipline. A key role of teachers is to direct their students "in the way [they] should go" (Pr 22:6). Teachers do so within an atmosphere of security, lack of fear, and mutual respect for others' dignity and property.

We may not forget that students through conversion and regeneration become *fellow workers* with God and *co-heirs* with Christ (1Co 3:9; Ro 8:17). When they turn their hearts to God, they can work with true purpose and meaning, although, like ourselves, they still fall short in their service. Our teaching helps them become transformed through the renewing of their minds (Ro 12:2). They learn to pitch in to help make God's creation a better place.

Despite their sin and weakness, God extends to students the gift and the mandate of His Kingdom. This makes their task in school and life a far richer one than that proposed by the traditionalist or the behaviorist. Seize opportunities to help students see how important and enriching it is to be touched by the Holy Spirit. Plan your pedagogy and choose content so that you encourage students to take up their intended calling as God's images.

The Bible also makes clear that persons are unique. All are able to contribute to life in community in a special way, using their distinctive gifts (Ro 12:4-8). In the classroom, expect that all students are actively engaged. Not all students, however, can achieve equally. Therefore use diverse approaches. Modify assignments for students with different abilities. Otherwise, you may not bring up children and adolescents in the training and instruction of the Lord. Rather, you will exasperate at least some of them (Eph 6:4).

Build on students' strengths! Enable them to understand their particular gifts and develop them. Encourage them to do things they can do well. Thus students may acquire and maintain a sense of worth. All of us need success before we can confidently explore unfamiliar or difficult areas. When you give students tasks that they successfully complete, you enhance self-confidence and future growth. Give all students meaningful roles as participants in class-room and school activities and events. They need to know that you appreciate them for being contributing members of a learning community where they image God in all aspects of their lives.

◆ACTIVITY 4-2

This section outlines (but does not exhaust) what being an image of God means for students. What is central is that God calls each student (and teacher!) to commitment and being His co-worker on earth. Discuss the classroom implications for each of the following student characteristics:

- *multidimensional and yet holistic*

- *uniquely gifted*

- *responsible and accountable*

- *sinful but living under God's common grace, with the possibility of redemption*

Are there other important aspects of being image bearers that have implications for the classroom? For a more detailed description of a Biblical view of the child and its implications, see Fennema (1977).

Experiential background and developmental layers

One of the marvels of childhood is the powerful ways in which young human beings learn through their everyday experiences. Before children attend school, they have already learned an amazing amount about quantity and space, movement and speed, warmth and light, rocks and water, plants and animals, human emotions and interrelationships, rights and wrong, and beliefs and faith.

It is also humbling for teachers to realize how much school-age persons learn without being taught, both inside and outside school. Once they attend school, pupils continue to develop their insights through the countless experiences they have at home, on the street, in parks, in church, and in shopping malls. They also learn through exposure to printed, visual, oral, and computer-based materials.

That does not mean that schools are unimportant for learning. They are more than just institutions that socialize students. The more formal, focused learning that schools provide plays an important role in students' development. But teachers need to take into account what their pupils have learned and are learning experientially. Use students' experiential knowledge as a starting point for more focused learning. Through guided questioning, deepen and formalize what students already know. Ask them to stand back and study God's world as a place with structure, patterns, and relationships. Help them apply resulting insights to various life experiences.

Teachers cannot assume, of course, that all students have similar experiential knowledge backgrounds. Homes vary greatly in how much and what type of stimulation occurs. This affects both the readiness and the ability of students to learn. For instance, some children enter school without any experience with books. Such children know nothing of the rewards of reading. They are not ready to learn decoding skills. If their experiences have not given them any reason for needing or wanting to read, decoding for them may be a rote activity with little point except to please the teacher. A defeatist attitude easily results.

Therefore plan many experiential activities, especially for pupils with meager backgrounds. Base more formal, focused school learning on students' own background knowledge, whether gained outside school or as a result of activities you provide. Neglecting this will result in rote learning that is not personally meaningful.

Nurture a learning context for students by giving rich experiences with the primary "stuff" of reality. Provide activities with concrete, manipulative and imaginative materials. Before you formally teach new content and skills, give your students activities where they themselves explore, generalize and make informal inferences. Meanwhile, observe, interact with, and guide them. Note how they think and whether they are ready for more focused learning. Try to find out whether they are gaining meaning. Allow inexact thinking and products early on. Kindergarten teachers, for instance, give many opportunities for emergent reading and writing and informal exploration with numbers and shapes. Grade 10 science teachers will encourage students to experiment with lenses and prisms. Students draw interim conclusions before the concepts are formally taught.

It is easy to fragment learning to the point where students see little relevance in school learning. They experience life as a whole.

The mathematical, physical, emotional, social, aesthetic, and moral dimensions of life all impinge on real life situations. They can be separated for the sake of analysis, but pupils do not experience them separately. Therefore teach even specialized topics in a meaningful context. How does the topic relate to other aspects of knowledge? To life in culture? How does the topic relate to Biblical themes and norms that set the direction for our lives? Can the topic help students see the unity of creation and of life? How can students respond to and use the knowledge gained in a personal way?

Be sensitive not only to the traits and backgrounds of your students, but also to their developmental levels. Effective learning activities take into account pupils' current conceptual and thinking abilities. In school, Piaget has pointed out, students' thinking ranges from concrete, perception-dominated reasoning to formal abstract reasoning. Avoid labeling pupils too soon, however. Some students develop early; others, late. Some pupils learn to read slowly and find the early years of school difficult. Yet they may be very intelligent in other ways and become perceptive and creative persons.

Developmental stage theories are not as helpful as sometimes assumed. Teachers do not know precisely the level of students' cognitive development. Even if they did, they would still face a wide spectrum of stages in their classrooms. Moreover, developmental theories usually describe *what* is the case, not *how* the learning should proceed or what we ought to teach. Piaget's theory concerns itself mainly with logical thinking which "represents only a small part of the intellectual equipment children bring to making sense of the world and their experience" (Egan 1983, p. 96).

Kieran Egan (1997) suggests three developmental "layers of understanding" that may help you in planning: *mythic, romantic,* and *philosophic* understanding. Successive layers do not replace previous ones but fuse with them, giving deepened understanding and insight. At the mythic or primary level of understanding (up to 8 years of age), students can already deal with deep and abstract concepts and themes, according to Egan. To do so, teachers design topics as "stories" that communicate meaning and values in terms of "binary opposites" such as love and hate, honor and selfishness, or dominance and submission. He adds that what intrigues children at this age is the remote and the imagined that expands their horizons. Stories or "myths" provide children with causal explanations, prediction, and control.

Once students move into the romantic layer (ages 8-15), they do not lose their interest in story or narrative formats, but now look for adventure, imagination, and idealism. They enthusiastically explore the world and their experience in it. They are fervent in their quest for knowing about the extreme and the exotic. Facts and explanations of how and why things happen fascinate them. Teachers make the familiar strange. They stimulate romance, wonder and awe. At the same time, they develop units around basic "transcendent" human values.

In the philosophic layer (ages 15-19), students understand and develop causal chains of reasoning and interrelationships within networks of concepts and knowledge. Here students move beyond detail into drawing general conclusions. They want to explore and understand what causes phenomena in the world around them. Teachers focus their planning on underlying questions and issues.

Consider teaching about honeybees, for instance. In kindergarten you may emphasize the cycle of life and death. The children may experience how each bee has a special function in the life of a hive. While the activities are concrete, the unifying "story" may be how over one year a hive cares for and renews itself. In grade 5 you may have students explore the unexpected order and intricacies of the life of bees in a hive. God's gracious provision for pollination and honey becomes the underlying value that students learn to appreciate. In grade 11 teachers would put the study of bees in the context of genetic developments and our ecosystem. What will be the effects of African bees slowly moving north in North America? How will beehive devastation caused by mites impact crops and our ecosystem? Can genetic engineering develop mite-resistant bees? Is this desirable? What are the genetic differences between various types of bees and how can we classify them?

Students have different experiential backgrounds and operate at varying levels of cognitive, social, and moral development. Observe your students and listen to them carefully to check whether their learning is meaningful for them. At the same time, do not trivialize educational content because of dubious claims made about children's cognitive development. Children can enjoy, deal with, and learn from profound motifs and values, as long as these are presented in concrete settings, and as long as we don't expect them to reason about them in as formal a way as adolescents and adults.

◆ACTIVITY 4-3

Choose a topic that can be taught at different grade levels (for example, the family, Mexico, magnetism and electricity). Discuss how you would teach the topic in grade 1, grade 6, and grade 11. How do your suggestions relate to Piaget's stages of development and Egan's layers of understanding?

Motivating learning

Learners are images of God, created to respond to His call. This implies two guidelines for motivating them to learn. First, help students appreciate the value of their learning activities. Second, enable students to achieve success if they put forth reasonable effort (Good & Brophy 1994, p. 214). In other words, the best motivation for students is to master tasks in a supportive setting. Either such tasks should have inherent interest or value, or shown to be useful in attaining further goals. We advance mastery when we set tasks with high but realistic expectations that take into account both students' developmental level and their unique giftedness.

Within such a context, use the following specific strategies to motivate students (Good & Brophy (1994, pp. 235ff.):

- *Model interest in learning and project enthusiasm. Convey that what is learned is important.*

- *Treat students as if they already are eager learners, and induce interest or curiosity. Keep them actively involved!*

- *Ask students to list what they already know about a topic and what they would like to learn.*

- *Encourage students to succeed and learn from mistakes. Build their confidence.*

- *Make content personal, concrete, or familiar, and bring out the unusual and unexpected.*

Note that intrinsic motivation is more effective in the long run than extrinsic motivation such as, for instance, giving students rewards. The suggested strategies are effective mainly when learning is inherently meaningful. Students want to learn about things that matter to them. On the basis of brain research, Caine & Caine claim that the source of most intrinsic motivation is the "deep meaning" that shapes what we are willing to look at and how we interpret it. That is, intrinsic motivation comes about largely when teachers deal with what children believe to be important and relate it to their sense of purpose and values. A regard for student purposes and values is the essential glue for meaningful learning (1997, p. 112). As images of God, students intuitively know that God's reality has meaning and purpose. They want their learning to relate to the meaning they have experienced and to deepen and broaden their perspective.

In the remainder of the chapter, I develop a model for meaningful learning. This model allows you to take into account that your students are uniquely gifted images of God who learn to walk with Him as they use and develop their diverse gifts.

◆ACTIVITY 4-4

Think of occasions in school where you were motivated to learn. List the factors that led to a high level of motivation. Compare your list with those of others, and try to find common patterns. How does your list compare with the items mentioned in this section?

Learning styles

Students differ greatly in their preferred learning styles. It is neither feasible nor desirable to provide all pupils with experiences during each class that match their particular learning style preference. Yet knowing the features of diverse learning styles makes you sensitive that pupils approach learning best in different ways. For each unit or unit section, provide some learning activities in which students can use their own favored learning style. Also, help students feel more at ease with activities that involve less favored learning styles. Students need to become comfortable with diverse learning strategies. That helps them progress toward their personal goals and become balanced persons. Analyzing your own preferred learning style(s) helps you plan a balance of learning experiences, including ones that do not match your own preferred style(s).

◆ACTIVITY 4-5

No one classification of learning styles captures all the nuances of differing preferred approaches to learning. Some emphasize that learners favor visual, oral, or kinesthetic means. Others base their classification on the fact that pupils may prefer kinesthetic, logical, linguistic, interpersonal, or aesthetic learning (Armstrong 1987). One learning style survey involves more than twenty factors in four areas: cognitive skills, perceptual responses, and study and instructional preferences (Keefe 1988).

Think of a topic with which you are unfamiliar but that you would like to know more about (for example, how to compose a song, the early history of your community, the effects of ocean currents on climate). How would you prefer to go about learning? Why? Compare your preferences with those of others. Are there "better" or "worse" ways of learning? Why or why not? Should we allow all students in a class to learn in way(s) they prefer? Why or why not?

A person who has synthesized and categorized learning style research for application to classroom learning in a helpful way is Bernice McCarthy (1981, 1997). Her work has its roots in the Myers-Briggs classification of personality types as well as the work of David Kolb (1984). McCarthy begins by considering how humans *perceive* and how they *process* experiences as they learn. Her first dimension of learning establishes that humans perceive reality differently. Some perceive new situations more intuitively, by sensing and feeling them concretely. Others analyze experiences more abstractly, thinking and reasoning about them. McCarthy then describes a second dimension of learning: how persons process experiences and information. Some process or internalize experiences by actively jumping in and trying things out. Others stand back and reflect on their experiences (or those of others). Schools, in general, have favored abstract perception and reflective processing. Yet students need to feel as well as think, do as well as reflect. Society needs persons with all these different abilities. If we superimpose these two dimensions of learning, four learning style categories result, as shown in Fig. 4.2.

The upper right quadrant includes learners who tend to perceive information concretely and process it reflectively. Learners favoring this style are *intuitive* learners (I am using my own terms;

McCarthy uses innovative, analytic, common sense, and dynamic learners, in clockwise order). Intuitive learners are personally involved in their learning. They view concrete situations from different perspectives, reflecting on their own experiences to seek meaning and reach conclusions. They enjoy social interaction and involvement, and learn by listening and sharing ideas. They are good listeners. They ask questions and learn through responding to and discussing their perceptions. A key question for intuitive learners is, "Why?" Teachers need to give such learners both problems in concrete settings and help them explore reasons. Counselors, psychologists and many elementary school teachers fall into this category.

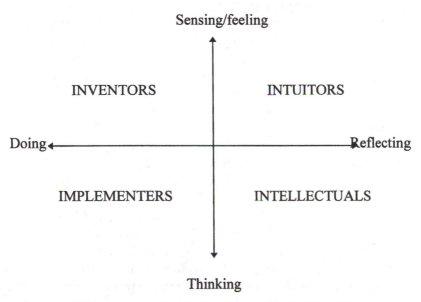

FIG. 4.2. LEARNING STYLE CATEGORIES

The lower right quadrant contains *intellectual* or *analytic* learners who perceive information abstractly and process it reflectively. They are more interested in concepts and ideas. They collect and analyze information and conceptualize material. They find satisfaction in thinking through problems and issues and in determining the validity of a thesis. They learn well in traditional classrooms, from lectures, objective explanations, and reading. A key question for intellectual learners is "What?" Teachers help them gather, digest and process facts and concepts. Unlike intuitive learners, they may not enjoy working in groups or open-ended tasks. Planners, research scientists and mathematicians often favor this learning style.

The lower left quadrant includes *implementers* who perceive information abstractly and process it actively. They revel in hands-on experiences and in solving concrete problems. The want to know how things work, and how they can apply concepts in everyday situations. They enjoy learning by testing theories and applying ideas to practical situations, rather than by being given answers. The key question for implementers is "How?" Teachers must let them do things and move around as they construct, manipulate, experiment and tinker. They tend to act before they reflect. Implementers include many nurses, technicians and engineers.

The fourth category is that of *inventive* learners. These perceive information concretely and process it actively. They are also people of action, but rather than implementing the ideas of others they prefer to let their own ideas take flight. They work with people but others sometimes see them as too pushy in their enthusiasm and drive. They are entrepreneurs who like to make things happen. They test experience and excel in situations that call for flexibility, improvisation, and creativity. They seek out possibilities through trial and error and experimentation, often reaching accurate conclusions without linear, rational argumentation. Inventive learners ask, "What if?", and teachers must let them discover and seek out hidden possibilities. Many marketing and sales people as well as artists are inventive learners (McCarthy 1980, pp. 37-43; 1997).

Students may lean heavily toward one orientation, have two or even three strong ones, or be balanced in all four. Moreover, learning style preferences may well change with age and with different types of experiences. Analytic high school learners, for instance, may have preferred a hands-on approach in kindergarten. There is some research evidence that indicates that at the high school level slightly more students lean toward intuitive and inventive learning than the other two categories (McCarthy 1980, p. 81).

Traditionally schools have emphasized learning activities that particularly fit intellectual/analytic learners. Yet if we are to pay more than lip service to students being unique images of God, then students should, on a regular basis, be able to use their own preferred learning style. They should also become more comfortable with other ways of learning so that they develop and use their gifts in diverse ways. Furthermore, building a learning community in the classroom requires the contribution of each student. By providing activities for all learning styles, each has opportunities to do well at some point and help others in their learning.

◆ACTIVITY 4-6

Choose a unit topic for a particular grade level (for example, weather and climate). Find activities that would suit learners who prefer:

- ◆ intuitive learning

- ◆ intellectual/analytic learning

- ◆ implemental learning

- ◆ inventive learning

◆ACTIVITY 4-7

Obtain one of the standard learning style inventories and complete it. What implications do your results have for your own teaching?

Phases of learning

◆ *The apostle Peter's teaching on Pentecost morning described in Acts provides an example of four more-or-less distinct phases of learning: setting the stage, disclosure, reformulation, and transcendence. Peter first provided the setting. He waited until the people had experienced the morning's strange events and asked each other, "What does this mean?" He then related his remarks to what people were thinking: "These persons are not drunk, as you suppose . . ." (Ac 2:15). Next, he provided disclosure, analyzing and building a conceptual structure. He recounted that the events were taking place in historical context, showed that they fulfilled prophecies of old, and proclaimed the Good News of Christ. The listening learners then reformulated the concepts themselves. Their thinking and reflection led them to be "cut to the heart." They asked, "What are we to do?" (Ac 2:37). Finally, they had an opportunity for transcendence, for moving beyond what they had learned. Many accepted the message. They were baptized and devoted themselves to the apostles' teaching and to the fellowship, and they gave to everyone as they had need (Ac 2:41-47). Biblical knowledge involves commitment and leads to obedient action.*

Many years ago Alfred North Whitehead (1929) wrote about the fact that there is a natural rhythm in learning. It moves from what he called romance, to precision and, finally, to generalization. In thinking about this I came to the conclusion that a better categorization for the phases of learning would be a four-fold one: setting the stage (*preparing*), disclosure (*presenting*), reformulation (*practicing*), and transcendence *(responding by going beyond)*.

A few years later, I saw McCarthy's categorization of learning styles. I realized that I could superimpose her template on my four phases of learning. Each phase lent itself to activities particularly suited for one of McCarthy's learning style categories. I also saw, however, that learning is too complex to categorize completely. I do not intend my phases to represent a rigid, foolproof formula for lesson planning. But the schema is helpful to check that in teaching a topic you provide for all phases of learning and for all learning style categories. The "four phase" model stands independently of a consideration of learning styles, but is enriched by it. It encourages students to use their diverse gifts to exercise responsive obedience to God's call in life, no matter what their learning style may be.

◆ACTIVITY 4-8

For the example below, pick out activities to fit each of the four phases of learning. How do these relate to McCarthy's learning styles?

◆ *The grade 7 teacher first engages her students by reading a number of pages of the novel* A Wrinkle in Time *to them. The students read the rest of the novel themselves. They respond to their reading by drawing a picture of a favorite scene, creating a collage showing their feelings about the novel, or writing another ending to it. Later, as an introduction to more formal work on characterization in the novel, some students dramatize certain scenes to show the uniqueness of the characters. Others do an interpretive reading. The activities are open-ended and allow for much exploration and imagination before the novel is discussed formally in class. The activities emphasize the students' own enjoyment and personal reaction. The teacher encourages informal reflection by asking questions.*

The teacher then introduces a handout, "A Way of Responding to Literature." Using this, the class develops a plot graph, discusses the conflicts in the novel, and learns what is meant by the plot climax. The students then write a paragraph organizing their reasons for believing that the climax occurs at a particular point in the novel. Later, the teacher analyzes with the class how the author portrays love and evil, writing the main points brought out on an overhead transparency. In a small group discussion the students compare this with what the Bible says about evil and love. The students then make a summary statement comparing and contrasting the two views.

At the end of the unit, the students write an essay on the characteristics of the evil that exists on the planet Comazotz. The teacher asks the students not only to compare the author's and a Biblical view of love and evil, but also to state how they would respond to the Comazotz-type evil we find on earth. The class holds a discussion about how people in society and the students themselves can be more accepting of each other as unique images of God. The teacher invites them to write one or two specific ways in which they will try, during the next week, to show Christian love in an area where they have a difficult time so doing. Finally, the unit provides personal choice and open-ended response about other novels and poems by the same author.

Phase 1: Setting the stage *(preparing)*

The first phase of learning attempts to make the learning that is to take place personally meaningful. It makes use of the students' experiential knowledge. It encourages them to enjoy, to discover, to imagine, to search for relationships, and to draw conclusions without approaching a topic deductively and formally. This phase of learning is a time for exploring, for asking questions, for delight in immediate response.

In this phase, provide a meaningful setting by encouraging your students to react, to express their feelings, to make suggestions, to draw their own conclusions—even if those are unpolished at this stage. Help them reflect on the knowledge they already have and explore the limits of such knowledge in non-threatening ways. Dialogue with students to find out what they are thinking so that you can plan the other phases of learning to meet their needs.

In this phase all students should experience, as Whitehead called it, some "romancing" with academic content. Especially here make use of imaginative materials, real-life objects and situations, field trips, and film and drama. Seerveld (1980) calls this phase the one of *surprise*. He suggests that you "imaginatively arouse the students to grab hold of [your] hand as they go pioneering, detecting, imagining . . . unfamiliar things." While surprise is not always necessary, use this phase to motivate students to become involved in and excited about the learning that is to take place. The students' informal work during this phase prepares them for more complex formal work.

Intuitive learners especially shine in the "setting the stage" phase. Here students check out their feelings and ideas, often interacting with other students. Students try to answer "Why?" questions in personal ways. They step into and reflect on concrete situations, integrating personal meaning with the experience. You encourage them to use their imagination and innovation. You are the facilitator and motivator who helps students analyze concrete experiences in meaningful ways.

♦ *A unit on the natural history of the British Columbia coastal forest begins with a class activity where students answer the questions "What do we know?" and "What do we want to know?" The students categorize their answers and then plan a field trip where they begin to seek answers to some of their initial questions. During this trip, on the basis of their previous knowledge and present information, they also record the relationships they discover between plants, animals and their physical environment. They discuss their experiences and findings as they draw an informal web showing forest relationships, one that they expand and correct as the unit progresses. Other unit sections start with an open-ended investigation of the properties and importance of water, and a film and subsequent discussion of communities of living things.*

The setting the stage phase may last one or several days at the beginning of a topic, or may consist of short activities at the start of individual lessons. Its length or when activities take place varies considerably. What is important is that the students themselves become engaged in their learning. They need to reflect on their own experiential knowledge, their present action, their own feelings, and their own beliefs.

Phase 2: Disclosure *(presenting)*

It is insufficient for schools to have students do no more than explore and reflect informally using their experiential background, even when you structure and guide such activities. To understand God's complex creation and the role of humans in serving God in it, schools must systematically disclose and analyze significant aspects of that creation and how humans respond to their calling. If learning does not go beyond the setting the stage phase, students will have hazy insights, fuzzy thinking, and be unable to distinguish peripheral from central concepts. Precise, well-organized instruction must follow the first phase of learning.

The second phase of learning, *disclosure*, builds on the students' experiential knowledge, including that gained in the first phase. In this phase the topic is unfolded and disclosed to the student in a carefully structured manner. You supersede the explorative nature of Phase 1 with systematic and focused teaching modes: oral and visual presentations, demonstrations, class discussions, readings, computer-based instruction, collaborative small group work, tutoring, and so on. This phase emphasizes careful conceptual development.

Avoid two pitfalls here. First, do not *close* the topic instead of *disclosing* it. Continue to involve and challenge your students. Ask penetrating questions. Encourage them to ask questions in turn. Phase 2 is not just a one-way presentation. Students are not passive receptors of information. They must actively process concepts and ideas. Meaningful learning demands active involvement.

Secondly, most teachers know how to organize, present, and explain concepts and information very well. Therefore they may be tempted to overemphasize Phase 2. Yet disclosure may not become the sole or principal focus of learning. Gradually, as students get older, teachers may give more time to this phase. Yet even college students regularly and legitimately complain that instructors shortchange them when a course consists mainly of lecture presentations. At higher grade levels, students can do more Phase 3 and 4 activities outside of class. However, always strive for an appropriate balance of the four phases of learning. Regularly ask whether you are not putting too much stress on Phase 2 learning. Remember that fewer than one-quarter of our students prefer this type of learning, and that even they need to process and apply and extend the ideas themselves in what for them are original ways.

An important and integral part of disclosure is *conceptualization*. Students abstract concepts from experiential knowledge. They expand and develop them during disclosure, building their conceptual structures. You present information selectively so that you highlight core concepts. You consciously relate main and subordinate concepts within each discipline and throughout the curriculum. You help students assimilate concepts in a meaningful, non-verbatim way (Steensma & Van Brummelen 1977, p. 21).

Precise conceptualization involves hard work. Often you must take concepts out of context to develop them further, resulting in an additional level of abstraction for students. You and your students need self-discipline and patience. However, if you regularly include all four phases of learning, your students will understand the purpose and place of conceptualization. They will recognize that it is a necessary prelude for further generalization and application.

It is the intellectual/analytic learners who delight and excel in the disclosure phase of learning. They enjoy learning and thinking about new concepts and their implications. They have the inclinations and good facilities in analysis, classification, drawing conclusions, and theory construction. They examine and critique ideas. Often they are "trivia" collectors. In the past, because schools have emphasized Phase 2, and, to an extent, Phase 3 of learning, it is these students who have been especially successful in school.

The disclosure phase of learning may take five minutes or several weeks, depending on the topic and the students' developmental level. It leads directly into Phase 3, reformulation. Usually, in fact, reformulation activities are closely integrated with or closely follow each disclosure activity. Therefore the example of the forest unit continues in the next section.

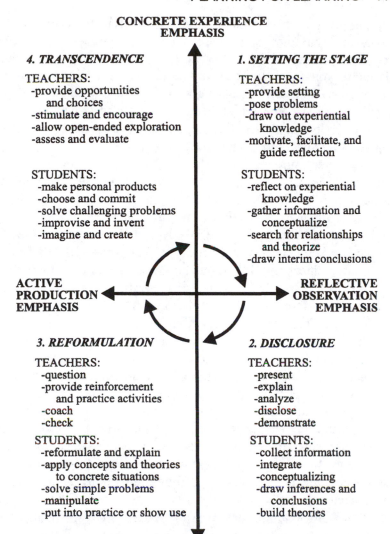

CONCRETE EXPERIENCE EMPHASIS

4. TRANSCENDENCE

TEACHERS:
-provide opportunities
   and choices
-stimulate and encourage
-allow open-ended exploration
-assess and evaluate

STUDENTS:
-make personal products
-choose and commit
-solve challenging problems
-improvise and invent
-imagine and create

ACTIVE PRODUCTION EMPHASIS

3. REFORMULATION

TEACHERS:
-question
-provide reinforcement
   and practice activities
-coach
-check

STUDENTS:
-reformulate and explain
-apply concepts and theories
   to concrete situations
-solve simple problems
-manipulate
-put into practice or show use

1. SETTING THE STAGE

TEACHERS:
-provide setting
-pose problems
-draw out experiential
   knowledge
-motivate, facilitate, and
   guide reflection

STUDENTS:
-reflect on experiential
   knowledge
-gather information and
   conceptualize
-search for relationships
   and theorize
-draw interim conclusions

REFLECTIVE OBSERVATION EMPHASIS

2. DISCLOSURE

TEACHERS:
-present
-explain
-analyze
-disclose
-demonstrate

STUDENTS:
-collect information
-integrate
-conceptualizing
-draw inferences and
   conclusions
-build theories

ABSTRACT CONCEPTUALIZATION EMPHASIS

FIG. 4.3. FOUR PHASES OF LEARNING

Phase 3: Reformulation *(practicing)*

The presentation and analysis of the disclosure phase does not become personally meaningful until students can *reformulate* the main concepts. That is, they must demonstrate that the concepts are integrated into their conceptual schema. That does not mean that they can just parrot what has been disclosed. Rather, it means that they have fit the pieces into their conceptual framework, and can use and respond to what they have learned in their own way. During this phase you follow up (and often intersperse) your disclosure with interpretation and inference questions. You ask for general and specific reactions. You ask students to explain their new knowing and use it in simple applications. During this phase students "reinvent" and begin to use the disclosure phase.

During disclosure and reformulation you may use resource materials and reinforcement activities to good advantage. These materials can clarify concepts, give further information, pose questions, and, especially, provide activities to strengthen and sharpen what has been learned. Exercise material gives students opportunities to reformulate key concepts in a variety of ways, and supplies necessary reinforcement and drill. You should be careful not to use such exercises as the basis of a course or program. They have a legitimate place in furnishing reformulation experiences, but they are only one part of meaningful learning. If such work becomes the main focus of learning, you impoverish education. Students then tend to become passive rote learners, not responsive images of God.

Students who learn best as implementers appreciate the reformulation phase. They are the ones who like to do things themselves. They try out and apply concepts and theories. During this phase, therefore, provide activities in which students apply concepts and theories and solve related problems. Allow them to manipulate and experiment, to do things on their own in a step-by-step fashion. Facilitate students' progress by giving directions and constant encouragement. Involve them actively, usually individually but sometimes in small groups. In this phase students manipulate prescribed materials related to the disclosed concepts. Their knowledge grows in small steps. They make the material their own, and begin to add something themselves and use it in personal ways.

◆ *The unit on the natural history of the British Columbia coastal forest contains many disclosure and reformulation activities. In a discussion, for instance, the class lists the characteristics of all ecosystems and classifies the characteristics into major concepts (disclosure). When finished, the students use the creatures found in the forest during Phase 1 of the unit to draw a large model ecosystem to show these characteristics (reformulation). The disclosure phase in the section on the food pyramid involves doing a number of experiments and readings. The reformulation phase consists of a class question-and-answer section and individual student summary diagrams of the food chain.*

Phase 4: Transcendence *(responding by going beyond)*

The final phase in the rhythm of learning is *transcendence*. I use the word in its original meaning of "going beyond." In this phase students move beyond and rise above disclosure and reformulation. During transcendence theoretical reflection becomes reflective action. It is an integral and crucial part of meaningful learning.

Without transcendence, schooling may fail to touch students personally. They are less likely to develop the dispositions and commitments we cherish. Learning may then be little more than controlled regurgitation. Without this phase, your students are unlikely to exercise their talents in school in the full, rich way God intends them to be used. Yet, as teachers we easily leave out transcendence. Many of us like the neat packaging that is possible for disclosure and reformulation. We may find it difficult to find time to do justice to this phase. That is partly the case because of the traditionalist overemphasis on Phases 2 and 3.

Nevertheless, transcendence is as important as the other phases of learning. During this phase students may respond in deeper and more creative ways with what they have learned. They apply concepts and principles in their own unique ways, often in what for them are original situations. They develop personally meaningful products and choose responses that affect their own lives. They commit themselves to certain dispositions, values, and courses of action. Students now offer to others the results of their learning and thinking in various forms. They have frequent opportunities to share and display the results of their learning. Especially in this phase students may experience how humans can live in obedient response to God, and accept the mandate of God's Kingdom for themselves. Their work may reflect their understanding of their religious calling and set out their own positions.

The products that students create during this phase should be their own, reflecting reality and their place in it as they perceive it. Such response may involve answering open-ended questions in class: What does this mean for you? How can you use it? It may be applying mathematical concepts in new contexts. It may be a science investigation that goes beyond class discussions and demonstrations. It may involve writing an essay, doing a project, or making an object. As teachers we ask initial questions. We provide guidance and incentive for thinking and exploration to continue when needed. We recommend resource materials.

At the same time, especially in the transcendence phase, students need to share in choosing and planning their responses. Enable them to capitalize on using and developing their unique gifts. Encourage them to use not only conventional but also new, expressive representations. Support them in creating new perspectives of seeing and responding to God's Word and world. Writing and painting, for instance, are means through which students refine and transcend the reformulation phase. Students may also share or teach their knowledge to others.

Inventive learners do well in this phase of learning. They are able to compose and fashion products with imagination, using learned concepts in singular and original ways. They enrich reality and animatedly try out new possibilities. As teachers we stir interests, make suggestions, guide thinking, and evaluate products. On the whole, however, inventive learners want to learn by themselves. They take their own initiatives, and develop ideas on their own.

♦ *The coastal forest unit has far more transcendence activities than students in a particular class can do. Of the fifteen learning activities on the role of government management of the forest, the whole class does three or four activities that involve the first three phases of learning. Individual or small groups of students then choose several others. (Having a choice helps to make those chosen personally meaningful.) Most of these activities include several phases of learning besides transcendence. For example, "Debate the statement: The only good wolf is a dead wolf," asks students to read a book and see some videotapes (setting the stage and disclosure), identifying and analyzing the issues (reformulation), and responding personally to them (transcendence). Other parts of the unit suggest meaningful transcendence products that will appeal to students with different interests and abilities. Students may write or give reports. They may write psalms similar to Psalm 104 using forest creatures. They may draw a scale diagram of a model garden landscaped with plants native to the forest, or experiment*

*with different kinds and cuts of wood from the forest and inves-
tigating their use.*

A model for meaningful learning

The four-phase model of learning described in the previous section
is summarized in Figure 4.3. The model assumes several Biblically
based premises:

♦ *students are responsive and unique images of God.*

♦ *knowledge entails far more than learning concepts. Knowledge
involves dispositions and commitment. It intends to lead to
service.*

♦ *the dimensions of teaching embody guidance through unfolding, structuring, and enabling.*

Note that the *type* of structuring tends to differ in the four phases of
learning. As learning moves from the first to the second phase, the
learning activities become more teacher-directed. As it moves
toward transcendence, the classroom structure allows for more
student initiative and choice. Also, while the four components of
teaching occur in all four phases, there is more emphasis on unfolding in the first two, and more on enabling in the last two.

The four-phase model of learning does not put teachers and students into a straitjacket. Rather, it allows them to use the flexibility
and freedom in teaching and learning that God provides in their
particular situation. You can use a great variety of strategies and
techniques in each phase. Your choice depends on the subject
material, your personality, the nature of the class, and the time
available. While some types of learners seem to "fit" into one
quadrant better than the others, there is no precise one-to-one
correspondence. Students never exhibit learning characteristics
solely in one category. Moreover, each phase of learning can include some activities that are suitable for each type of learner.

Further, despite a natural rhythm, the phases described do not
necessarily always follow each other sequentially, nor are they
always given equal weight. The phases also operate at different
levels. In the whole school curriculum, we gradually move through
the years from a greater emphasis on setting the stage and reformulation to more on disclosure and transcendence. In particular
courses, early units may set the stage, with later ones stressing

transcendence. Each unit, if well designed, has a cycle that moves from setting the stage to disclosure and from reformulation to transcendence. And, in a more limited way, many lessons quickly set the stage, involve some disclosure and reformulation, and at least hint at some transcendence. Thus the phases may overlap, occur in a variety of forms, and not always follow each other in exact sequence.

What is important, however, is that teachers deliberately plan learning to include all four phases of learning. Provide an adequate, experientially based setting. Accompany disclosure with a variety of reformulation activities that help students assimilate and reinforce new concepts. Give students opportunities to transcend the precision learning by applying their learning to new situations and responding in their own distinctive ways.

Traditional schools have emphasized Phases 2 and 3, downplaying Phases 1 and 4. As a result, often learning did not become personally meaningful. Constructivist approaches, on the other hand, easily overemphasize Phases 1 and 4, with students not sufficiently developing an understanding and appreciation of our cultural heritage, or clear conceptual frameworks that they need to function well in society. Regular inclusion of all four phases is most likely to lead students to knowledgeable, insightful, reflective, and committed involvement and action.

◆ACTIVITY 4-9

Choose a unit topic and suggest learning activities for each of the four phases of learning. Discuss whether each activity also suits the type of learner that, according to the previous sections, "fits" that particular phase. If not, why not?

Now consider two or three specific class periods in the unit. Which phases if learning would be included in each period? Is it possible to include all four phases of learning? Is it desirable? Why or why not?

◆ACTIVITY 4-10

Is the structure of the chapters of this book effective in recognizing the four phases of learning? Should textbooks be written to
take into account the four phases, or should they focus on disclosure, with instructors providing activities for the other three
phases?

Multiple intelligences

Howard Gardner argues that persons possess eight different types of
intelligences. These are the *verbal-linguistic, logical-mathematical,
visual-spatial, bodily-kinesthetic, musical-rhythmic, interpersonal-
social, intrapersonal-introspective,* and *naturalist-physical world.*
Most students, he claims, develop some intelligences highly, other
modestly, and the rest hardly at all. The intelligences are only
slightly interdependent. Gardner indicates that there may be other
intelligences that still need to be verified (such as spiritual and
intuitive intelligence). Also, controversy exists about whether the
bodily-kinesthetic and intrapersonal categories are actual intelligences. Further, students' intelligences and how they use them
shift, grow and vary over time (Hatch 1997, p. 28).

What becomes clear from Gardner's theory, nevertheless, is that
learning is complex and needs to take into account not only students' learning style preferences, but also the intelligences or ways
of knowing they favor. Gardner's followers reject the question,
"How smart are you?" They replace it with, "How are you smart?"
That is, they rightly point out that all students have specific gifts of
intelligence. They then design learning to take into account the
diversity of intelligences and to enable students to capitalize on
their strengths. Gardner's work reminds us that teachers need to
celebrate diverse patterns of intelligence gifts. They need to try to
arrange learning contexts where students feel free to develop their
personal ones.

Because the relationship between learning styles and Gardner's
intelligences is as yet unclear, most curriculum planners take into
account either a certain learning style categorization, or Gardner's
intelligences, but not both (but for one interesting attempt to do so,
see Silver, Strong and Perini 1997). As we have seen, the four

phase model of learning relates closely to learning styles, not to modes of knowing. However, the curriculum planning chart in the next chapter includes twelve aspects of reality, and most of these reflect a mode of knowing that links to one or two of Gardner's intelligences. In other words, using the curriculum planning chart together with the four- phase model of learning should mean that you use strategies that suit a wide diversity of students.

◆ACTIVITY 4-11

This section is too brief to do justice to Howard Gardner's work. If you are interested in pursuing his theory and its classroom application, look up one or two of the following books: Armstrong (1994), Fogarty & Stoehr (1995), Weber (1995), or Fogarty (1997), or the September 1997 issue of *Educational Leadership*. Weber's book applies the theory at the high school level. As you read, ask yourself about the strengths and weaknesses of the approach. For instance, do the authors have in mind basic aims other than the promotion of diverse intelligences?

Meaningful learning

Meaningful learning does not just happen in the classroom. It presupposes careful planning. It doesn't occur by just following a textbook or by providing learning activities. As a teacher you must consider all aspects of the learning environment. Take into account the characteristics and needs of individual students and of the whole class. Consider the community and governmental context of the school. Be sensitive to students' experiential backgrounds, developmental levels, preferred modes of knowing and learning styles. Plan for the phases of learning and motivating students. Reflect on the positive and negative effects your own personality may have on the learning atmosphere.

For meaningful learning to occur, create a classroom atmosphere where students feel secure enough to take risks in the course of their learning. Recognize students for the contributions they can make to the learning community. Encourage reciprocal trust, respect, and responsibility. Further, as described in chapter 5, give the learning content a clear focus for your courses, units, and individual lessons.

Even with all this in place, learning will be successful in helping students be responsive disciples only to the extent that the Holy Spirit takes hold of you and your students and enlivens both. When that happens, learning will truly enable your students and you to walk in God's truth with undivided hearts (Ps 86:11).

◆ACTIVITY 4-12

This chapter has not said anything about the place of technology in learning. Yet the use of computers and other technologies has become common in the schools. Make a list of the types of technologies that are frequently used in the classroom. In what phase(s) of learning can each be used most effectively? Why? Consider the advantages and disadvantages of the use of each type of technology. Ask questions such as the following:

◆ *In what ways can the technology contribute to meaningful learning? Is the technology being used effectively in classrooms with which you are familiar? Why or why not?*

◆ *In what ways is the technology changing learning and the curriculum? What are the positive and negative aspects of such changes?*

◆ *Could the funds spent on the technology be spent in more effective ways? Are there times when less or no technology better?*

◆ *Is the technology available equally to schools in diverse socioeconomic neighborhoods? What are the implications?*

◆ *How does the technology enhance communication? In what way does it curtail meaningful communication?*

Reviewing the main points

1. *Metaphors* that look at learners as blank slates, trainable objects, unfolding plants, and primary agents of social change contain some kernels of truth but give limiting representations.

2. *Learners are images of God.* They are total, integrated, uniquely gifted, and responsible and accountable beings. Sin affects all humans, but within an atmosphere of supportive security, most learners will contribute to the classroom community in a special way.

3. *Learning must take into account the learners' developmental phases, motivational needs, modes of knowing, and learning styles.* A model that helps teachers plan involves four phases of learning: setting the stage, disclosure, reformulation, and transcendence.

REFERENCES

Armstrong, T. 1987. *In their own way: Discovering and encouraging your child's personal learning style.* Los Angeles: J. P. Tarcher.

Armstrong, T. 1994. *Multiple intelligences in the classroom.* Alexandria, VA: Assoc. for Supervision & Curriculum Development.

Caine, R. & G. Caine. 1997. *Education on the edge of possibility.* Alexandria, VA: ASCD.

Egan, K. 1983. *Education and psychology: Plato, Piaget and scientific psychology.* New York: Teachers College Press.

Egan, K. 1997. *The educated mind: How cognitive tools shape our understanding.* Chicago: University of Chicago Press.

Fennema, J. 1977, 1996. *Nurturing children in the Lord.* Sioux Center: Dordt College Press.

Fogarty, R. 1997. *Problem-based learning: Other curriculum models for the multiple intelligences classroom.* Palatine, IL: IRI/Skylight.

Fogarty, R. & J. Stoehr. 1995. *Integrating curricula with multiple intelligences: Teams, themes, and threads.* Palatine, IL: IRI/Skylight.

Good, T. & J. Brophy. 1994. *Looking in classrooms.* 6th ed. New York: HarperCollins.

Hatch, T. 1997. Getting specific about multiple intelligences. *Educational Leadership* 54(6): 26-29.

Keefe, J. *Profiling and utilizing learning style.* Reston, VA: National Association of Secondary School Principals.

Kolb, D. *Experiential learning: Experience as the source of learning and development.* Englewood Cliffs, NJ: Prentice-Hall.

McCarthy, B. 1981. *The 4MAT system: Teaching to learning styles with right/left mode techniques.* Barrington, IL: Excel.

McCarthy, B. 1997. A tale of four learners: 4MAT's learning styles. *Educational Leadership* 54(6): 46-51.

Seerveld, C. 1980. *Rainbows for a fallen world.* Toronto: Tuppence.

Silver, H., R. Strong & M. Perini. 1997. Integrating learning styles and multiple intelligences. *Educational Leadership* 55(1):22-27.

Steensma, G. & H. Van Brummelen (eds.). 1977. *Shaping school curriculum: A Biblical view.* Terre Haute, IN: Signal.

Weber, E. 1995. *Creative learning from inside out.* Vancouver: EduServ.

Whitehead, A. 1929. *The aims of education and other essays.* New York: Macmillan.

Chapter 5

SHAPING CURRICULUM

*I*n a unit on trees, Mr. Traditionalist asks his students to
learn, reproduce and apply knowledge about trees. He
presents details about the parts of trees and their functions. He
explains the process of photosynthesis, and how humans have
classified trees. He asks them to think critically about abstrac-
tions related to classification. He thoroughly discusses the properties of trees in diverse biomes and how each suits its
environment. He regularly checks whether his students have
grasped the content. He largely ignores how the study of trees
relates to his students' own lives or to life in society. For him,
personal commitment is not a part of learning. He ensures that
he "covers" the science curriculum. His students must thoroughly know the facts and concepts listed in the prescribed curriculum guide.

   Ms. Constructivist, on the other hand, holds that students'
intellectual processes are all-important. Her students learn to
construct knowledge themselves. Her role as a teacher is to facilitate inquiry and problem solving. What *she teaches is not as
important as* how *her students construct personally meaningful
knowledge, including their own values. She asks her students
what they want to learn about trees. She then helps them develop
strategies to answer their questions. One group of students experiments to see how much a branch will bend when they hang
various weights from it. They try to establish a relationship between bending and branch thickness. Another group tries to
come up with a tree classification schema based on their observations of trees. A third group decides to investigate how trees
and forests affect their personal lives. Ms. Constructivist wants
her students to engage actively in diverse learning activities

where they construct knowledge. That is more important, she believes, than students learning a common body of concepts about trees. Her students are to become self-directed learners who choose their own meaning and values.

Ms. Critique prepares her students to serve the interests of society, especially by analyzing social phenomena. She stresses the economic, political, social and ecological aspects of trees and forests. Forests are webs of life that humans have used but, more often, abused. Who controls the power levers with respect to the use of forests? Who allows clear-cut logging or the destruction of all trees in an area in order to build a subdivision or shopping mall? What are the climatic and social changes occurring because of the destruction of forests? Not only Ms. Critique's content but also her classroom structure differs from that of Mr. Traditionalist and Ms. Constructivist. Ms. Critique wants her students to become critical agents of social change. She therefore involves them in field trips, debates, and projects that make them critically aware and able to respond to what is happening in their communities.

Christian teachers, both in public and Christian schools, have often accepted common approaches to curriculum without carefully analyzing their worldview roots. As a result, their teaching has not fully reflected a Biblical view of knowledge. That is true, for instance, for the traditionalist, constructivist, and critical theory orientations illustrated above.

That does not mean that Christian educators cannot learn from such orientations. Students ought to become familiar with basic concepts and use them to think clearly about reality. They also need opportunities to investigate and explore, and to test their ideas and interpretations against those of others. Further, if students are to be responsive disciples of Jesus Christ, they need to become active in applying Biblical principles to all areas of life and culture. Yet the three teachers described all fall short in providing the balance and structure suggested by a Biblical approach to learning and teaching.

A number of groundings determine how persons look at and plan school curriculum. Your *worldview*–your basic beliefs, assumptions, values, priorities, and biases–undergird how you view curriculum. This chapter develops an approach to curriculum based on Biblical views of knowledge, persons, and values. Because today we often see tugs-of-war between traditionalist and constructivist approaches, we will first look more closely at them. [My book *Steppingstones to Curriculum: A Biblical View* (1994) deals more extensively with the topics in this chapter.]

◆ACTIVITY 5-1

We seldom find curriculum orientations in their "pure" form in the classroom. Teachers often use aspects of several orientations, depending on the subject matter, school and community expectations, and the nature of their class. Yet most teachers lean more toward one than to others. Assuming that Mr. Traditionalist, Ms. Constructivist, and Ms. Critique usually teach as indicated, outline the strengths and weaknesses of each approach. If you had to choose just one of these three approaches, which would you choose? Why?

Traditionalism and constructivism

What we think of as traditional education is, paradoxically, the result of what is often referred to as modernism. The underlying faith that sustains modernism is faith in the triumph of technology over nature and in economic and social progress. Schools exist to enable students to play meaningful roles in an ever-improving society. This is done by carefully sequencing skill and knowledge learning, applying educational research results, using new technologies, and testing frequently to ensure content mastery.

This type of approach has led to difficulties, however. Learning seldom takes place in linear fashion. True, carefully structured, step-by-step teaching and learning strategies may improve test scores temporarily. But often they do so without taking into account long-term effects or the basic purpose and nature of schooling. They may suit the needs of certain students. But they frustrate many others who learn better in different ways.

Traditionalists focus on the transmission of knowledge and skills. They frequently teach as if students receive learning passively. Generalization, evaluation, and application may stay at a low level. Often traditional education fails to address the ecological, social, ethical and spiritual problems that affect students and society.

Throughout the 20th century, educators have suggested alternatives to traditional education. Many have implemented more child-centered approaches that, they hoped, would overcome the shortcomings of traditionalism. The most common alternative as I wrote this book was *constructivism*. Constructivism proposes pedagogical strategies that actively involve students. It gives them a meaningful voice in their learning. Students experience and participate in reflective and creative activities. Teachers, rather than supplying information, facilitate independent learning. They coordinate and critique student constructions. They lead learners to dialogue and explore and generate many possibilities. They do so through challenging, open-ended investigations, especially of problems and contradictions. The students themselves play an active role in selecting and defining learning activities. Constructivism recognizes that students in the same classroom learn different things, and interpret what they learn differently (Fosnot 1996; Van Brummelen 1997).

While this may sound attractive, few constructivist teachers realize the theoretical basis or the practical pitfalls of constructivism. Constructivism breaks radically with our Western–and Christian–tradition that knowledge can be gained through the senses and leads to pictures of the real world. It holds that humans do not *discover* knowledge or "read the book of nature." Rather, it claims that humans *construct* all knowledge. They do so either individually or through social interaction in order to cope with their experiences. Order in reality is arbitrary, imposed on the world by humanly constructed knowledge. That is what creates personal meaning and significance. No ultimate knowledge exists that is true for everyone.

In the classroom, therefore, learning begins with children's own ideas and explorations. Teachers seek and value learners' constructions, viewpoints, and solutions. Teachers support learning. They do not control it. They value meaningful activity over right answers. Indeed, there are no single right answers. There are only discrepancies that students may analyze and resolve in a variety of ways: "Right answers are not possible in a constructivist textbook. It goes against the philosophy" (Baker & Piburn 1997, p. xv; see also Steffe & Gale 1995). When students discuss a poem, each person's interpretation is valid. The study of literature is important not so much to understand important issues in life, but to help us develop tools for meaning making. We create our own reality, our own answers, our own values. For this, language is an important tool. But it does not transmit common meaning or concepts (Fosnot 1996, p. 7).

Moreover, there cannot be a general curriculum model because both teachers and students create and transform knowledge and meaning as learning takes place. Course outlines and unit plans are therefore indeterminate. The curriculum organizes itself from students' personal experiences and interests.

◆ACTIVITY 5-2

The last four paragraphs outline the basis of constructivism. Discuss how the worldview perspective at its basis leads to certain curriculum approaches. Now add other strengths and weaknesses to your list of Ms. Constructivist's classroom. To help you, here is an example of a constructivist unit:

A grade 7 teacher asks her class, "What is your greatest concern in the world?" and "What is your greatest fear?" Student answers range from "failing at school," "dying of AIDS," to "going to Hell." Most responses revolve around their own death. The teacher wants her curriculum to focus on "a desire to hear students' voices." She therefore has her students make a topical framework for a unit on death and dying. She asks them to answer, What will you study? How will you approach it? What materials will you use? What will be your responsibilities? The students choose novels that different groups will use. They decide on group and individual activities. Journal writing begins with the question, "What do you expect to learn in the next six weeks?" Students' own questions move the unit on (e.g., How has my past affected my future? Is there a heaven and a hell? Why do people choose to die?). The resulting projects are diverse in design and execution. Students arrive at their own conclusions in independent, self-directed ways. (McNeil 1995, pp. 8-9)

The foregoing unit on death and dying no doubt motivated students. It provided a forum for learning about important life issues. As such, much meaningful learning likely took place. Yet, if used often, this approach contains pitfalls. First, it takes an immense amount of time. Teachers must find suitable themes and activities that relate to and spark student interests. They must respond to the views of all students in open-minded and enriching ways. They let initial activities evolve into many different questions and investigations. They let students figure things out for themselves without giving explicit directions (Aurasian & Walsh 1997). Student interests may also severely truncate the scope of the curriculum or make it lopsided. Books and articles on constructivism generally limit themselves to examples of how teachers implement constructivist strategies. That is deliberate since the specific content is not as important as the process.

The basic problem with constructivism, however, is that the question of truth is no longer meaningful (Baker & Piburn 1997, p. 115). Since people construct their own knowledge and meaning, many possible realities exist. Ultimately, then, we no longer have to recognize common human bonds and values. The most we can say is that some constructions may be more feasible than others in a particular context and time. All personal choices are legitimate. One model of reality is as good as any other. Everyone can choose their own truth, their own meaning, their own way of life. Personal views replace authority and a sense of community.

What results is self-centered individualism and relativism. Constructivists reject the notion that universal norms and values govern life. Therefore they also implicitly reject the value of our cultural and Christian heritage. Many constructivists will admit that some student constructions are better than others. That, however, means that they apply certain standards. In other words, then they compromise their own basic tenets. Indeed, then they no longer give students full freedom to construct meaning for themselves. That is how constructivists ultimately contradict themselves.

Constructivists reject that there is a created reality governed by God-given laws for both physical reality and human interaction (Ps 19). They overlook the evidence that we live in a well-ordered reality, not one that results just from human construction. They ignore that there are universally held values such as integrity, respect, compassion, responsibility, and stewardship without which a democratic and just society cannot function. True, we develop descriptions and interpretations of such values as well as of our physical and social surroundings, both personally and communally.

And those are open to revision since our understandings are incomplete. Some interpretations are more right than others, however—and some can be shown to be false.

Finally, note that students do not always have to form their own "constructions" to be active learners. That is both too complex and too time-consuming. Teachers also need to *in*struct students about basic concepts and skills. They need to teach God-given universal values. And they can do so using strategies of active learning that constructivists try to co-opt for themselves!

In short, constructivists are right. Traditional education falls short. It does not do justice to specific classroom contexts nor to the diversity of unique students in those classrooms. But constructivism also fails. It does not allow teaching to define a common vision with a moral purpose that transcends personal construction of knowledge.

◆ACTIVITY 5-3

The foregoing section implies that there is no such thing as a neutral approach to curriculum planning. Do you agree or disagree? Why or why not? Give some specific examples to defend your view.

A Biblical view of knowledge and its implications

This section describes how a Biblical view of knowledge affects school programs in four ways:

♦ *Knowledge is rooted in God's revelation.*

♦ *Knowledge points to God's providence and marvelous deeds, and instructs us in His ways.*

♦ *Knowledge involves a person's whole being, not just the intellect.*

♦ *Knowledge leads to response, commitment, and service.*

"The fear of the Lord is the beginning of wisdom," says Solomon. The rest of Proverbs makes clear that knowledge, discernment, and wisdom are closely intertwined (Pr 1:7; 14:6; 24:3-4). Knowledge of God and of his riches and power comes through "the Spirit of wisdom and revelation" and the enlightenment of "the eyes of your heart" (Eph 1:17-19). Complete understanding comes about not just through reason and empirical evidence. We possess true knowledge only if the Spirit of Truth enlightens us (Jn 14:17).

The life of Samuel is instructive here. When God called Samuel in the night, Scripture says, "Now Samuel did not yet know the Lord" (1Sa 3:7). Samuel had already ministered before the Lord and found favor with Him (1Sa 2:18, 26; 3:1). He knew a great deal about God's attributes and what serving him entailed. Yet he "did not yet know the Lord." Why not? Scripture continues, "The word of the Lord had not yet been revealed to him." The end of the chapter makes clear that Samuel became a recognized leader after God's heart because God revealed himself to Samuel through his word, and Samuel acted on that word (1Sa 3:19-4:1).

God is the origin, sustainer and redeemer of all human knowledge. God reaches out with his Word and reveals himself to us. He does so through his created physical world (Ps 19:1-4), through his written Word (2Ti 3:15-17), through his Son (Jn 1), through special revelation (Ac 9), and through the mediation of other people (2Ti 3:14). God's revelation makes clear to us who he is and his calling to us. God calls us to be committed to use our thoughts, words, deeds, and affections to serve him and our neighbor obediently and responsively. True knowledge does not exclude or contradict reason and empirical evidence but becomes the ladder by which faith climbs higher and higher (Stott 1979, p. 67).

Knowledge in the Biblical sense reveals the praiseworthy deed of the Lord. It also reveals God's ways of righteousness. That is why Samuel in his farewell speech as civic leader of Israel said that he would continue to teach the Israelites the way that is good and right. He encouraged them at the same time to consider the great things God had done for them (1Sa 12:23-24). Our science, art, and history lessons must proclaim God's marvelous handiwork. At the same time, they must help and encourage children "to act justly and to love mercy and to walk humbly with their God" (Mic 6:8).

Scripture also makes clear that knowledge involves our whole being, not just our intellect. Knowledge is more than absorbing facts and concepts. In Hosea 4:6, for instance, God accuses his people of being destroyed from a lack of knowledge. That does not mean that they didn't know their Bible lessons or were school dropouts. Rather, they had rejected what they had learned. They ignored God's law of life. They were unfaithful to God and to each other. They failed to integrate their "mind knowledge" into their everyday life. Lack of knowledge in Scripture means a lack of commitment, a failure to put learning into practice.

Knowledge that does not include committed service is no more true knowledge than faith without works is true faith. God searches hearts and minds. He evaluates how we act on what we know (Rev 2:23; Jer 17:10). In the last five chapters of Job, God teaches Job that his knowledge was too cognitive, too intellectual. Job needed to transcend his conceptual learning, see the greatness of God, and respond with his heart. In school, the content we choose, how we think about situations and issues, and the attitudes and dispositions we engender through what and how we teach–all these must reflect our dedication to hear and do the Word of the Lord.

◆ACTIVITY 5-4

Discuss how the examples below illustrate (or fail to illustrate) the four marks of a Biblical view of knowledge described in this section.

♦ *Jason Szabo, in his grade 4 unit on weather and climate, shows that weather is not just part of closed-off, autonomous world of cause and effect. Rather, it functions in all aspects of created reality. His students learn how weather acts upon our environment and therefore on plants, animals, and human life. They discuss how weather affects people's feeling and moods. They explore how weather and climate influence transportation, human survival, and agriculture, as well as planning daily and seasonal life. Jason teaches the basics of the physical aspects of weather and climate. He does so, however, in a context that makes the topic personally meaningful for the students. At the end of the unit, his students make a large mural in the hall of the school that they call, "Living with our weather."*

♦ *Elaine Brouwer teaches a grade 6 unit called* The Book Company. *The students explore what the Bible says about God's norms for economic life. They use this to operate a book company that produces and markets a book. The students buy shares for ten cents each. They raise additional capital for materials by visiting and making a loan at a local bank. They decide the content of the*

*book. Elaine helps students see that a business intends to serve
people by making and selling things that help them, such as dura-
ble toys, healthy foods, and worthwhile books.*

*Once the students have decided the book's content, they col-
lect, write, edit, organize, typeset, and illustrate the material.
They design a cover and make plans to print and bind the books
themselves. They decide how many books they need to produce
and plan a marketing strategy. Elaine makes suggestions about
using resources responsibly. She guides them in setting the price:
businesses may make a profit but may not charge exorbitant
prices. At the end of the unit, the students decide how to divide
and use their profits. Throughout, Elaine stresses that if we
really try to serve God in business, we must love our customer as
ourselves. The students learn not only how a business operates,
but also how their attitudes and ways of going about business can
obey or disobey God's norms.*

Toward a Christian curriculum orientation

A Christian curriculum orientation finds its basis, first of all, in
three Biblical injunctions. First, God gave us His creation mandate
to care for and be stewards of the world (literally, to keep it holy!)
(Ge 1:28; 2:15; Ps 8:6-8). However, humans fell into sin, and no
longer ruled in the just and loving way God intended. God therefore
also gave us the Great Commandment to love him above all and our
neighbor as ourselves (Lk 10:27). Subsequently, Jesus "tasted death
for everyone" so that we could again take on God's calling (He 2).
Jesus specified as part of that calling his Great Commission. It
enjoins us to make disciples of all nations and teach them everything that he commanded us (Mt 28:18-20).

What do these injunctions mean for school curriculum? First,
schools emphasize focused learning to enable students to care for
their world. This learning includes cognitive content ("knowledge-
that") and abilities ("knowledge-how"), as well as problem-solving
and creative activities that are rooted in their own experiences.
Such learning helps students experience both the unity and diversity
of God's marvelous creation, and to see its relevance and application to life in society. Students also recognize that humans have
distorted God's creation mandate, and that the earth will not be
fully restored to God's original intent until Christ returns.

Secondly, the Great Commission demands that we confront students with the importance of committing their lives to Jesus Christ, and to recognize the implications. Together with our students, we explore what Jesus commanded us. That means we investigate a Christian vision of life as it relates both to personal and to societal issues and phenomena. We do not choose learning experiences just for the sake of attaining cognitive and ability outcomes. Our aim is to develop tendencies and dispositions that encourage students to believe, value, and act on the basis of the Biblical principles that Christ taught us. In the gospel of Matthew, for instance, Jesus promoted humility, mercy, generosity to the needy, peace, justice for the oppressed in society, forgiveness, and faithfulness to your

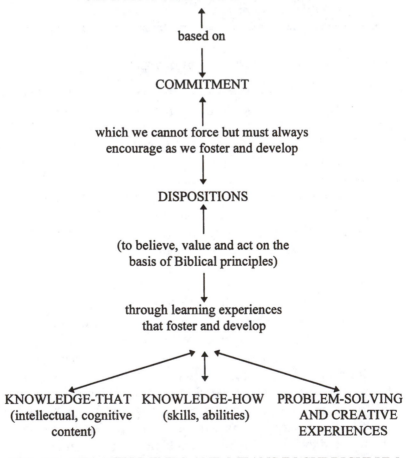

AIM: RESPONSIVE DISCIPLESHIP

↑

based on

↓

COMMITMENT

↑

which we cannot force but must always
encourage as we foster and develop

↓

DISPOSITIONS

↑

(to believe, value and act on the
basis of Biblical principles)

↓

through learning experiences
that foster and develop

KNOWLEDGE-THAT   KNOWLEDGE-HOW   PROBLEM-SOLVING
(intellectual, cognitive   (skills, abilities)   AND CREATIVE
content)   EXPERIENCES

FIG. 5.1. RELATING ENDS AND MEANS IN CURRICULUM

marriage partner. Such dispositions, in turn, foster a commitment which, if the Holy Spirit grants conversion and regeneration, en ables students to take on their God-given calling. In other words, in planning courses and units, we choose knowledge-that, knowledge-how, problem-solving and creative experiences as a means to an end–the ultimate end being responsive discipleship.

Finally, the Great Commandment indicates that students should not just learn *about* a Christian vision of life, but also *experience* it in the way teachers plan and implement learning activities. The curriculum makes clear what it means to love God and neighbor in strategic areas of society such as politics or business. But Biblical love also characterizes the classroom itself. Teachers give students meaningful responsibilities in a setting where they nurture respect and support. The curriculum helps students unfold their gifts to serve each other, to share their joys, and to bear each other's bur-dens. Teachers foster Christ-like learning communities.

A Christian approach to curriculum thus views the world as a place where God, through the power of his Spirit, calls his children. He calls them to be faithful in doing the truth, in reconciling what sin has distorted and ruined, and in influencing their neighbors and cultures. The curriculum shows that all creation proclaims its Creator. It equips students to respond to that Creator. Students acquire the discernment and abilities necessary for standing in the world as dissenters and reformers. Graduates should be able to offer fundamental critiques of secular society, its institutions, and its values.

Moreover, a Christian curriculum orientation fosters knowledge that leads students to active service. Students relate to others. They develop a Christian lifestyle. They serve society without compro-mising their commitment. They develop their abilities and insights in order to become vibrant Christians as family members, friends, consumers, workers, citizens, and church members. They learn and experience the rightful place of science and technology, leisure and labor, communications and aesthetics, and justice and love.

In all learning, teachers model that submission to the Lord is the beginning of wisdom. That is the starting point for the focused learning that takes place in the classroom. Christian teachers do their planning while wearing the "spectacles of Scripture." The knowledge they teach points their students in the ways of the Lord.

Then, by God's grace, students' knowledge will become heart knowledge, used for Christian service and action.

=====

◆ACTIVITY 5-5

Discuss in what ways the examples below exemplify a Christian curriculum orientation. Are there any changes and/or additions you would make? Why or why not?

♦ *In a grade 4 unit in trees, students first explore and learn to appreciate trees as an essential part of the whole of God's plan in creation. They observe the function of trees in their own lives, as well as in the life of their communities. They investigate what products we obtain from trees, and their role in soil enrichment and conservation, water control, and oxygen replenishment. They also investigate how forests provide a home for wildlife and other plants. In the disclosure phase of learning, they learn about ecosystems with different trees, tree classification, parts of trees and their functions, the growth and reproduction of trees, and tree diseases. The students then use this background knowledge to investigate how humans have used trees and forests. They conclude by considering human and their personal responsibility as stewards of God's creation. Using the norms found in texts such as Deuteronomy 20:19-20, they seek Christian answers to social issues involving trees. They write some local politicians about the results of their investigation and reflection..*

♦ *A grade 11 and 12 week-long mini-course makes students aware of stewardship and lifestyle responsibilities. They learn about transportation, land use and shelter, food and nutrition, clothing and appearance, and time and leisure. By studying specific issues in everyday situations, the students explore and experience what it means to respond positively to God's Word for stewardly living.*

The students begin to realize that Christians do not have all the answers to the many problems faced by our technological culture. But they begin to ask penetrating questions. They make everyday decisions using God's Word to guide them in stewardly use of time, talents, and resources. By the end of the week, the students critique their own lifestyle and explore some positive alternatives. Through a hunger awareness dinner, they learn to understand that our personal and communal decisions affect people throughout the world. They also plan and experience a Christian celebration. The unit clarifies some important components of a Christian vision of life.

◆ACTIVITY 5-6

In a one or two page statement, outline your own personal curriculum orientation. Don't just copy the ideas presented in the last section, but think through what *you* believe!

The teacher as curriculum planner

◆ *Wilbur Kowalski, a high school social studies teacher, spends several weeks each August planning for the next school year. He updates his yearly overviews, organizes the first unit of each course in detail, and plans for the use of new resource materials. If he is dissatisfied with last year's outcomes of a unit, or if he feels that the same approach may result in tedium, he revises it as well. Most years, he also joins other teachers in preparing a multi-disciplinary unit (such as the role of technology in culture), in sponsoring a field trip, or in planning a combined major assignment (such as a research paper for social studies and English).*

Wilbur's careful planning contributes to students appreciating his teaching. His textbooks do not determine his program. Rather, he sets intended learning outcomes that fit the school's aims. He chooses learning activities and resources accordingly. He tries to meet the needs of students with different abilities and learning styles. He uses a variety of resources: textbooks, reference books, articles from magazines and newspapers, audiovisual materials, and CD-ROMs. In most classes as well as on tests he challenges his students to think critically and explore causal relationships.

It took Wilbur a number of years before he felt satisfied with his organization and planning. During his first year or two of teaching, he made extensive use of outlines and textbooks that were available in his school. He just did not have enough time to do justice to his long-term planning. He kept up his day-to-day work conscientiously. Often, however, his courses and units did not fully attain his goals. But gradually, he was able to choose, adapt, organize, and prepare his teaching and learning activities more deliberatively. He set out to develop several units for each course each year.

Today, while Wilbur feels "on top" of his teaching, he still works at least 50 hours per week. He has developed a personal schedule that usually enables him to do his day-to-day planning and evaluation before and after school and on Saturday mornings. It was not until he had several years of experience and had learned to use his time well before and after school, however, that Wilbur was able to leave most evenings free for his family and other responsibilities and interests.

Curriculum is a dynamic, ever-changing series of planned learning activities. It is framed by basic worldview beliefs as well as by the context of the school: its socioeconomic makeup, government expectations, and so on. Nevertheless, the curriculum constantly changes as teachers re-interpret, revise and adapt programs as they implement them. Different teachers interpret the formal government or school district curriculum differently. And students in a classroom experience it differently again. Governments and school boards intend certain curricula to be taught. Schools and teachers revise these as they plan implementation. And the actual attained curriculum differs from the planned one.

While planning your program, keep in mind your overall goals, but revise your plans as you teach. Capitalize on unexpected opportunities ("teachable moments"). Adjust as needs arise. Your intents and planned learning activities will change as you organize, implement, and evaluate classroom learning. Curriculum is not a static document that gives rigid step-by-step formulas. It is more like a dynamic organism such as an ameba that keeps its basic identity but constantly changes as it moves to fit particular circumstances.

Published curriculum documents are *guides* only. They keep you on track as you plan to provide a balanced program. You yourself bear the final responsibility for your classroom planning, however. Of course, you do so within a given framework. But the most crucial curriculum planning takes place at the school and classroom levels.

Jesus himself holds you responsible for what you teach. He graphically warns persons against causing little ones to sin (Lk 17:2). Teachers may do so, for instance, by teaching content that hinders children from knowing and doing the truth. Jesus reminds us that teachers of the law are like stewards who produce from their storerooms new treasures as well as old (Mt 13:52). You are a "teacher of the law." God calls you to teach his laws that undergird his creation order and his precepts for life. Jesus instructs you to teach what is worth learning, things both old and new. Children learn the old that is legitimately time-honored. They also re-order, analyze, and refine new insights and knowledge, however. Like the traditionalists, Jesus fully upholds eternal truths. Like the constructivists, he also wants us to help students discover and explore new knowledge and how it affects contemporary society.

In short, Jesus expects teachers to choose and design and adapt curriculum with care. You depend, of course, on the work and insight of other educators. You cannot yourself develop or even analyze all curricula. Work to implement programs that point children to the Kingdom of heaven. Refer back regularly to your overall aims of schooling to see whether your more specific planning relates to those aims. Don't expect ever to reach perfection, but improve your program each year. "Those who hope in the Lord will renew their strength . . . they will run and not grow weary" (Isa 40:3).

◆ACTIVITY 5-7

In view of Wilbur Kowalski's experiences, discuss how teachers, especially new ones, can use their available time best to plan their daily and long-term program. Is Wilbur's approach a good one? How would you change it to satisfy your personal traits and preferences?

Planning classroom units

As a teacher, you likely plan your curriculum at four different levels. First, you develop yearly overviews for each subject or time block. Such outlines generally contain overall goals, topics and skills, main resources, a time line, and general methods of assessment and evaluation. At a second level, you plan "units" that may take anywhere from one week to two or even three months. These usually focus on a particular theme. Third, you do your daily preparation and lesson planning within the framework of your yearly and unit plans. Finally, you make on-the-spot decisions as you teach on the basis of student reactions or flashes of insight.

It is probably at the unit level that your planning best comes to grips with implementing a Christian vision of life (or another worldview). Such units should be *integral* ones in that they possess internal unity. That is, give your units a clear rationale or thematic statement that contains the key idea(s) toward which you direct all thought and activity. Make such a statement reflect Biblical norms and thinking. Ensure that each learning activity supports one or more of the unit's learning outcomes. If you do this, your students will see more clearly the central thrust of the unit. They will be more likely to respond personally and commit themselves to live by what they have learned. Without internal unity, a unit becomes a sequence of possibly interesting but disjointed or even purposeless activities.

Units should also be *integrated* ones. That is, avoid dealing with concepts in isolated, fragmented fashion. Rather, seek out significant, natural interrelations that exist between the unit's central concepts and subject disciplines that are not the unit's main focus. You then help students experience the wholeness of life and how different dimensions of life affect each other. Situations in everyday life are usually multifaceted. Building bridges in this way helps children analyze phenomena holistically even when the topic involves several disciplines.

Before writing a thematic statement and learning outcomes for a unit, you want to think about its scope. What concepts, skills, and values do you want students to learn? Make a webbing diagram or complete a planning chart such as the one shown. The planning chart is a working document that you can use in four ways. First, use its suggested key values as a starting point to choose those you want to include in your unit. Second, consider which abilities and skills you want your students to learn. Indicate them in the appropriate categories. Third, check which "aspects" of reality relate to your topic in a natural way. For some, it may be only two or three; for others, eight or nine. Finally, you have no doubt already thought

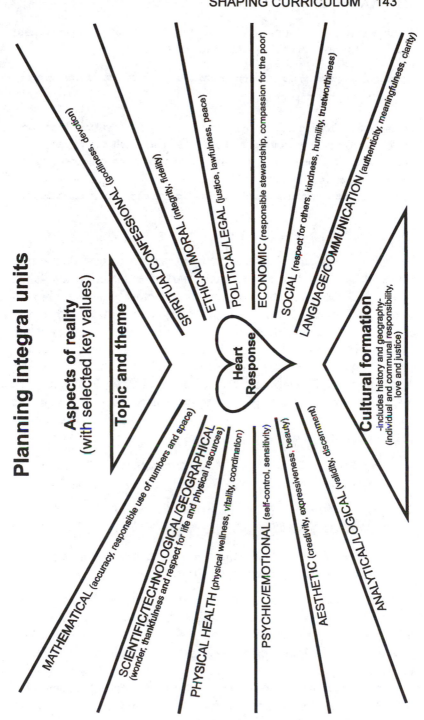

Planning integral units

Aspects of reality
(with selected key values)

Topic and theme

Cultural formation
--includes history and geography--
(individual and communal responsibility,
love and justice)

Heart Response

SPIRITUAL/CONFESSIONAL (godliness, devotion)

ETHICAL/MORAL (integrity, fidelity)

POLITICAL/LEGAL (justice, lawfulness, peace)

ECONOMIC (responsible stewardship, compassion for the poor)

SOCIAL (respect for others, kindness, humility, trustworthiness)

LANGUAGE/COMMUNICATION (authenticity, meaningfulness, clarity)

MATHEMATICAL (accuracy, responsible use of numbers and space)

SCIENTIFIC/TECHNOLOGICAL/GEOGRAPHICAL
(wonder, thankfulness and respect for life and physical resources)

PHYSICAL HEALTH (physical wellness, vitality, coordination)

PSYCHIC/EMOTIONAL (self-control, sensitivity)

AESTHETIC (creativity, expressiveness, beauty)

ANALYTICAL/LOGICAL (validity, discernment)

if some suitable learning activities. Insert them in the appropriate "spokes" on the chart so you don't forget them.

◆ACTIVITY 5-8

Complete a planning chart for a topic at the grade level you teach or intend to teach. You may want to use your photocopier to expand the chart from the book. This activity is best done as you brainstorm with three or four people.

Thematic Statements

Usually it is not necessary to start from scratch in planning a unit. You will have various resource units and other materials available. It is useful, however, before looking too closely at available resources, to complete your own planning chart and compose your own thematic statement. In this way you will put your own stamp on the unit. You are then more likely to meet your intended learning outcomes. Your thematic statement indicates the main values, dispositions, and commitments that you want to foster. It gives the major concepts and skills you want your students to acquire and the creative experiences in which they will participate. Sometimes it helps to ask the following questions:

♦ *What did God intend for the particular area of creation or society that we will investigate?*

♦ *How have sinful humans distorted this intent? How does God want us to respond?*

♦ *How can this unit contribute to a deeper understanding of and commitment to a Christian way of life?*

Consider, for example, a grade 5 or 6 unit on government. Its main theme is that God intends governments to render justice and allow citizens in society to exercise responsibility in an atmosphere of peace and freedom. Regrettably, governments have often abused their power. Corruption may exist. Leaders may have seized undue powers. They may let people carry out unjust economic or unethical acts. They may limit basic freedoms. God calls Christians to witness to government leaders about what it means to rule with justice and righteousness. They also need to obey lawful authorities. This unit should therefore help students begin to take on their role as citizens who contribute to their nation according to the Biblical guidelines and values that relate to life in society:

♦ *God instituted government in order to preserve order and harmony in our society. The task of governments is therefore to provide and coordinate services that (1) promote and develop justice, (2) uphold good, and (3) restrain and punish evil caused by brokenness and sin on society. God calls Christians to be responsible citizens who strive for just laws and who obey governing authorities. In this unit students learn about the three levels of democratically elected governments and their respective tasks: federal, state or provincial, and local. The students also investigate why and how governments raise funds for their services. Finally, they explore some current political issues and present their views on one to a political leader.*

One more example. Business and government uses statistics regularly to make decisions. Statistics gives us powerful tools to collect and analyze data. It is often applied and used, however, in questionable ways. For example, government leaders may decide an issue on the basis of fickle public opinion rather than trying to guide opinion in order to be able to do what is right and just. Statistics can also be used to distort reality, for instance, by asking leading questions in surveys. God wants us to gather and apply statistics in ethically responsible ways, and base decisions on aesthetic, social and moral factors that go beyond statistics:

♦ *In a grade 11 unit on statistics students experience how statistics is used to gather and interpret large quantities of numerical data. They read and draw statistical graphs. They calculate averages and standard deviations. They use sampling techniques, and explore normal distributions and their uses. They discern underlying patterns and trends and how to draw conclusions from them. The students examine how statistical analyses and conclusions are applied in various everyday situations. They investigate how statistics is used as a foundation to make economic, social and political decisions. The unit shows that statistics can be used in both ethically responsible and irresponsible ways. The students design a project in which they use and apply statistics in a relevant setting.*

◆ACTIVITY 5-9

Write a thematic statement for the unit topic you chose in Activity 5-8.

Learning Outcomes

Once you have written a thematic statement, you prepare your intended learning outcomes. Some of these you write yourself. Others you select or modify from curriculum guides and available units. Learning outcomes elaborate your thematic statement and further articulate what you intend your students to learn. They provide direction for choosing learning activities and resources, and for the nature and means of your student assessment and evaluation.

Learning outcomes have different emphases. Some focus on *cognitive knowledge*; some on *abilities* (mental or physical); some on *solving problems* (which is also an ability); and some on *creative experiences* where the specific outcome may be uncertain. Note that all of these may take place at varying levels of complexity. There should be cognitive knowledge objectives, for instance, at the recall and comprehension, the interpretation and simple application, and the complex application and evaluation levels. Learning, in other words, should be well balanced. It should not overemphasize recall and comprehension.

Learning outcomes should not be so general that they do little but restate your thematic statement. Nor should they be so specific that you get swamped in details. The latter problem can occur with performance outcomes that reflect a reductionistic view of learning and a deterministic view of the person ("the student will identify at least three deciduous and five coniferous trees in the coastal forest").

Here is a set of learning outcomes for a grade 1 unit on the seasons. They are categorized into three general ones, each with several related more specific ones.

It is the intent of the unit that students will:

1. **Recognize that God provides seasons with special conditions.**
   a) *Identify the four seasons in their order.*

    b) *Observe God's faithfulness in the reliable order of the seasons.*

    c) *Contrast weather conditions in different seasons, both locally and elsewhere in the world.*

2. **Investigate the effects of seasons on the local area.**

    a) *Determine which special days and events occur in each season.*

    b) *Investigate how seasons affect water, plants, animals and humans in the local area.*

    c) *Find out how and why the length of days and nights changes with the seasons.*

    d) *Observe how the colors of nature change with the seasons.*

    e) *Survey how the seasons affect the food we eat.*

3. **Recognize that each season gives unique opportunities to enjoy and work in God's world.**

    a) *Share and record why people like (or do not like) winter, spring, summer and fall.*

    b) *Enjoy poetry, art, songs, drama, and music related to the seasons.*

    c) *Identify how the seasons affect the bodies, clothes, and activities of children and their parents.*

    d) *Share seasonal activities, and delight in doing some of them together as a class.*

    e) *Make a scrapbook about what they have learned about the seasons.*

◆ACTIVITY 5-10

Check whether this set of intended learning outcomes provides a balance of different types of outcomes. Can you suggest any improvements?

Now write a set of intended learning outcomes for the topic you have been working on in this chapter. If available, compare yours with those given for this topic in a curriculum guide or in a teacher resource unit.

Choosing and organizing learning experiences

Once you have defined your intents, you are ready to develop and choose learning activities. Probably you already had many activities in mind, and your sources will give you additional ideas.

There is no "right" way to organize activities. Some teachers list activities in the order in which they plan to use them, checking afterwards whether all outcomes have been "covered" (and whether some activities go beyond the outcomes). Others prefer to develop activities relating to each objective in turn, adding broader intro-ductory and concluding activities. Some teachers write out the activities below each other. Others structure each page into three vertical columns: intended learning outcomes; learning activities; materials and resources. Develop a format with which you are comfortable.

Include the development of appropriate skills in your units. In units that focus on social studies and science you can easily incor-porate language arts, art and music, and, on occasion, mathematical skill development. As much as possible, make skill learning an integral part of your units. You can use skill development checklists in language arts and mathematics. While studying a novel unit you might incorporate the teaching of certain composition skills as well as the identification and use of adjectives. However, you will still need to set aside a regular daily time period for systematic skill development and reinforcement. Don't, however, let skill instruc-tion become the main focus of learning. If you do, schooling be-comes mechanical training.

Once you have what you believe to be an effective set of learn-ing activities, check or recheck a number of things:

♦ *Do you have activities for each learning outcome? Have you included effective introductory and concluding activities?*

♦ *Did you include activities for all four phases of learning and for students with different learning styles? Are there recall, in-terpretation, application, and more open-ended problem solv-ing and creative activities? Have you balanced whole class, small group, and individual activities?*

♦ *Do you like the overall order and structure of the unit? Do the activities flow well from one set of learning activities to the next? Is the unit unified in direction and perspective?*

♦ *Are your expectations high but realistic for your particular class?*

♦ *Have you included a time schedule? Student assessment strategies? (for the latter, see chapter 6)*

♦ACTIVITY 5-11

For the unit topic that you chose, design an introductory activity that sets the stage and a concluding activity that pulls together the main unit's theme.

Now develop or find activities that emphasize recall, skill reinforcement, interpretation, application, and more open-ended problem solving and creative activities. Again, use available curriculum guides or resource units. For your topic, what would be a good balance of these types of activities?

Suppose you planned your unit for a four week time period. Under what circumstances and to what extent might you deviate from your planned time framework?

Choosing and using resources

The resource materials you choose should contribute to your learning outcomes. Textbooks and other available resources should not determine your teaching content or your methods, however. Resources are tools, not masters. True, your learning activities sometimes depend on the resources you have available. But as a teacher *you* decide when, where, and which curriculum materials contribute to your intended learning outcomes goals.

Carefully consider the appropriateness of materials for your classroom. Some books promote ethical relativism. These suggest that students should choose their own values. Science books usually present an evolutionary explanation of human origins and development. They also often assume that through science and technology we control our destiny. Christian textbooks also need careful examination. Some are excellent but others are poorly designed or too difficult. Sometimes their authors seem unaware of a Biblical view of the person and knowledge. Here are some questions to ask as you examine curriculum materials:

♦ *What values, commitments, and goals do the authors state or assume?* *What do they think is important in society, in the way we live, and in the way we view the world? Does my faith and worldview correspond or conflict with that of the material? (Look especially at introductions and endings, and the choice of content. Note also what is missing: history books may minimize the importance of religion, for instance. Books whose worldview differs from yours may still be useful. But think about how to use them effectively.)*

♦ *Does the type of learning suggested encourage responsive discipleship?* *Do the books actively engage the students, or, at least, can you use the material to plan a variety of activities that suit different needs and that help children take on responsibility for their learning?*

♦ *How is the material put together?* *Is it motivational? Are the important themes and concepts highlighted and reviewed? Do the layout and illustrations promote learning or do they just "decorate" the print materials?*

♦ *Do* **mathematics** *materials teach new concepts in a meaningful setting, showing the relationship between mathematics and culture? Do* **science** *materials develop a sense of excitement about science as an exploration of a wonderful reality? Do they also show the limitations and dangers of uncritical application of science and technology? Do* **reading and literature** *materials present significant content with role models that reflect Biblical lifestyles, or content that leads to discussions of basic values? Do* **social studies** *materials show cultures as embodiments of worldviews based on a system of beliefs and values? Do the materials state biases openly or do they remain hidden?*

Often teachers do not have the luxury of choosing or being involved in choosing their main resources. The school may have purchased materials some time ago and for budgetary or policy reasons cannot change. Examining the books carefully is still useful, however. You will see the strengths and weaknesses of the materials more clearly and plan accordingly.

◆ACTIVITY 5-12

With a small group, examine one or two commonly used textbooks in a subject and at a level of your interest. Use the questions above to draw conclusions about the suitability of the books and the ways in which you would make use of them (if at all).

To what extent should schools and individual teachers be able to choose their own curriculum resources? Is there a need for common textbooks so that children in different communities receive similar content instruction? Or should teachers use various resources rather than one textbook even in one classroom?

Day-to-day planning

Appropriate unit planning makes your daily preparation easier and more focused. The format of your daily plan, often called a lesson plan, might include the following:

1. *Intended learning outcome(s):* These are taken from the unit plan, or closely related to them. You do not need a long list of very specific learning outcomes. Those will be self-evident from your learning activities. They also take much time to write. You do need to state your main intents, however, so that you can keep them in mind as you teach. Make clear what you expect your students to learn. Can you achieve the outcomes? Take into account the dynamics of your classroom. Be flexible if things just don't work the way you had hoped.

2. *Introduction.* You need an introductory activity (a) to motivate students, (b) to help them see the value of what they are to learn, and (c) to relate the learning to previous experiences. Phase 1 ("setting the stage") activities are often useful here.

3. *Learning activities.* Ask yourself what type of activities will attain your learning outcomes. Include activities suitable for diverse learners. Do you want activities in all four phases of learning? Or does this lesson call for only one or two phases? Will you actively involve your students throughout the lesson? Plan a variety of activities for longer time blocks. Even in high school, a "disclosure" presentation should normally not exceed

ten minutes. Note any independent work and follow-up that needs to take place after the period.

Write down the key questions you will ask. Include ones that go beyond recall and simple comprehension. Ask students to give reasons, to draw conclusions, and to support or refute arguments. Also ask them to extrapolate ("What would happen if . . .?"), to assess, to justify viewpoints and opinions, and to suggest solutions. Give students enough time to think about their answers, and ask follow-up questions to help students develop their insights.

4. *Conclusion.* Don't leave your lesson "hanging" at the end. Pull together the main points that you want students to learn. Ask the students, for instance, to write down the two most important things they learned. Or conclude with some review questions that give will indicate whether the class has attained your intended outcomes.

5. ***Resources and materials needed.*** List the resources you need: books, pamphlets, computer files, physical materials, chart paper, audiovisual equipment, and so on. Use a variety of resources but choose them judiciously.

6. *Assessment.* How do you plan to assess students' learning both during and at the conclusion of the lesson? Sometimes this may involve little more than informal observation. Plan to monitor student interest and response. Also plan to check the quality of assignments done prior to, during, and after the lesson. Leave some space on your planning sheet to jot down what went well—or poorly–in the lesson.

7. *Notes and reminders.* You may want to design your own photocopied (or computer file) lesson planning outlines with the above headings. This last heading is useful for reminding yourself about special notes and instructions that you must give to the students, contacts you must make with specific students, special supervisory duties, and so on.

◆ACTIVITY 5-13

Talk to one or two teachers about how they make day-to-day lesson plans. When do they develop them and how much time do they take?

Which of the above points do they include? How much detail do they include? Do they refer to the plan as they teach? How do they feel about the usefulness of written daily plans?

◆ACTIVITY 5-14

Pick a topic for which you have some resources available, perhaps within the same unit you have been working on in previous activities. Develop one or two daily lesson plans for the topic, using the outline given above. Include your key questions.

Once you have written the plan and discussed it with several other persons, teach the lesson to a small group. Afterwards, analyze with the group how successful you were in attaining your intended learning outcomes. Revise your plan accordingly.

Subject area considerations

The Bible does not contain "recipes" indicating what content we should or should not teach. It helps us understand the basic motifs for life: creation, fall, redemption, the coming Kingdom of God, the calling of human beings. We infer that the school curriculum should also help students develop their God-given office. The content we teach should encourage children to respond in righteous obedience to God's mandate.

More specifically, curriculum content should point to the *vertical unity of knowledge* proclaimed in Colossians 1:16-17, "All things were created by [Christ] and for him. He is before all things, and in him all things hold together." It is in Christ, Paul continues in Colossians 2, that all the treasures of wisdom and knowledge are hidden. Secular approaches to education often ignore or reject this unity. Yet to make this unity clear to students and to show that Christ is pre-eminent and gives us direction for all aspects of life is not an easy task. Nevertheless, many Christian teachers do plan individual units that make clear how God's Word is "a lamp to [our] feet and a light for [our] path" (Ps 119:105). You can see this, for instance, from the examples in this book, most of which are based on actual classroom situations.

Often we teach curriculum content most easily within the framework of established school subjects. We must also make clear to our students, however, the *horizontal unity* of knowledge. Many topics and issues cut across disciplines. They become significant parts of the curriculum when we study them in a focused, academic way. Furthermore, our content must also expose the many natural interrelationships between different disciplines. In science, for example, mathematics is not only an essential tool but also a vehicle for interpreting scientific phenomena. Further, economics and ethics proclaim limits to the applications of science.

Since most knowledge arises from and is applied to multidimensional phenomena, not all learning should take place within well-defined "subjects." Too much discipline-focused fragmentation of knowledge prevents students from interacting with reality in a meaningful way. Then their knowledge can easily become sterile formalism. Nevertheless, when teachers are aware of this danger and plan accordingly, subject disciplines often provide useful organizational foci, especially at the higher levels.

♦ *Three Christian schools in British Columbia pooled ideas to develop a grade 8 humanities curriculum. Humanities is an integrated study of past and present human relationships and actions. Students learn to see the connections between themselves and the world around them by exploring and examining their relationship with God, each other, the past, their own and other cultures, and creation. The content comprises themes and issues from Biblical studies, English and social studies. Three units in the program are* Community and Culture, Kingdom Building, *and* Taking a Stand *(Society of Christian Schools 1996).*

For the last unit, the teachers defined the thematic statement, intended learning outcomes, and focus questions as follows:

> In each generation and culture the Spirit of God moves people to take a stand in pursuit of truth. Taking a stand involves personal commitment and a willingness to question those traditions which distort the discovery of truth. A personal relationship with Jesus Christ is the foundation of all truth: His world illumines all human understanding.

The unit is intended to help students:

♦ understand the Gospel's message of salvation by faith alone as expressed in Paul's letters.

- understand that the pursuit of truth, which drives many individuals to observe, question, challenge, experiment and defend their convictions, often involves personal suffering.

- see the sovereignty and love of God as He continually calls His Church to repent and to proclaim His message through a walk of faith.

The focus questions for the unit are:

- How do people's beliefs influence their lives?

- What are the characteristics of individuals who make a difference?

- What kind of stand does Christ call us to take?

The unit consists of four main parts:

- *Paul's life, how he took a stand, and, specifically, his letter to the Galatians.* The study of Galatians does not only provide the link between Paul's writings and Martin Luther's Ninety-five Theses, but also confronts students with questions about their own life: How did Paul take a stand? What is the depth of Paul's message for you, and us, today? Which of the following beliefs and practices do you think are necessary to being a Christian? (e.g., praying to God, baptizing believers, marrying a Christian) One student assignment is to create a brochure promoting the Christian faith using the theological themes of the letter of Galatians.

- *The Renaissance and Reformation, focusing on why individuals such as Wycliffe and Luther took certain stands.* Students write a research paper and a biography. They also write a report on how a historical or current religious leader has made a difference in people's lives, and how a religiously based group such as World Vision has improved the lives of others in our world.

- *the novel, Cue for Treason.*

- *the television play, Twelve Angry Men,* with students learning about television as a medium and focusing on the statement of one juror, "It takes a great deal of courage to stand alone."

A concluding activity is entitled, "How should we then live?":

We seek to discover the patterns, themes and trends. We would like to learn from the victories and the mistakes of others. Begin by thinking about the things that interested you most about the areas that we studied. Then search for an underlying theme, for example: loyalty, cowardliness, courage, perseverance, compassion, integrity, creativity, godliness, etc. You will use the theme you choose for both your position paper and your speech. The examples you use come from the cultures we have studied. The application should be specific to what you feel is important for us to remember in the way we live our lives today. Choose a topic that is important to you. Your speech and position paper will be more powerful if you believe in your topic. [Topic ideas included "It is more fun to live today than at any other time in history . . .," "I believe our society has lost the faith that Christ, Paul and the Reformers died for . . .," and "We need to follow the example of our Christian forefathers and make a difference in our world . . ."]

Without going into details, note how the unit takes a very different view of knowledge and values than does constructivism, and yet allows for a great deal of student response. God's Word is held central as the authoritative truth for our lives. History is looked at in terms of human response to God's creation mandate and His Great Commandment. While human interpretation and bias are not denied, the unit recognizes the importance of actual historical happenings and cultural development. It holds that history is more than arbitrary human constructions. Students grapple with their personal beliefs and values. They do so within the context of the existence of certain absolutes which they can follow or rebuff in their lives. Yet the learning goes much beyond passive memorization or simple interpretation. The unit includes a wide variety of learning activities and continually calls for personal response and action. In that sense it is soundly rooted in a Biblical understanding of knowledge.

The development and use of this humanities program is also instructive. First, teachers in each school worked on school-based programs, with several principals giving pairs of teachers some joint planning time a couple of times a week. Once teachers had tried various approaches, they then saw the benefit of getting together for a couple of weeks and pooling insights and experiences. They drew up a joint program with the help of a curriculum coordinator. The joint program was superior to any of the three original parts. But note that the three schools, while working together, still maintained their individuality. For instance, one school substituted a study of Romans and Corinthians for Galatians. Another put more emphasis on the importance of the Great Commission in the lives of heroes of the faith, and had an extensive service project as an integral part of the unit. In all cases, however, the implemented program reflected Biblical views of knowledge and the person while avoiding the secularism and relativism of our age. (Van Brummelen 1997)

◆ACTIVITY 5-15

Discuss, if you were to teach the *Taking the Stand* unit, what changes you would make. Would you integrate Biblical studies, English and history as described, or would you teach the subjects separately? Give reasons. How would you revise the unit to be able to teach it in a public school?

◆ACTIVITY 5-16

Below are some basic guidelines for teaching various subjects. In each case, what are some implications for teaching and learning? For one or two subjects, find out some currently discussed issues. Do the guidelines help set a direction for dealing with those issues? Are there alternative guidelines you would prefer? [For more detail, see Steensma & Van Brummelen 1977 and Van Brummelen 1994.]

♦ Biblical studies *helps students read and interpret the Bible in a more meaningful way. It steeps them in the Bible as God's revelation of his plan of redemption. They practice Biblical hermeneutics, studying the literary forms and cultural background of individual Bible books as well as tracing significant Biblical themes. In addition, they apply the Biblical message to their personal lives, to their relationships with others, to contemporary issues, and to life in the community. Throughout, teachers face students with the Biblical call to personal repentance, faith, and discipleship.*

♦ Language arts/literature *helps students grow as they enhance their ability to relate to and communicate with others in positive, meaningful ways. Language is a beautiful and exciting means to serve God and our neighbors and build community. Students learn to listen thoughtfully, speak effectively, read critically, and write creatively. In literature, students develop spiritual, moral and social maturity as they learn to discern the worldview visions that are presented and promoted.*

♦ *In* science *students learn that their inquiry about physical reality assumes that God's laws and precepts are trustworthy (Ps 111 and 146). They observe, experiment, and draw conclusions about our creation structure. They also begin to recognize, how-*

ever, that human investigation and formulation reflect the unchanging laws of God only in limited ways and that science can never be our ultimate authority in life. Moreover, they see how God created each living being to fit the environment in which he placed it, with each having a special purpose in God's plan for life. Through science, students become aware of their personal and our collective roles as caretakers of our planet: to maintain healthy bodies, make stewardly lifestyle decisions, maintain harmony among living things and their environment, and deal responsibly with social issues that have a scientific component.

◆ *The basis for mathematics lies with God's wise and orderly decrees (Ps 33:6-11; Jer 33:25). Children initially discover God's created order about number and space from concrete, hands-on, real experiences. Only slowly do teachers introduce and reinforce more precise conceptualization, formal reasoning, and algorithms. Even then, they continue to show how society uses the methods and conclusions of mathematics as an essential tool in various areas of life.*

◆ *In the fine arts (visual art, music, drama, creative movement, film) teachers provide children with rich experiences in which they look, listen, and feel. They introduce students to the artistic statements of other people, both past and present. Students experience the power of aesthetics to shape people and their values. They respond artistically, with originality, within a framework of purposeful conceptual and skill development. In music, for instance, the students listen, perform, compose, and improvise. They learn to appreciate how music is an important part of life and culture. They learn how to use music in praise to their Creator as they express joy and sadness, faith and doubt, obedience and disobedience in imaginative ways.*

◆ *The starting point for physical education is the belief that God calls us to honor him with our bodies as well as our minds (1Co 6:20). Human beings are a unity and their physical health affects their emotional, mental, and spiritual state. As such, physical involvement is part of a Christian lifestyle. Therefore the aim of physical education is that students develop and maintain acceptable motor proficiencies, health fitness, and physical skills in a variety of activities. Physical education encourages and enables all students to incorporate wholesome physical activities in their everyday routines.*

◆ACTIVITY 5-17

For your grade level, discuss which subject disciplines you consider essential and which could be optional. Give reasons.

A spectrum of subject integration is possible in schools. Schools can teach school subjects in completely separate time blocks. On the other hand, they can have an "integrated day" in which all learning is thematic, without any subject distinctions. At the grade level you teach or intend to teach, how much subject integration is desirable? How much is realistic?

Reviewing the main points

1. *Traditional education* does justice neither to the unique giftedness of learners nor to the response and commitment demanded by a Biblical view of knowledge. On the other hand, *child-centered approaches such as constructivism* lead to self-centered individualism and to relativism of knowledge and values.

2. *A Biblical view of knowledge* affirms God's revelation, providence and acts, and acknowledges that knowledge must lead to response, commitment and service.

3. *A Christian curriculum orientation* takes into account *God's three basic injunctions* to humans: (a) *his creation mandate,*(b) *the Great Commandment,* and (c) *the Great Commission.* It holds that all learning activities, including cognitive- and ability-focused ones, ought to foster dispositions and commitments consistent with Biblical guidelines and values.

4. *Teachers plan at four different levels: yearly overviews, unit plans, daily lessons, and making modifications while teaching.* It is at the unit planning level that they can best develop a distinctively Christian approach. Units should have a clear focus stated in a thematic statement and corresponding intended learning outcomes. They should also draw in natural interrelations with other subject areas to avoid an artificial fragmentation of knowledge.

5. *Daily lesson plans* include intended learning outcomes; introductory, main, and concluding activities; a list of the resources used; how you assess learning; and notes and reminders. *Evaluate resources* for both content and structure.

REFERENCES

Airasian, P. & M. Walsh. 1997. Constructivist cautions. *Phi Delta Kappan* 78(6):444-449.

Baker, D. & M. Piburn. 1997. *Constructing science in middle and secondary school classrooms.* Boston: Allyn and Bacon.

Fosnot, C. 1996. *Constructivism: Theory, perspectives and practice.* New York: Teachers College Press.

McNeil, J. 1995. *Curriculum: The teacher's initiative.* Englewood Cliffs, NJ: Merrill.

Steffe, L. & J. Gale (eds.). 1995. *Constructivism in education.* Hillsdale, NJ: Lawrence Erlbaum.

Steensma, G. & Van Brummelen, H. (eds.). 1977. *Shaping school curriculum: A Biblical view.* Terre Haute, IN: Signal.

Stott, J. 1979. *God's new society: The message of Ephesians.* Downer's Grove, IL: InterVarsity Press.

Van Brummelen, H. 1994. *Steppingstones to curriculum: A Biblical path.* Seattle: Alta Vista College Press.

Van Brummelen, H. 1997. Curriculum development is dead–or is it? *Pro Rege* 26(1):14-23.

Chapter 6

EVALUATING STUDENT LEARNING

*G*rade 7 teachers Connie Clements and Jim Vance are in the teachers' workroom discussing their students' report cards.

"My students did poorly this term," Connie laments, "I'm afraid quite a few parents will be upset with all the D's and the euphemism we now use for F's, the I's for "in progress." But it's better to give these marks now than at the end of the year. Maybe they'll shock my pupils into better effort."

Jim asks, "But isn't positive reinforcement more effective if you want to stimulate effort?"

Connie ponders the question. Then she answers, "Well, that may generally be true. If my pupils have done poorly, though, then their parents must know the truth. And parents can put on some pressure to see that their children do their work."

Jim persists, "All right, so parents need to know. But what about parents who say—or think—that if so many of your kids have poor marks, it's you as the teacher who's the problem?"

"I'll give them a piece of my mind," Connie shoots back. "My students generally did well on daily seatwork. There I could supervise them closely. But their test results were poor. They sure didn't focus on their work consistently."

Jim replies, a bit hesitantly since he risks some collegial friction, "But couldn't a parent then ask, 'Did you teach the concepts thoroughly? Did you review enough? Were the tests valid ones?' Or even, 'Are you putting too little emphasis on everyday work for assigning grades?' I don't know your class all that well, Connie. But it does seem to me that parents may have some legitimate questions if the marks of the whole class have dropped sharply."

Connie, stung, quickly recovers, "Well, maybe some of their questions are valid. But shouldn't report card grades show how much my students actually know? And I believe mine do!"

Jim doesn't want to prolong the discussion. Like Connie, he must finish his report cards before the deadline. He still has to think through what comments he will put on them. So he says, appeasingly, "Well, you know, for a long time our staff hasn't discussed how we should assign grades or what they reflect. Our principal accepts what we put on our reports. He only asks us about an unusual number of high or low marks, or about comments that don't seem to match our grades. We all do our own thing. I myself, for instance, emphasize informal observation and assessment of daily work more than you do. And your "B" does not mean the same thing as mine, I suspect. I'm not saying that either of us is right or wrong. But should we suggest a staff discussion about this? After all, students and parents do have a right to expect some consistency, especially if we expect them to interpret our evaluations properly."

As this discussion shows, assessment of student learning is controversial. It may be done without a good understanding of its aims or even of how it can advance learning outcomes. Should we have anecdotal reports rather than grades in primary grades? Is it meaningful to assess effort as well as achievement? Should we use a pass/fail system? What weight should we give to final exams? How do we use student portfolios, if at all? Is marking "on the curve" fair at the high school level? Should we use criterion-referenced assessment where students pass if they achieve 80% on a unit test and otherwise review the material until they succeed? Is it possible to evaluate compositions and reports fairly? Is there a Biblical approach to assessing and evaluating learning that leads to better relations among teachers, students, and parents?

The list of questions is inexhaustible. This chapter does not give all the answers or lay all the arguments to rest. Rather, its intent is to stimulate thinking and suggest some Biblical principles that we need to keep in mind as we assess learning.

◆ACTIVITY 6-1

Outline what you consider to be some basic guidelines for a Christian approach to student evaluation. Save your sheet. At the end of the chapter review and refine what you wrote.

Aims of assessment and evaluation

Assessment means gathering information about student learning. Teachers set, give and grade assignments and tests, for instance. *Evaluation* involves interpreting the information and making resulting judgments and decisions. To what extent have your students achieved both your intended and other learning and behavioral outcomes? What does this mean for your future classroom learning?

Summative assessment sums up student achievement at the end of a unit or year. Final exams at the end of high school, for instance, assign students a mark but give no feedback or help for future improvement. *Formative* assessment and evaluation is more valuable for student learning. It diagnoses student learning and growth in order to improve learning. A teacher may, for instance, give helpful comments on a draft of a composition. The student then uses the comments to set personal goals and write a final draft. The formative and summative aspects of assessment and evaluation overlap when teachers provide useful feedback but also assign a mark.

◆ACTIVITY 6-2

Assess the balance between formative and summative assessment in your elementary and your high school experiences. Then evaluate whether the balance was appropriate. Would you strive for a similar balance in your own classroom? Why or why not?

Teachers constantly assess student characteristics: their behavior, aptitudes, interests, achievements, and dispositions. They base such assessment on their own and society's beliefs about the nature and function of schooling. Both *how* and *what* they choose to assess—and how they evaluate the results—reflects what they hold to be important. Teachers who emphasize short-answer factual test questions, for instance, value different things from ones who give students questions that require critical thinking. Also, teachers may evaluate a score of 80 on a science test in electricity quite differently. One may interpret it to mean that the student has mastered the material thoroughly. Another may conclude, however, that the student has memorized the content well but has not grasped well enough how to apply concepts in new situations. The teachers implicitly value different dimensions of learning. They therefore interpret the results differently. Assessment and evaluation always are *valuing* activities.

The importance teachers attach to assessment and evaluation and how they go about it *creates* meaning for them and their students. Some teachers make recall the focus of their assessment on tests. They impress on students that memorization and recall are of prime importance in learning and in life. Other teachers may usually ask students to evaluate and apply what they have learned. Their students likely conclude that knowing concepts and skills is only a basis for solving further problems or analyzing issues. Assessment has a substantive effect on students. Therefore, it ought to reflect a Biblical understanding of the nature of persons and of knowledge, as described in earlier chapters of this book.

Assessment and evaluation are means to an end, not ends in themselves. That may seem obvious. Too often, however, North American educators put the horse of learning behind the assessment cart. Many school boards use externally developed tests to impose a central curriculum. The results rank schools and students. Teachers, in turn, teach to the tests. This may help teachers to concentrate on some important "basics." However, usually such tests reflect only a small portion of a school's desired achievement outcomes. Yet the tests often become the main focus of student learning.

◆ACTIVITY 6-3

It is not only outside agencies whose assessment limits learning. As high school teacher Don Aker put it:

[When I began teaching], I thought that . . . teachers assessed for three reasons: to bring about closure to a unit of work ("We'll fin-

ish this off with a test on Friday"), to maintain control of the classroom ("You'd better pay attention because this could be on the test"), and to reward or punish students for learning or not learning ("Maybe next time you'll study harder for the test"). For me, assessment was something that ended with a mark in my record book and on a report card. Fortunately for my students, I know better now. (Aker 1995, pp. 11-12)

In what ways was Don Aker's view of assessment a limiting one? How do you think his views of assessment changed over the years?

Appropriate assessment tries to find out how well students have attained the intended learning outcomes. Not all learning outcomes can be fully measured. Take, for instance, an outcome in a unit on multiculturalism such as "to exercise respect and compassion toward others." Its realization will not become clear unless a teacher happens to observe an unsuspecting student in a real-life, relevant setting. Also, assessment should take into account that learning activities may have outcomes that were not intended. Suppose students develop and put on a skit to show differing attitudes toward forestry practices. In some circumstances the activity may run aground unless the teacher helps students develop conflict resolution skills. The latter may even become the focus of the learning activity.

Assessment of learning helps teachers to evaluate the effectiveness of the curriculum, teaching strategies, and learning activities. Since it is an integral part of the instructional process, assessment needs to be continuous. It helps students be more responsive in their learning and teachers more responsive in their planning and teaching. Specifically, the purposes of assessment includes the following:

1. *To encourage and improve student learning.*
   a) *To assess the extent to which students have met the intended learning outcomes, and to look for and evaluate unintended outcomes.*
   b) *To recognize achievements and diagnose learning difficulties so that students learn to build on their strengths and overcome or cope with their weaknesses.*
   c) *To help students develop and practice self-appraisal and self-understanding skills about their learning.*

d) To help students set meaningful and realistic learning goals and assume responsibility for their own learning.

e) To refine instruction and other learning experiences in order to improve both individual and class learning.

2. **To communicate meaningful information to students, parents, and school authorities about student learning.**

a) To give realistic and helpful feedback about achievement, capabilities, behavior, attitudes, and dispositions.

b) To put teachers, students, and parents/guardians in touch with each other about progress over time.

c) To provide guidance for educational and vocational choices.

d) To account for the learning that takes place to school authorities such as school boards and governments.

◆ACTIVITY 6-4

Are there any assessment and evaluation goals that you would revise or add?

Before going on to the next section, jot down some of the implications of these goals for the classroom. How would assessment and evaluation differ from what you experienced in school?

Some guidelines and hazards

Assessment inevitably puts values on certain behaviors and achievements. Therefore some basic premises guide a Christian approach:

> ◆   *Assessment and evaluation must enable students to respond as images of God.* Response is an integral aspect of knowing and of being an image of God. Therefore use assessment and evaluation to lead to further learning. Help students reflect on and refine their learning. Also, encourage them to learn from mistakes.

> ♦ *Assessment recognizes accomplishments and challenges students to further learning and growth.* With respect to student behavior and achievements, God calls teachers, like pastors, to "correct, rebuke, and encourage-with great patience and careful instruction" (2Ti 4:2). We evaluate, give feedback, and correct in a loving, helpful, and patient way, within a context of supportive but persistent and well-planned instruction. In both 2 Timothy and in Titus, Paul states that encouragement must always accompany correction.

Education calls forth three different kinds of student responses. Teachers assess each differently. They assess *definite responses* with relative ease. They can use straightforward questions and answers because only one or two responses are right. In *non-prescriptive responses*, students display their unique abilities and creativity. Although teachers still use defined criteria, their assessment is more subjective. Here teachers give students thoughtful feedback that helps them grow.

Our ultimate aim in schooling includes positive *internal response*. We can evaluate this only partially, and usually not immediately. Yet we continue to encourage positive internal dispositions and commitments, even when not measurable. For some of the most important ones we may not see immediate results and yet be the Holy Spirit's instruments. For instance, I was disappointed with my lack of meaningful interaction with a troubled and troublesome grade 12 student. I met him ten years later on a city street. He said it was only during the last year, after he had committed his life to Christ, that what other teachers and I had taught him about life became personally meaningful. After drifting for many years, what he had learned a decade earlier led him to a career in social services. He now helped others facing problems similar to those he had had.

Assessment and evaluation become more subjective as we move from definite to non-prescriptive to internal student response. Yet assessing non-prescriptive responses, while time-consuming, is usually more valuable for student growth than definite responses. Further, teachers and staffs ought to review from time to time the effect of their program on students' values, dispositions, and commitment to a Christian way of life. A balanced student assessment program goes beyond grading definite responses.

The positive use of assessment and evaluation helps students discover, develop, and use their talents. This requires far more than "pigeonholing" students. The latter, research shows, can easily become a self-fulfilling prophecy, especially for weaker students. It is possible for our evaluation methods to lead "little ones to sin," especially by discouraging them from using their abilities in enriching ways. Jesus points out that teachers bear a heavy responsibility in this respect (Lk 17:2; 19:20-22).

Today's education system requires student grading. Unavoidably, implicit or explicit ranking accompanies such grading. But grading and ranking may not be not the main focus of assessment and evaluation. Therefore, from time to time, honestly discuss differences in aptitudes and achievements with your students. Stress that all are special and all have special callings. Don't put some students on mountain tops or in deep valleys because of their grades.

A former student, now a senior pastor, shared with me an experience in high school. I had long forgotten but it affected him a great deal. I had made a written comment on a math test on which he got an "A-." My comment was that he needed to start using his God-given abilities more effectively. I said he was just marking time, and should turn his life around–and he did. An "A" does not necessarily show excellence for a particular student!

On the other hand, many students give up because they cannot seem to progress beyond a "D," no matter how hard they try. In such cases grading diminishes eventual chances for success (Van Dyk 1997, pp. 105-106). Richard Edlin (1994, pp. 156ff.) argues that the parable of the talents shows that the class plodder would have received Jesus' approval long before the "smart kid" who with little effort still achieved an "A."

You will not be able to overcome completely students' perception that letter grades indicate their worth as persons. However, try to minimize it. Discuss with your students how all of them are images of God. Help them experience and use their personal talents and resulting responsibilities. For projects, give students your comments and discuss them before giving them their final grade. Display the work of all students when it represents their best effort. Do so without indicating grades publicly.

Note, finally, that assessment and evaluation have limited functions. In God's sight, what students *are* counts much more than what they *know*. Jesus makes clear that it is not our role to judge a person's heart (Mt 7:1). Therefore, be careful to evaluate student behavior and products, not their personhood. Don't leave students with the impression that they are of little worth and not valued because they are "below average." A real and verified danger is that low assessments and resulting low expectations become self-fulfilling prophecies. They often lead to low motivation and low achievement (Good & Brophy 1994, pp. 83-127).

In short, do justice to the Biblical notion that each student is an image of God. Use assessment and evaluation to strengthen students' sense of worth and calling of students even when God has not given them superior academic talents. Assess in order to encourage further learning, not to judge personal worth.

◆ACTIVITY 6-5

For a curriculum topic (preferably one for which you have learning outcomes available), suggest some assessment procedures for activities involving both definite and non-prescriptive students responses. To what extent should a school try to evaluate students' internal responses?

Classroom observation

Formal and informal observation is the most used and often the most valuable method of assessing student learning. You can use various effective methods. Ask frequent questions to check whether students understand a concept. Check their facial expressions for puzzlement, frustration, or boredom–reactions that may call for different teaching strategies or activities. Walk past students to check whether they can apply the mathematical algorithm just taught. Observe students at learning centers to see what processes and skills they use. Look around the playground to understand pupils' interactions and to help those with special social or emotional needs.

To help your observations be systematic and beneficial:

♦ *Regularly record anecdotes about students' progress, special achievement difficulties, and behavior patterns.* Record only what happens, not your inferences or interpretations. Keep a notebook handy. Alternatively, jot down notes about students on "post-it" notes. Transfer these to student files at the end of the day. At the elementary level, choose two students each day that you will observe with special care.

♦ *Use your observations to revise your teaching and to provide extra help for students who need it.*

♦ *Periodically complete language arts, mathematics, fine arts, and social/emotional development checklists for each student.* In higher grades, use mastery charts for subjects that involve many skills.

♦ *For learning center work or major projects, prepare a sheet on which students indicate the completion of specific tasks.* Hold students responsible for keeping track of their progress, but also monitor it yourself using their sheets.

♦ *Give frequent oral feedback.* Discuss observations with your students to help them improve performance. Require students to do their best, but be positive. When you need to confront students about work not done well, continue to encourage them even as you criticize.

◆ACTIVITY 6-6

Discuss with a teacher how she uses observation as a daily assessment tool. Are there things she would like to assess but for which she does not have time in her regular routine? If you can visit a classroom, ask whether you can help to observe and assess some aspect of learning of an individual student or of the class.

◆ACTIVITY 6-7

Look at some resources that contain assessment checklists that you can use to observe and conference with students. Two good sources are the British Columbia Primary Teachers Association's *Evaluation: Techniques and Resources* (1995) and Cornfield's *Making the Grade*

(1987). Discuss how, when, and to what extent teachers might make effective use of such checklists.

Assessing student products

Both during and after students have performed a learning task that, you believe, leads to desired learning outcomes, you assess the learning product(s). You may want to consider the following questions (Aker 1995, p. 55):

1. *What do I consider a successful response to the task? What criteria will I use to assess student achievement? Do my students know and understand the criteria? Do the criteria relate to my intended learning outcomes?*

2. *Will I assess all students according to the same criteria, or do my expectations vary according to student giftedness?*

3. *Will I assess the final product only, or also the process and/or some intermediate steps?*

4. *If students collaborate on this task, will all group members receive the same mark, or will I also assess each students' individual contribution? If the latter, how will I do so?*

5. *Would I want to be assessed in this way? Would it allow me to demonstrate fully what I know and can do?*

How teachers assess student products depends on the intended learning outcomes, the nature of the product, and the amount of available time. It is not appropriate to assess a map drawn by a student for effective use of color when your intended learning outcomes and the work in class dealt only with accuracy of scale and how to designate physical features. Similarly, assess a project on the basis of the criteria that you discussed with your students.

Use comments and simple scales to mark class work or overnight assignments. I often use a +, ✓, - , or 0 to indicate exceptional, satisfactory, unsatisfactory, or no effort. I then supplement this with comments. Here I try to be positive and encouraging, but also honest ("You did a good job in listing the main points. Your answers, however, just repeat those points. You failed to give your personal views."). Focus comments on students' strengths and on how they can improve achievement. From time to time, review your comments to see whether they encourage students. For example, "You have written good sentences but try to improve your neatness" will accomplish more than "Messy writing."

To assess major assignments and presentations, you require a table of criteria. I give a condensed sample in Fig. 6.1. An alternative to a table of criteria is a *rubric*. A rubric gives a scale of values to assess student work. Rather than teachers assigning subjective scores, a rubric lists set points for specific performance in a cate-

HISTORY PROJECT ASSESSMENT SHEET		
Name:_____ Title: _____ Date: _____		
Main merit(s):		
CRITERIA	MARK	COMMENTS
GRASP OF CONCEPTS AND ISSUES: perceptive, thorough	/25	
EXAMPLES: prudently chosen, consistent with position	/10	
JUSTIFICATION OF CLAIMS AND VIEWS: clear, careful, logical, complete	/15	
ORGANIZATION AND WRITING EFFECTIVENESS: coherent, unified, effective development and flow, lively style, creativity	/20	
EXPRESSION, DICTION AND MECHANICS: clear, controlled, fluent, precise, correct spelling and grammar	/20	
USE OF RESOURCES: variety, relevance, merged into whole	/10	
TOTAL	/100	Additional comments on reverse side

FIG. 6.1. TABLE OF CRITERIA FOR PROJECT ASSESSMENT

gory. The descriptions usually describe a continuum of achievement. Consider the "justification of claims and views" category in the table, for instance. The rubric might list four possible standards: expert (clear logic and strong supporting evidence), proficient (absence of contradictions and basic supporting evidence), beginner (no major contradictions and general evidence that lacks specificity), and novice (inconsistent, little or no supporting evidence). The teacher then assigns student work a 4, 3, 2 or 1 respectively for this as well as each of the other categories with defined standards. For some detailed examples see Chapter 11 of Stiggins (1997).

Assessing and evaluating assignments is time-consuming, especially for non-prescriptive responses. At higher levels, you may sometimes want to spot-check. For instance, collect all student journals but respond with comments for only five or six students. You then rotate this to different ones every ten days or so. The use of rating scales and rubrics reduces time spent writing comments and still gives meaningful feedback to students. In composition, use peer editing for specific skills that students have learned. This reduces your marking time, reinforces what you have taught, and develops student responsibility (even if at first you need patience!). Manage your time well. Schedule time for observation, for recording information, and for conferring with students when they do activities that require little intervention. Use peer writing conferences to have students assess first drafts of compositions.

Self-evaluation and peer assessment cut down the time you need to spend on assessment. More importantly, it makes students more responsible for their own learning. Paul enjoins all persons to test their own actions (Gal 6:4). Self-assessment enables students to actively participate in their learning. They learn to set appropriate learning goals and develop realistic self-concepts. Give students weekly logs, for instance, on which they write their daily goals. Ask them to indicate for each whether they were done, almost done, or not done. Make some comments about their successes and how they might improve. For projects, ask them to describe the project in writing and then complete open-ended statements such as

◆ *What I enjoyed most about this project was . . .*
◆ *In this project I learned . . .*
◆ *If I were to do this project again I would . . .*
◆ *I would like to find out more about . . .*
◆ *What I found difficult about this project was . . .*

Student portfolios are organized collections of sample student work, usually kept in folders or envelopes. They help students assess their daily work as well as their long-term progress. Students who use portfolios frequently reflect on and revise their work. They experience their assessment as instruction for improvement. They recognize the expected standards as aids for further learning (Gordon and Bonilla-Brown in Baron & Wolf 1996, pp. 38ff.). As students add products, their portfolios show their growth over time. They can set goals that fit their individual abilities and achievements. Portfolios can also strengthen ties between home and school.

To use portfolios effectively, discuss with students the purpose of the portfolio and which (dated) work samples they should include. Have students ask with you, "Why is it important to include this product? What does it reveal about my learning?" Evaluate the included work. Some teachers prepare cover sheets for portfolio entries. On these students give reasons for choosing each item. The teacher, in response, then indicates some positive features as well as one or two areas on which the student should work. Review the items with the students from time to time, keeping only those that show significant growth. Portfolios provide a meaningful basis for teacher-student, teacher-parent, and student-led parent conferences. Invite parents to peruse portfolios and make comments before a conference (BC Primary Teachers' Association 1992, pp. 11.09-11.10). Students do need careful training for effective use of portfolios. Also, they are time-consuming if you have many students.

For group work, it is best to rotate various roles such as leader, clarifier, encourager, checker, and recorder (you need to teach and model these roles!). Observe students in each role. Assess whether they perform their assigned roles and whether they attain the intended learning outcomes. When appropriate, ask the recorder to hand in a sheet with a summary of the group work. Assess this the same way you assess day-to-day assignments.

◆ACTIVITY 6-8

Assessment and evaluation can affect the relationship between students and their teacher both positively and negatively. Have you had any assessment experiences that affected your relationship with a teacher negatively? If so, how could the teacher have used assessment in a more positive way? For the grade levels you teach or intend to teach, discuss the assessment strategies that teachers can use with daily assignments in order to maintain good classroom rapport and improve student learning.

Constructing, administering, and scoring classroom tests

◆ACTIVITY 6-9

Before reading this section, discuss in what ways tests and examinations can be negative experiences. Is it possible for them to be positive learning experiences? Write down four or five key points that you believe teachers should keep in mind when administering tests in order for them to be effective experiences for students.

Ideally, tests help students reinforce, consolidate, and integrate what they have learned. They make connections between concepts, issues, and topics that previously may have appeared disjointed. Like other means of assessment, they serve formative and summative functions. Formatively, tests help teachers diagnose learning so that they can improve follow-up instruction. Summatively, tests inform students, parents and teachers about learning accomplishments. Test results should lead to self-evaluation. Use them to help your students focus once again on the essentials of what they have studied and learned. As a teacher, interpret the results in relation to the other assessment and evaluation methods you use, including your conclusions from observing and listening to students. How can you improve future results?

Testing is often a stressful occasion for students. I base the suggestions that follow on my belief that testing must be done in love and fairness, and must help students, not just rank them. To do so, keep in mind the following when preparing and giving tests:

◆ *Use your intended learning outcomes and a description of the unit's content and skills to decide the types of questions you use and their balance.* If your learning outcomes stress problem solving and critical thinking, don't emphasize low level multiple choice questions, for instance—even if such a test requires more time to write and score.

♦ *Use a clear, logical format.* Provide space for the students' name. Indicate how much each item is worth. Group all items of the same format together. Give clear instructions for each section. Within each section, sequence items from easy to more difficult ones, or in the same order as the learning took place. Arrange items on the page clearly for easy answering. Don't use separate answer sheets; they make tests more complex. Phrase questions and problems carefully.

♦ *Test what was important in the unit.* Avoid questions that trick or deal with obscure points. Before finalizing a test, check whether the items represent a fair sampling of the unit content. Provide a proper balance of questions among recall, comprehension, and application of knowledge; reasoning proficiency and problem solving; abilities and skills; creative activities; and dispositions. Also check the growth of value judgments and dispositions to the extent that is possible.

♦ *For optimal response, put students at ease as much as possible during a test.* Beforehand, give sample questions from previous tests so that students know what to expect. Acquaint young students beforehand with unfamiliar types of questions. For review, have small groups of students write sample test questions. Include one or two of these on the test. Suggest strategies that minimize stress such as doing the easiest questions first and briefly outlining an answer before writing it. Give tests reasonably frequently so that the result of any one test does not carry too much weight. Ensure that ventilation, lighting, and noise levels are acceptable. Tell students what they may do when they complete the test.

♦ *Monitor problems with tests and note what you can improve next time.* Speed tests are designed to check how much work students can do in a given time. Otherwise, however, if more than 20 percent of the students do not finish a test in the allotted time, the test was too long. If many questions arise during test writing, you need to clarify some things for next time. If some students who do well on everyday work but poorly on tests, observe them while writing the test. Perhaps they have special difficulties that can be overcome. Some students may know the work but need to be tested orally, for instance.

♦ *Mark tests quickly and fairly.* Feedback within one week is necessary if the test is to enhance learning. Develop a detailed scoring key. For longer questions, outline what you require for a full score. To maintain a consistent standard, score all students' answers for one question before going on to the next. Avoid bias by not looking at students' names. Shuffle papers between questions so that a particular test is not, for instance, always near the beginning or after the best student in the class. Score only positive points. Correcting for guessing is wasted effort.

♦ *Before you file away the test and forget about it, analyze how students answered questions.* Write down what you can do to help your instruction and improve future tests.

Standard books on measurement and evaluation contain many suggestions for writing effective test items (e.g., Stiggins 1997). Each type of question has strengths and weaknesses. The main advantage of true/false, matching, short-answer, and multiple choice items is that they are quick to score. Such questions almost always focus on low-level content, however. They also ignore the importance of writing to communicate insight. True/false questions are particularly unreliable because of the guessing factor.

Good multiple choice items are difficult to write, especially ones that go beyond recall and simple comprehension. Also, creative and divergent thinkers see possibilities besides the ones listed and therefore may have difficulty with this type of question. If teachers give many multiple choice questions, students conclude that they value pre-determined answers more than students' own expression and thought. It follows that the number of multiple choice questions should not exceed 25 to 30 percent of a test. If you use them to save marking time, create a bank of multiple choice items and reject or revise those that prove to be unsatisfactory.

Longer answer questions take longer to score. They do allow students to analyze and evaluate as they formulate and organize ideas, however. They evaluate composition and critical evaluation skills, as well as the ability to assimilate, organize, and apply knowledge in new settings. State questions so that they present a clear, definite task (describe, explain, compare, interpret). For long answers, define the direction and scope of the response and the criteria used for scoring. Indicate the length of answer you expect and how much time students should spend on it.

Use some creative questions that require students to apply and transcend knowledge learned in class. In a unit test on Australian government, for instance, you might ask the students to write a letter to the Australian Prime Minister: "Describe the advantages and disadvantages of Australia becoming a republic. End your letter with a reasoned personal conclusion and advice for the Prime Minister." Such a question assumes that you have discussed with the students the characteristics of a good persuasive letter, and that you give them the criteria you will use to score their answers.

Remember, finally, that tests alone do not give a valid basis for assigning report card grades. Tests have a valid but limited role in assessing learning. Don't make decisions about students too quickly on the basis of one or two tests! Testing cannot take the place of day-to-day teacher observation and evaluation.

◆ACTIVITY 6-10

Obtain some sample tests, preferably ones that have been scored. Analyze their effectiveness in view of the suggestions given in this chapter.

Using standardized tests

Standardized tests are developed by test publishers or government agencies. They can provide a benchmark and help diagnose learning strengths and weaknesses. In almost all cases they should be used in a formative rather than a summative way. That is, use them to improve your program or your instruction. Their intent is not to "grade" your school's program. Regrettably, the media nevertheless uses them in that way.

Standardized tests have some shortcomings. Often they take much class time to administer. Also, most make use of multiple choice formats with their inherent limitations. This format prevents such tests from adequately measuring critical thinking, creativity, or the ability to express thought. Yet it is crucial that schools develop such important God-given gifts. Moreover, the reliability of standardized tests is questionable, especially for younger students. In fact, teachers' own grades continue to be better predictors of later success in school than standardized achievement test results.

This is true both because teacher assessment is continuous, and because teachers base classroom tests on what they actually taught.

Nevertheless, if used and interpreted with care, some standardized testing can be useful. Diagnostic tests, especially in reading and mathematics, pinpoint areas of learning difficulties. They may help teachers to design special strategies to suit the needs of individual students, or to decide to refer the child to an outside consultant.

Standardized achievement tests, especially if they "fit" a school's curriculum, may identify strengths and weaknesses in a program, or in a particular class. Some years ago, for instance, Christian schools in British Columbia participated in provincial mathematics achievement tests at the grades 4 and 8 levels. The results showed that Christian school students achieved well in all areas of the curriculum except geometry and probability. The schools took steps to improve their geometry programs. Results four years later showed that they had done so successfully. Interestingly enough, the schools also decided that probability was not a desirable topic for young students. In other words, they used the test results to improve the attainment of the schools' own goals, but they did not change the program just to improve scores and "look better."

Government examinations at the end of high school are defended because they maintain and improve "standards"–and they do. A difficulty, however, is that the standards are ones set by the government. Those standards may limit the scope of learning. They may also be at odds with the aims of Christian schools in subjects such as English, history, and biology. From this point of view, the more general American Scholastic Achievement Tests are less objectionable. While they also suffer from the shortcomings outlined above, they do provide colleges a nationally-normed benchmark when academic standards are inconsistent from one school to the next.

Grading and reporting

The primary goal of grading and reporting is communication. You want to keep not only students but also parents informed. Parents have the primary responsibility for their children's nurture. Good communication helps them to support you, and this in turn helps student learning. Communicate with parents more often than at report card time. Send home school products and communicate general results through a class newsletter. Contact parents about special achievements and problems. The former especially pays off for learning. Try to phone one or two parents a week with a specific positive observation.

Grades communicate less information than most parents assume. Grades (as well as single scores on major assignments) "average out" the assessment of very different qualities. In the process, those who see the composite mark get little idea of achievement in specific elements, or even what standards a teacher used to assign the grade. Moreover, grades are subjective. A "B" given by two different teachers may mean quite different things. In fact, a "B" given by the same teacher on two different assignments or to two different students may not mean the same thing. Once I asked a group of principals who taught language arts to grade a photocopied grade 7 student composition. Their assigned grades ranked from a D- to a B!

Grades are norm-referenced; they compare students against each other. A "B" usually indicates somewhat but not exceptionally above average. Some schools also use *criterion-referenced* or *performance* assessment. It gives students and parents a detailed list of specific learning outcomes that students have successfully attained in each subject, but no grade. One advantage is that teachers base assessment on set criteria, rather than against other students. With criterion-referenced assessment, you expect your students to learn all the concepts and skills that the school deems important. You do more than just let them "pass." This type of assessment has less danger of becoming solely summative.

Criterion-referenced assessment does not tell parents how their children are achieving in relation to other students. Yet most parents still want to know this. That is why they like grades, especially when the average class grade is also shown. If assigned with care, grades can provide a useful indicator to parents. For, despite their limitations, grades do provide quick, symbolic summaries of overall student achievement. They may help to give students a realistic self-concept of their abilities in diverse areas. As well, they can be used to recognize excellence.

To minimize the hazards of grades, clearly explain the meaning of grades to students and parents and how they should interpret them. Have established criteria, even if they are informal ones, for giving specific grades. Ensure that their use is relatively consistent throughout the school. Since grades present an incomplete picture, accompany them with comments on essays, projects, and report cards. Avoid giving grades in the first few years of schooling. If young pupils get "pigeonholed" too quickly, research shows that weaker students perform more poorly in the long run.

If you use numerical percentage categories for assigning grades, do so flexibly. If a major test turns out to be too difficult (or easy), your pre-set scale has little validity. Further, if four or five students are all grouped right at the border of "B" and "C," there is no defensible reason for giving some a B and some a C. While a scale may provide a basic guideline, use "natural breaks" between groups of scores as well as the difficulty of tests and assignments to adapt the scale to a specific situation.

For completing report cards, use your anecdotal notebook, your checklists, and your mark book. Then you can be specific and give helpful feedback about significant aspects of student progress. Balance positive comments with constructive criticism. At parent-teacher interviews, have sample work available for parents. Point out specific strengths and weaknesses of students' work. Both your reports and your parent-teacher interviews should develop a "we-together" attitude of mutual cooperation.

◆ACTIVITY 6-11

In the history of western civilization, the use of grades such as A, B, C, D, and F is a relatively recent phenomenon. At times, such grading has been controversial. Educators have suggested using a pass/fail system instead. However, research shows that grades do motivate many students to learn more. Debate the pros and cons of grading, and whether and how they can be used in positive ways.

◆ACTIVITY 6-12

Photocopy an unassessed student assignment. Ask each person in your group to assess and grade it. Discuss the results, drawing conclusions about the consistency of criteria and standards used.

Using assessment to improve learning

♦ *Connie Clements' and Jim Vance's school staff decide to re-*
view their student assessment procedures. Connie and Jim be-
come part of a committee that considers what a Christian
approach to assessment and evaluation should involve. The
committee does not find a large number of Bible texts with a di-
rect bearing on evaluation. But they do conclude that a number
of Scriptural givens are relevant.

First, each child is a unique image of God. Therefore teach-
ers use assessment to keep track of each pupil's progress and
responses. They do not use it just to rank them. Ideally, assess-
ment leads students to boost their learning, not to hinder it. It is
not always done by the teacher. Students learn to assess and
evaluate their own work. They also learn to contribute to the
learning of others through peer assessment.

Secondly, the fruit of the Spirit must be evident in student
assessment. Ideally, teachers are motivated by love and fair-
ness. They patiently reassure students and animate their learn-
ing as they assess and evaluate. They help their students strive
for excellence. But excellence for the Christian does not mean
being first or second academically. Rather, it means developing
all of one's gifts and abilities optimally for service to God and
neighbor. That means that assessment takes into account effort
and progress as well as achievement.

The committee shows that much of the school's assessment
has focused in giving summative information to parents. Also, it
points out inconsistencies. For instance, some teachers use
mainly student work to grade students and give mostly B's on
report cards, while others put a heavy emphasis on tests and
have a wide spectrum of grades.

After some initial discussion, the teachers write a coherent
student assessment and evaluation policy. They develop sample
skill checklists, project marking guides, and student profile
charts. They discuss how they can maintain the motivation of
weaker students while giving students and their parents realis-
tic information about performance and growth. They consider
how assessment can take place on a daily basis. They share
ideas on giving corrective yet positive feedback on assignments.
They discuss how evaluation can be an integral part of class-
room instruction, and how they should use the results of

teacher-made and standardized tests. They revise their report cards in order to give more specific and detailed information to parents.

The teachers establish a common understanding. They now seek out methods that help their students develop and use their abilities without disheartening them. They move away from allowing their teaching to be governed by their summative assessment. Instead, they consider how their intended learning outcomes can determine their assessment. They regularly ask themselves how their assessment strategies affect student attitudes and learning, and whether they are in touch with students' needs. They try to maintain high but realistic expectations, and to give much formative feedback. And now they use a summative grading guideline that clearly spells out what each grade means.

Of course, the teachers' different personalities and varying grade levels still mean that each goes about assessment and evaluation somewhat differently. It is still difficult to interest and motivate students frustrated by years of academic lack of success, or to be patient with lazy or uncaring ones. But the change of emphasis from summative to formative assessment and from judgment to encouragement improve student learning and achievement as well as classroom relationships.

◆ACTIVITY 6-13: **Reviewing the main points**

List the main points about assessment and evaluation arrived at by the staff of Connie Clements' and Jim Vance's school in the previous section. Are there any points you would add from the remainder of the chapter?

REFERENCES

Aker, D. 1995. *Hitting the mark: Assessment tools for teachers.* Markham, ON: Pembroke.

Baron, J. & Wolf, D. *Performance-based student assessment: Challenges and possibilities.* 95th Yearbook, Part 1. Chicago, IL: National Society for the Study of Education.

British Columbia Primary Teachers' Association. 1992. *Evaluation: Techniques and resources Book II.* Vancouver: British Columbia Teachers' Association.

Cornfield, R. et al. 1987. *Making the grade: Evaluating student progress.* Scarborough, ON: Prentice-Hall.

Edlin, R. 1994. *The cause of Christian education.* Northport, AL: Vision.

Good, T. & Brophy, J. 1994. *Looking in classrooms.* 6th ed. New York: HarperCollins.

Stiggins, R. 1997. *Student-centered classroom assessment.* 2nd ed. Upper Saddle River, NJ: Merrill.

Van Dyk, J. 1997. *Letters to Lisa: Conversations with a Christian teacher.* Sioux Center, IA: Dordt College Press.

Chapter 7

NURTURING STUDENTS IN COMMUNITY

*T*he first bell of the Faith Christian Community School *rings at 8:35 AM. Pupils flock to the doors. Teachers greet them with a cheery "Good morning!" while making sure that they enter in orderly fashion. The custodian, broom in hand, congratulates some grade 4's on the hall display they made about their current science unit. The school secretary helps several students. She says to one boy, "Kevin, I appreciate that you came in to tell me right away. But I am disappointed that you forgot your money again. Let's think of a way you will be sure to remember tomorrow."*

Principal Hall is the last person to come in. As usual, she spent the past fifteen minutes circulating through the school and playground. She talked with and gave words of encouragement to teachers, students, volunteers, and parents. She made a mental note to speak with two teachers. One of Ms. Brown's grade 2 students was troubled about the breakup of her family. And she wants to compliment Mr. Wood. His grade 8 students are excited and perceptive about a model they are making of an "ideal" community. Ms. Hall quickly delivers birthday cards to the two rooms where students have birthdays today. She also stops in the grade 5 class to thank it for organizing yesterday's chapel. There she finds students sharing prayer requests. She stays a few minutes for devotions.

Later in the day, she speaks with a prospective parent who has spent some time in the school. The parent remarks on the warm atmosphere of the school. "Everyone here seems to feel part of a close-knit community. People care for each other."

Ms. Hall replies that the school consciously works at this. She says, "All of us stand in relation to God as well as to each other. Our school tries to be a community that provides a supportive setting for developing everyone's gifts. That includes students, teachers, volunteers, secretaries, janitors, and, yes, our school board and committee members, too. We want to help each member of our school community to live as a responsive disciples of Jesus Christ."

"But many schools might make such claims," the parent says. "What, specifically, makes you different?"

"Well, what is basic is that all of us work together to develop an atmosphere of respect and responsibility. Everyone must feel and experience that they play an important part in making the school a pleasant and worthwhile place. Our parents helped us develop a 'school covenant.' It applies to everyone. One of its statements is that we treat people with love, respect, and compassion.

"As teachers we make this code part of our school's daily life. At the start of the year, we explain the covenant. Then we have our students help develop three or four general classroom rules that reflect the covenant. 'Be on time and prepared,' for example. Students also help in setting classroom procedures. The class reviews and practices the rules and procedures, both to give students a sense of security and to develop good habits."

"What does that have to do with being a Christian *school? Don't many schools do this kind of thing?"*

"Yes, they do," agrees Ms. Hall. "But our sense of community is rooted in our faith commitment. Our school covenant reflects God's covenant of grace with us, as described in Psalm 111. We are neither teacher-centered nor child-centered, but Christ-centered. Jesus allows us to live as responsive disciples. Jesus offers redemption to each person in the school, and allows us to use God's creation for his glory. That is why we work at developing a sense of spirituality. You've seen our prayer bulletin board in the hall and attended our weekly student-led chapel. On Monday mornings parents are encouraged to join our staff devotions in the school foyer. On Fridays be-

fore closing teachers and students review what God has done this past week. They pray specifically for personal and class needs for the next week. After school, the teachers together share joys and concerns and pray for each other and their students."

"I noticed some students in the hall working out some kind of disagreement," says the parent, "What is that all about?"

"Well, we have implemented a school-wide program of problem and conflict resolution. Right from kindergarten on, students learn and implement the steps of resolving problems themselves in a peaceful and loving way. Our trained student mediators help prevent problems, especially on the playground. We also team up younger classes with older ones to plan weekly 'buddy' activities. At each grade level some units address aspects of what it means to live as followers of Christ in community. And students put this into practice not only in their academic learning, but also in yearly service learning opportunities both inside and outside the school."

"But with all this going on, do you have time to teach all the academics?"

"When schools are places where people really care for each other, research shows that students like school more. Their attendance is better. They interact better socially, with fewer behavior problems. Not only that, but students are more motivated to learn. They work harder and achieve more (Lewis, Schaps & Watson 1996). We have a sound curriculum and set high expectations for our students. But more than that, our school works hard at implementing what Paul says in his letters about living as a Christian community. That helps us be a place where students learn well. Moreover, we also work at students learning to harness and use their emotions in socially effective ways. That is as important for how they will function in life as their academic achievement."

"What else I should know before I decide whether to enroll my child?"

"We believe that open communication is a key for making the school a community. We listen carefully to all students—our school exists for them! We try to be loving and positive. At the same time, we set high expectations for students to do likewise. We want our parents to have regular and open contact with our

staff. I will give you a copy of our school information package. Then, if you have any more questions, give me a call."

Along with parents and the mass media, schools are primary agents for enculturating children into society. We live in a pluralistic age where Biblically based values are often derided. Moreover, children and adolescents often endure serious emotional, social, and ethical problems. These may be brought about by factors such as little parental time for children, family breakdown, increased mobility, hedonistic individualism, waning of religious beliefs, and abuse of various kinds. Moreover, the media's commercialism is "a corrosive phenomenon that comes between parents and children, threatens nonmaterial human relationships, and undermines democratic values" (Molnar 1997, p. 164).

In the last twenty years, children throughout the world show more unhappiness, overdependence, anxiety, depression, inability to concentrate, loss of temper, hostility, aggression, moral insensitivity, and disobedience. Daniel Goleman calls this slide "a new kind of toxicity seeping into and poisoning the very experience of childhood, signifying sweeping deficits in emotional competences." He adds that within this context, schools have to go beyond their traditional mission to help children live with emotional, social and moral proficiency (1995, p. 233, 279). We therefore have to provide schools where students learn to live in and contribute to compassionate, just, and dependable communities.

Effective schools are *communities* for learning. They are more than collections of individuals going about their own tasks. School communities are united in common ideals and purpose. Their members commit themselves to each other. They recognize that unity and mutual support strengthens the whole school while allowing students' and teachers' individualities to flourish. They share with those in need, are faithful in prayer, and live in harmony with each other (Ro 12). They strive to make learning purposeful and effective for all. Teachers and students appreciate each other's gifts. They encourage their use and development for service.

No school community is perfect. The power of sin affects both teachers and students. That is why building school communities requires commitment and work. We put structures in place that encourage respect and responsibility. We develop policies that serve the welfare of students, not just administrative convenience. We strive to create a positive atmosphere in the staff room, halls, gym, library, and classrooms. We model and insist on courtesy and respect. We teach the steps and interpersonal skills for resolving conflicts. We pay attention to the emotional, social, and ethical dimensions of learning. While caring and supportive, we do not make learning painless. However, we do allow students to tackle new topics, overcome challenges, take risks, venture opinions, and make mistakes without feeling threatened or judged. We encourage students to help and collaborate with classmates. We give them a genuine say in the life of the classroom. We hold them responsible for the community they help shape.

Bob Frisken of the Christian Community Schools in Australia points out that in today's society "the task of the Church in discipling its students is a difficult, almost impossible task. I believe God has raised up Christian schools for this very purpose" (Frisken 1996a, p. 3). He adds that the school's culture, what it considers important in life, and the meanings it gives to words and actions all influence students' values, attitudes, and behavior in society.

Therefore school communities, Frisken concludes, should examine whether their stated values agree with those lived by teachers, parents, and students. Prescribing values does not work. Then students do what we want them to do, but only when we see them. We should work closely with homes and churches to strive to "display characteristics of a godly community." A balance of righteousness and mercy experienced in such a community will encourages students to walk responsively and responsibly with God and fellow creatures (Frisken 1996b, 1996c).

◆ACTIVITY 7-1

Describe your understanding of the term "learning community." Make a list of the four or five characteristics that you believe to be particularly important. Compare this list with the points mentioned by Ms. Hall in describing her school, and with lists made by two or three other persons. Can you reach a consensus?

◆ACTIVITY 7-2

Ms. Hall mentions the importance of open communication in a school. Describe and discuss several ways in which each of teacher-student, principal-teacher, and teacher-parent communication can enhance or detract from a sense of community.

◆ACTIVITY 7-3

David Purpel is a consultant for a network of nineteen American Roman Catholic schools. The fourth main goal of these schools is to "commit themselves to educate to the building of community as a Christian value." Specifically, adults model and teach skills needed to build community, with opportunities to exercise these skills. Further, the school provides experiences of diversity that develop an understanding and appreciation of all people.

Interestingly, many goals listed in other categories also emphasize the importance of community. The schools promote individual as well as communal prayer and reflection. They awaken a critical consciousness that leads its total community to reflect on society and its values. All members of the school community are to show concern and respect for one another. Students have opportunities to share their knowledge and gifts with others, to practice responsibility and decision making, and to exercise leadership. The schools are linked in a reciprocal manner to ministries with the poor and marginalized (Purpel 1991, pp. 54-55).

Imagine a day in the life of a grade 10 student in one of these schools. What would it be like? In what ways would it differ from the school you attended in grade 10? What would be the advantages and disadvantages of such a school?

Educating for character

Character education is nothing new. The Greek philosopher Aristotle already argued that communities will be strong only if children are habituated into appropriate virtues and then later learn the rationale for them. Strong communities cherish and perpetuate their traditions. "Wherever community is emphasized," says Nell Noddings, "character education will be important" (in Molnar, p. 8).

Therefore strong communities acquaint children with their traditions and value systems. God instructed the Israelites to do so (Dt 6:4-9; Ps 78:1-8). Paul also encouraged leaders to teach not only the basics of faith but also values such as temperance, self-control, love, respect, endurance, honesty and integrity, soundness in speech, peacefulness, obedience, humility, and doing good (Tit 2 and 3).

Character education develops moral and ethical behavior and habits. It promotes the virtues that Paul mentions in Titus as well as the fruit of the Spirit: love, joy, peace, patience, goodness, faithfulness, gentleness, and self-control (Gal 5:22-23). Virtues often mentioned today overlap with these: respect, responsibility, care, and compassion. All these traits are more than just personal ones. They also refer to a community's understanding of social justice and equality. They relate, for instance, to treatment of visible minorities and the economic disadvantaged. Thus character education goes beyond striving for improved personal morality. It also helps students to participate in creating a just and loving society (Purpel in Molnar 1997, p. 152). It also addresses, for example, communal economic greed, ecological devastation, and the cruelty of armed conflict. Character education affects individuals as they, in turn, affect their communities. "What does the Lord require of you? To act justly and to love mercy and to walk humbly with your God" (Mic 6:8).

In view of our current societal context, it is little wonder that character education has once again come to the fore. Its proponents want to teach morals and values explicitly in the schools. Schools do influence students' values, dispositions, and behaviors. Therefore they should try to do so directly and systematically (Lockwood in Molnar, p. 179). However, values clarification and Kohlberg's moral reasoning, popular in the 1970's and 1980's, fell short. Values clarification rejected universal moral standards. It allowed students to choose their own values, leading to individualism and ethical relativism. Yet even among non-Christians there is widespread agreement on basic values that can be taught. These include respect, responsibility, fairness, empathy, compassion, and integrity. Effective moral education programs stress both knowledge of such values and acting on them. Kohlberg fell short in that his approach promoted moral reasoning but did address actual ethical behavior.

Christian schools involve, on the whole, fairly homogeneous value communities. Therefore they are able to plan and implement sound character education programs. But a positive school ethos does not happen by chance. Diane Berreth and Sheldon Berman suggest that each of the following is prerequisite to a school becoming a moral community (1997, pp. 25-27):

♦ *The school community collaboratively develops, clearly states, and celebrates core moral values.*

♦ *Adults exemplify positive moral values in their work with one another and with students.*

♦ *Students develop skills in and practice goal setting, problem solving, cooperation, conflict resolution, and decision making.*

♦ *Educators use a problem-solving approach for discipline.*

♦ *School communities provide opportunities for service—within and outside the school.*

♦ *Students and staff members appreciate the diversity in cultures and beliefs through both study and direct experience.*

♦ *At least one caring adult is personally connected with each child.*

◆ACTIVITY 7-4

Consider each of the points made by Berreth and Berman. How does each contribute to a school being a moral community? What difference would each make in the life of a school? Do you agree with all points? For instance, is it necessary for all students and staff members to "appreciate the diversity in cultures and beliefs"? How do you interpret the word "appreciate"?

Thomas Lickona is well known for his work in character education. He suggests twelve strategies to foster character development, nine for the classroom and three school-wide ones (Lickona in Molnar 1997, pp. 47-59):

♦ *Teachers serve as effective caregivers, moral models, and ethical mentors.* They love, respect and support their pupils.

They demonstrate moral sensitivity and responsibility. Also, they give moral instruction and guidance through explanation, storytelling, discussion, encouraging positive behavior, and corrective moral feedback.

♦ *Teachers create a caring classroom community.* They help students to get to know each other. They encourage them to respect, care about, and affirm each other. Also, they make them feel valued and accountable members of the class.

♦ *Teachers help students develop moral discipline.* They foster moral reasoning, self-control, and a generalized respect for others. Students learn to follow value-based rules because they respect the rights and needs of others.

♦ *Teachers create a democratic classroom atmosphere* where there is shared decision making that increases responsibility for the classroom climate.

♦ *Teachers teach values through the curriculum.* They deliberately choose curriculum content to encourage students to examine questions of morality and social justice.

♦ *Teachers implement collaborative learning activities.*

♦ *Teachers combine high expectations with high levels of support for student work,* so that students feel satisfaction with a job well done.

♦ *Teachers nurture ethical reflection.* They encourage students to apply general ethical principles to concrete situations and dilemmas, both in the planned curriculum and in issues that arise in the life of the classroom.

♦ *Teachers teach conflict resolution.*

♦ *The school community creates a positive moral culture throughout the school.* All this is done so that students commit themselves to and consistently act on a set of positive values. This may be a multi-year program. One school set objectives and strategies for developing and maintaining a positive school ethos in Year 1. It developed students' sense of responsibility for their work and behavior during Year 2. In Year 3 it emphasized conflict resolution. In Year 4 it focused on community service.

♦ *The school cares beyond the classroom.* It provides service opportunities with the potential to develop character. Kenneth Burrett and Timothy Rusnak add that the curriculum itself must allow students not only "to confront meaningful questions in the school and in the community," but must also "become involved in activities and actions to implement those solutions wherever feasible" (1995, p. 16). In other words, *responsible action* is a key ingredient of character education.

♦ *The school recruits parents and the community as partners in character education.* Parents are the primary nurturers of children, and schools need their input and support. Home-based activities (either school- or parent-initiated) are important for character education. The wider community (churches, businesses, local governments) are also often willing to cooperate in a consistent effort.

◆ACTIVITY 7-5

Develop some specific classroom activities for each of Lickona's strategies (if possible, brainstorm in a small group). Would all of Lickona's strategies be effective for all age levels?

Lickona has been criticized for emphasizing personal virtues rather than looking at social issues and problems. David Purpel believes that the type of character education proposed by Lickona is

> very much in the line of Puritan traditions of obedience, hierarchy, and hard work, values which overlap nicely with the requirements of an economic system that values a compliant and industrious workforce, and a social system that demands stability and order. There is an ideology here that puts very strong emphasis on control-adult control of children . . . The problems are acknowledged to be largely social but the proposed solutions are largely personal! (Purpel in Molnar 1997, pp. 145-46).

Is Purpel's criticism legitimate? Why or why not? How would you revise Lickona's strategies to satisfy Purpel? Would you prefer Lickona's original set of strategies or the revision? Why?

◆ACTIVITY 7-6

The Bible is clear that God calls communities to enculturate its youth into a way of life that upholds God's values. Some Christians disagree, however, that schools should play a role in this. Some argue that schools should teach academics, and leave the teaching of values to parents and churches. They claim that teaching values infringes on parental rights and responsibilities. Also, in a pluralistic society, a common value base no longer exists–even Christians differ on issues such as euthanasia and homosexuality. So, inevitably, students will be taught some values that undermine those taught in the home, especially in public schools.

If you disagree with this argument, construct a well-argued rebuttal for a public school setting. If you agree with the argument, which ones of Lickona's strategies would you reject for your classroom? Which ones could you still accept? Why?

Nurturing emotional and social health

Daniel Goleman in his 1995 book, *Emotional Intelligence*, argues that emotional and social "intelligence" is more closely linked to success later in life than academic achievement. He describes a study of four-year olds who were given a marshmallow. A researcher told the children that they could eat the marshmallow right away. If they waited until the researcher returned, however, they could have two marshmallows. About one-third ate the marshmallow right away. Another third waited a little longer. The remainder waited for the full fifteen to twenty minutes until the researcher returned.

When these same children were tracked down as adolescents, those who had been able to wait were more self-assertive and better able to cope with school and with life. Those who had eaten the marshmallow right away were not as well liked by their peers. They were easily frustrated, and provoked more arguments and fights. Also, they scored an average of 210 points lower on the Scholastic Aptitude Test than the ones who had waited. The main point made by Goleman is that particularly when children are young, they can learn emotional skills such as impulse control and accurately reading a social situation–with positive payoffs (Goleman 1995, pp. 80-83).

What has become clear is that students' emotional and social development affects their learning. That is why some schools are bringing emotional literacy into their curriculum. Most effective, according to Goleman, are small but telling lessons, delivered regularly over a sustained period of years (1995, p. 263). An example is a grade 5 lesson on identifying and distinguishing between feelings from pictures of a person's face. The students imitate and describe six basic emotions. Connecting facial expressions with feelings is important particularly for argumentative students who often misinterpret neutral expressions as hostile ones (1995, pp. 270-71).

There appear to be two crucial periods for emotional and social development: ages five and six, and the onset of adolescence. School discourages and frustrates young children who come to school without the social and emotional understandings necessary to cope with the classroom situation. Teachers can help students understand their own and others' motivations and intentions. Early adolescence is also a crucial time for learning emotional skills. It is a time when teens often suffer rejection or begin to experience depression. For intellectually able girls at this age, pressure to conform faces them with a serious conflict between their identity as achievers and their identity as females. Often schools give them little help in developing self-awareness, appropriate life goals, or a meaningful philosophy of life (Porath & Matthews 1997, pp. 7-10).

Certain insights and skills benefit students' emotional and social growth. Goleman points to recognizing and understanding feelings, managing and harnessing emotions productively, reading emotions with sensitivity and empathy, and handling relationships. The extent to which teachers should or are willing to involve themselves in this, however, is problematic. They have many other concerns. Also, they depend mainly on their own resourcefulness, since the few existing programs are not widely available. Again, some parents object to schools tackling what they consider family matters.

Yet students, as images of God, are holistic beings. Their emotional and social states and competencies affect their academic achievement. Teachers can be proactive in a number of ways, not the least of which is to be sensitive and respond to their students' feelings. Some courses such as health, guidance, or personal planning do address emotional and social development (for example, units on friendship). Also, many literary selections involve feelings and social interactions that can be discussed in class.

What is significant is that many of the strategies suggested for emotional and social growth are similar to those promoting character education. Both recommend teaching conflict resolution and using peer mediators. Both use stories such as "Frog and Toad Are Friends" or *Charlotte's Web* to discuss feelings, perspective-taking, caring, and the qualities of a good friend. Both use discipline "problems" as potential learning situations. Both employ class meetings to teach students to get along in a respectful way. Both ask students to role play difficult situations. Both promote service learning with follow-up seminars where feelings and positive social strategies are discussed.

The reason for this intersection is that character and emotional/social development are closely intertwined. Many primary emotions are closely related to Biblical commands. *Love* is part of the Great Commandment. *Anger* can lead to breaking the sixth commandment. *Envy* and *jealousy* are forbidden in the tenth commandment. *Disgust, shame* and *sadness* often (though not always!) arise from sinful acts; *fear,* from perceived or threatened sinful acts. Emotions such as surprise and enjoyment, or emotional disorders, are less directly linked to Biblical injunctions, of course. But those, too, affect people's behavior. Thus character education and emotional and social development overlap.

Research in character education as well as in social/emotional learning shows that both are important ingredients in enabling young people to take on their roles as responsive disciples in community. Students who do not act on sound ethical principles or whose emotional or social insights and skills are lacking will have difficulty functioning positively in their communities. They will break covenant with other persons and, ultimately, with God. Nevertheless, God still extends his grace to them. So if as teachers we walk with God in the classroom, we will show especially those students who lack moral commitments or emotional or social skills all the love and support we can muster, wearying as that can be.

◆ACTIVITY 7-7

Find some books or recent journal articles that deal with character education or emotional/social learning. It could be a classic such as Aristotle's *Nicomachean Ethics*. Or it could be a more recent best seller such as Thomas Lickona's *Educating for Character* (1991) or Daniel Goleman's *Emotional Intelligence* (1995). Journals such as *Educational Leadership* and *Phi Delta Kappan* also regularly discuss these issues, as well as journals dealing specifically with moral education. Report on the recommendations made by specific authors. If you are a member of a class, have some of you report on the latest developments in the field.

Service learning

The Bible makes clear that knowledge is more than the learning of concepts and skills. Faith, knowledge, and deeds are all intertwined (Ja 3). A Christian worldview cannot remain a theoretical thing; it must guide action. Schools can provide service learning opportunities as one way for students to exercise their knowledge and deepen their commitment while building community. Service learning allows students to follow Jesus' footsteps: "Now that I, your Lord and Teacher, have washed your feet, you also should wash one another's feet (Jn 13:14).

Schools plan service learning activities to enable students to improve community life. In well-designed programs, "students do more than ladle out soup to the homeless or pick up trash ... They apply what they've learned in the classroom, develop leadership and communication skills, become more caring and responsible citizens–and help community needs in the process" (Willis 1993, p. 4). Good projects involve direct experiences that connect students with their communities. They also stimulate reflective thought about their meaning, however. For instance, students may meet once a month for a "reflection session" to discuss students' experiences and explore related questions. Some projects may combine service and research. For instance, students may combine a renovation of a homeless shelter with research on poverty in the community.

Service learning provides hands-on experiences for students. Many students learn especially well from this type of experience.

Service learning is therefore most effective when it becomes an integral part of the curriculum. Kindergartners can prepare programs for senior citizens while studying a unit on "All people are special." Grade 6's may plant small trees along an eroding river bank as part of a unit on water and its effects. Grade 9's may use what they have learned in a unit on statistics to design and conduct a neighborhood survey on recreational needs in the community. Grade 11's may set up recreational programs for young offenders while studying crime and justice. In all such cases the community benefits, and the students' learning is motivated and enriched.

Pacific Academy, a large Christian school in British Columbia, involves all students from kindergarten to grade 12 in service learning. The purposes of its program are:

- *To "open students' eyes" to the needs of others in their community and around the world.*

- *To recognize that each of us has God-given abilities and to provide opportunities where students use them outside the classroom.*

- *To acknowledge that God has created us as part of the Body of Christ and to use our gifts and abilities to bring glory to God in community with others.*

- *To experience and appreciate the responsibility of world evangelism and to have opportunities to respond in obedience to Christ's call on their lives.*

Other goals might include to develop a sense of responsibility for life in the community, and dispositions for active community participation and service.

A large variety of service learning activities are possible, both inside the school and in the community. Here are some that teachers have shared with me:

- *Helping in the classroom:* Students help set up audiovisual equipment or science experiments, arrange bulletin boards, or are in charge of learning centers. Older students help younger ones by writing out stories told by younger ones and reading them back. Grade 1 and 2 classes make ABC or thematic "Big Books" that are shared with kindergarten classes. Students tutor their peers or mentor younger ones.

◆ *Helping around the school:* Students volunteer in the library of office. They are trained as peer mediators/counselors or as "kindersitters" during recess. Students organize and referee games and sports activities. They serve as monitors on the playground and on the school bus. They organize special events such as a grandparents' day or fundraising efforts for special projects. A class takes responsibility for the school's recycling program, the food bank support program, or the student newspaper.

◆ *Presentations:* Students present drama and music productions to senior residences and hospitals. High school students write children's plays or songs and present these to pre-school groups, children's wards in hospitals, and public libraries.

◆ *Service in the community:* Students "adopt" a grandparent at a senior citizen's home. They pay them regular visits, clean their apartments, read to them, and/or shop for them. Students set up maintenance programs for halfway houses or youth emergency shelters. Students maintain a bird sanctuary in a nearby park. An art class makes a mural or other art work for a homeless shelter.

Some schools make a certain amount of service work, say 100 hours, compulsory for graduation. Such schools argue that all students should benefit from the joy of serving. They claim that students who would never volunteer benefit most. They add that, after all, the projects are an integral part of the learning program. But other educators counter that forcing students to volunteer devalues the experience, and that community agencies will not want to use resentful students who are there just to fulfill a requirement. Some high schools allow unwilling students to complete an alternative project.

◆ACTIVITY 7-8

Design a service learning program for either an elementary, a middle, or a high school. Keep in mind the aims of such a program as well as the following criteria:

Do the activities relate to the present living experiences of the students? Are they consistent with their maturity level? Do they provide for differences in abilities and interests? Do they encourage students to want to actively participate in community life? Do they cultivate dispositions to serve others and improve human relations? Do students experience and reflect on basic trends and tensions of life today? Can students complete the activities with a minimum of adult dominance? (Richard Lipka in Schine 1997, p. 61).

Overall, does the program contribute to students becoming responsive disciples of Jesus Christ? Would you make the program a compulsory one for all students? Why or why not?

Building community through spirituality

Although not the main focus of a school, devotional times, worship, and Bible study can foster community through fellowship with God and each other, sharing faith insights, and reflecting on what lies ahead during the day. Such activities are part of the school's total learning experience. Through them, schools help students learn how to worship and pray. [This section and the next make extensive use of a report that had input from twelve Christian school teachers (Van Brummelen 1986).]

Christian schools can encourage special fellowship through staff-student and staff-staff prayer. Staff-student prayer can be meaningful in one-on-one meetings between students and their homeroom teachers or counselors. The need for prayer often stems from a concern or problem that a student shares with a teacher. Prior to prayer, time is spent discussing the concern. Beside personal prayer for each student and for their own teaching-learning situation, teachers will also want to pray with one or several fellow staff members from time to time. I have experienced meaningful prayer on the phone with a colleague when the tasks God had placed before me overwhelmed me. While not a cure-all for problems, prayer is powerful and changes individuals as well as the tone of a school.

Regular chapel services balance daily classroom devotions. The whole school community needs to worship God. Chapels may include Biblically based, interesting, and sometimes provocative presentations. These will challenge students to dedicate and rededicate themselves to serve their Savior and Lord, also as they learn and study. Enthusiastic singing also strengthens community.

In middle and high schools, a student committee can plan the chapel schedule. In some schools, including elementary ones, different classes are responsible for chapels each week. Speakers can be students, teachers, parents, Christian professionals and businesspersons, missionaries, or pastors (ask the latter to share, not preach!). Student-led chapels take teacher time and guidance to develop student leadership. Tuned-out fellow students often sit up and notice when they hear a peer attesting to the reality of Jesus Christ in their lives. Students who feel awkward about speaking may read a written devotion or excerpts from their own work. Classes may plan chapels to sum up their thematic units or to celebrate special occasions.

Today, spirituality and holiness are considered old-fashioned terms. Communities and schools, also Christian ones, often emphasize science and technology, the importance of effective communication, and employment skills. Scripture is clear, however, that we cannot be wholesome without being holy. The Bible rejects a dichotomy between sacred and secular activities. Even the bells of the horses and cooking pots were to be holy to the Lord (Zec 14:20-21)!

If we pray a lot but are indifferent to applying the guidelines of Scripture to structure our classrooms and plan our curriculum, we are not spiritual. If we worship God in devotions and chapel but this does not penetrate our everyday teaching and learning, we disobey God's Word. On the other hand, maybe we just emphasize the need to get good grades or to strive for academic excellence. If we do so but neglect to listen to God, to study our Bibles, and to praise God in word and song, then we implicitly reject that worship and praise are distinct and necessary activities wherever Christians gather for a common purpose. Then we are not spiritual.

Spirituality and holiness are the direct result of the work of the Holy Spirit in us. Spirituality depends on commitment, trust in God, faith, hope, and love. We cannot force spirituality onto our students. But schools *can* provide an atmosphere that encourages commitment leading to spirituality, model a spiritual lifestyle, and nurture spiritual maturity. Spirituality may not be an "add-on" that provides a Christian veneer. Rather, spirituality ought to direct, pervade, and support everything that is planned in a Christian school. That includes its policies, its learning structures and activities, and the moral, emotional and social development that we discussed earlier in this chapter. Only then will a school be a true learning community where teachers and students learn to walk with God.

◆ACTIVITY 7-9

Revisit the goals of Christian schooling outlined in Chapter 1. Do these goals reflect the claim of this section that "spirituality ought to direct, pervade, and support everything that is planned in a Christian school"? Why or why not?

Building school community through school-wide activities

Some Christian educators shy away from the phrase "school spirit" because they associate it with the superficiality of cheerleading and winning the "big game." Nevertheless, good student morale and pride in a school positively influence the life of the school and classroom learning. Students sense that they belong. They feel an integral part of a significant learning community. To encourage cohesiveness and enthusiasm, teachers foster a caring, Christ-like attitude throughout the school. True school "spirit" occurs only where the fruit of Christ's Spirit manifests itself. The root of the word "enthusiasm," significantly, is "God-inspired" or "God-possessed."

Schools have endless possibilities to foster community solidarity. Here are some examples:

♦ *Middle and high schools have active and meaningful homeroom systems, with students staying with the same "advisory" group for several years.* Such homerooms allow teachers to form bonds with a specific group of students. Together they have devotions and discussions about school and personal concerns. They plan occasional special events together. They have class meetings about school-related issues. Homerooms can also work together on projects such a writing a class song or doing a service learning activity. Teachers serve as role models as they work closely with a relatively small group of students. The sharing and caring that takes place in the homeroom setting is the basis of the sense of community in the whole school.

♦ *Students have meaningful audiences for projects* through displays, visits by other classes, and exhibitions in the gymnasium.

♦ *Schools have regular school-wide celebrations.* These might include school-community breakfasts, fine arts festivals, pajama reading sessions in the school library, special assemblies, and track meets where teams with students from all grades collecting points together.

♦ *Class outings such as field studies, swimming and skating excursions, science fairs and fine arts festivals, and special cross-grade integral units or exploratory mini-courses* are excellent ways for students and teachers to interact in different ways and in different environments. Outings become opportunities for cooperative planning. Some schools expect teachers to help plan one special event annually: an outdoor education camp, a math or chess contest, a science fair, a drama or musical production, a special school theme week, a student exchange program, or a service learning project.

♦ *Extra-curricular activities can foster a sense of belonging to the school community.* The Student Council can sponsor various clubs and organize special events. It may hold a snow sculpture contest after a heavy snowfall or a short pep rally before a school team goes away for a game. A school newspaper, yearbook, and intramural sport activities can also bind students together. Interschool sport teams should emphasize building team relationships, cooperation and sportsmanship. A winning-at-all-costs attitude has no place in a Christian school.

♦ *Schools consciously and consistently offer student leadership positions and nurture leadership skills.* Teachers help students work out and implement a vision through goal-oriented servant leadership. Teachers encourage and coach students to develop specific goals that they can accomplish themselves. Depending on their age and maturity, students can serve on committees that help organize safety patrols, choose school jackets, plan chapels, organize band trips, or revise the school handbook.

A Student Council gives students an opportunity to give leadership to the whole school. A Council can plan special events and outings, help organize hot lunches, and arrange sponsorships of a Third World orphan or a missionary. They can also address problems such as messy hallways or name calling, develop welcome programs for new students, or provide a child care service during parent-teacher interviews. Note that meaningful student leadership usually does not happen unless one or two teachers help students define their goals and deliberately foster leadership skills.

There are three other factors that affect the school as a community: the school's physical condition, its policies, and school size. First, *the school's physical environment* affects school "spirit." Is the facility well cared for? Are the classrooms tidy each morning? Is garbage picked up throughout the day? Are school and equipment repair dealt with quickly? At the high school level a lounge area adjacent to the office area (for unobtrusive but constant supervision) can be a valuable gathering place. An attractive guidance area, a library designed to welcome students, a corner for table tennis–all these help students feel that the school cares about them and for them. A well-kept, attractive school creates pride of belonging.

Second, *school policies* can enhance but also detract from a sense of community. My own institution opened a beautiful new cafeteria this year, with an enhanced food service. But a major controversy ensued. In an effort to keep part of the old cafeteria open, those in charge decided that microwaves for those wanting to heat their own food would be available only in the old cafeteria. Two mistakes were made. First, the students had not been consulted beforehand. Second, the importance of students–whether they bought a lunch or brought their own–to be able to eat together in community was overlooked. Thankfully, the decision was reversed.

One thing that becomes clear here is that as students get older, schools need to get their input when policy changes need to be made. Almost always, students make sensible suggestions when they recognize and understand a problem. Generally they will be more committed to the new policy when they have been consulted. This contributes to a healthier sense of community.

In order to provide a Christian environment, Christian schools nurture tendencies and behaviors that glorify God. Therefore, they have every right to expect their students to live by Biblical standards, whether or not the students have made a commitment to Christ. Guidelines are best written so that they point to the general principles God gives so that communities can function in positive and enriching ways. Very detailed and specific rules often cause resentment or defiance of the rules in spirit if not in letter. Codes of conduct in themselves do not create spiritual maturity. They do provide a context, however, that allows students to obey their God-given calling joyfully, in harmony with God's basic precepts. Many schools therefore require adolescents to sign a statement that they will support the school and its policies.

Finally, it is easier to build a sense of community in *schools that are small in size* (less than 250 students for elementary and 350 for high schools). Small schools require participation by teachers and students. In turn, they feel that they "belong." One research report showed that schools under 150 students had from three to twenty times more student participation than high schools of more than 2,000. In small schools, everyone senses that their contributions are important. They have a voice in decision-making and decisions are made more easily. Students develop far fewer self-interested social groups and cliques. Friendships are more flexible and non-exclusive. Teachers also feel more collegiality and support.

Most small schools have a coherent mission. Its simpler organization makes it more responsive to students. At higher grades, its diversity of course offerings is limited. Since teachers use more personalized approaches, however, especially students who are at-risk are much more likely to succeed. Small high schools can influence post-high school behavior positively, including college attendance. Also, parents are more willing to become involved (Gregory & Smith 1987; Meier 1996; Raywid 1998).

Whether any of the suggested approaches or school parameters help school cohesiveness depends on the general ethos of the school. Foremost in an enthusiastic ("God-inspired!") school is whether all people–students, teachers, and other staff–are treated with respect and have meaningful and rewarding tasks. It means that teachers will give and receive peer feedback voluntarily. They will discuss problems openly in order to improve teaching and learning. It also means that that teachers will advance students' personal welfare and engage them deeply in learning (Kohn 1996, pp. 110ff.). If done within an ethos of love and care, then the suggested activities will enhance the spirit of the school because the Spirit's presence will be felt.

◆ACTIVITY 7-10

This section lists many possible activities that can be used to enhance a sense of community in a school. For the grade levels you teach or intend to teach, list the three school-wide activities that you would prioritize as most effective for this purpose. Give reasons. Compare and discuss your list with that of another person.

◆ACTIVITY 7-11

Outline, with reasons, your views of the school policies below:

◆　An admission policy for a Christian school that accepts only students who are committed Christians or who have at least one parent who is a Christian.

◆　An attendance policy for high school students that suspends students after three unexcused absences from class.

◆　A dress code for a middle school that prescribes school uniforms.

◆　A mandate for a Student Council that makes all Council decisions subject to review by the principal or his/her designate.

◆ACTIVITY 7-12

Some people argue that interscholastic sports programs promote an individualism at odds with Christian community characteristics and force most students to be spectators rather than participants. Can an interscholastic sports program foster a sense of Christian community? Or should schools emphasize the involvement of a large proportion of its students in intramural sports?

◆ACTIVITY 7-13

Schools in North America have generally become larger between 1930 and 1980. Especially at the high school level, larger schools allow for more teacher specialization. It has therefore often been argued that larger schools can best meet the academic needs of individual and exceptional students. This section presented the other side of the argument. What do you consider a good size for an elementary school? a middle school? a high school? Why? Keep in mind that we want schools to provide quality programs and also foster supportive communities of learning.

Working as a team of teachers in community

♦ *Ms. Hall recognizes that as principal she has a leading role in forging the teachers into a unified team. While the school insists that its teachers agree with its vision and values, they have much flexibility within that framework. Ms. Hall respects each staff member's insights and abilities. She encourages teachers to take initiatives while she provides support. She is open to suggestions and has an "open door" policy. As much as possible, she tries to reach decisions by consensus. Ms. Hall delegates tasks according to teachers' expertise and preferences. Sometimes she relieves teachers so that they have the time to carry out special tasks. She also teaches an hour each day in order to stay in close touch with students and teachers.*

Ms. Hall and her teachers recognize the necessity of joint worship, prayer, and reflection. They get together for brief devotions every morning. They also hold an annual mid-year retreat to get away from their urgent concerns and focus on their spiritual growth. Such retreats include private devotion time; group Bible study, worship, and praise; and reflection on God's will for the school.

Ms. Hall and her staff also plan regular "sharing sessions." Teachers share their successes and frustrations. Some sessions have a specific focus. How can we improve parent-teacher communication? How is the art program going? Some sharing sessions are inconclusive, but others lead to proposed changes. Ms. Hall consults teachers about all policy changes. As a result, they have a sense of ownership and pride in the school. They are stakeholders rather than employees.

However, devotions, sharing sessions and consultations are not enough. Ms. Hall strongly feels her responsibility to help teachers develop their insights and abilities. She solicits input from her staff about the school's in-service program. The first sessions take place a week before the start of the new school year. These allow teachers to discuss the vision of the school and review how they can attain the school's goals.

The teachers of Faith Christian Community School have different abilities and insights. Some are gifted musicians. One has a special interest in athletics. Another gives leadership in curriculum planning. Several have expertise in specific subject areas. One teacher is a detail person who enjoys organizing special events. Two or three enjoy mentoring new teachers. Before the start of the school year, the teachers discuss how they can best use their special gifts and interests for the entire school community. The atmosphere of open discussion helps teachers commit themselves to being part of a school team working together for the good of the whole school without anyone becoming overloaded.

Ms. Hall's uses frequent short classroom visits for support and encouragement. For longer visits, she usually has a brief conference with the teacher beforehand to discuss what things will be useful to observe. Ms. Hall asks teachers to evaluate themselves. Post-visit conferences become forums for sharing feelings and insights—and setting mutual goals. Ms. Hall's annual evaluation reports describe these goals and to what extent they were achieved. Ms. Hall's approach shows that she uses her authority as principal to assist her teachers.

That doesn't mean that Ms. Hall's relations with her teachers are always smooth. Her teachers have different personalities with diverse views and expectations. They have a range of teaching styles. Some are more receptive to new ideas than others. Ms. Hall builds community but not uniformity. She encourages open discussion about differences. Nevertheless, she insists that all work be done within the framework of the vision of the school and its supporting community.

When hiring teachers, Ms. Hall assesses whether prospective teachers will model what it means to be a member of a Christian community. Do they display a naturalness and openness about their relationship with God and how God acts in their lives? Do they actively seek to live in communion with God? Do they study and use their Bibles to determine their lifestyle, to choose their involvement in Christian and other groups, and to make decisions? Have they witnessed for Christ in various spheres of life?

Do they model a neat and modest appearance? Ms. Hall knows that her teachers' personal qualities are important to the school. As a unit, her staff must be able to model Christian love, honor, and thoughtfulness. They must be sensitive to diverse views within the Christian community supporting the school. They must have an esprit de corps that supports the spiritual and community tone of the school.

Ms. Hall also investigates how teachers have treated students in the past. Did they deal respectfully with their students and show genuine concern for their personal and academic growth? Were they loving but punctual and firm? Did they follow up students' questions and concerns? Did they do something "special" with each child from time to time? Above all, did they demonstrate their commitment to Jesus Christ to the students? Ms. Hall also introduces promising candidates to her teachers for feedback as to how the applicant will fit into the "team." Once hired, Ms. Hall holds meetings with newly hired teachers to discuss the philosophy and goals of the school and how the school tries to implement them. The school requires teachers who lack a background in Christian approaches in teaching and learning to take courses to ensure that they understand the school's vision.

ACTIVITY 7-14

Make a list of questions that Ms. Hall might ask a prospective teacher in an interview. Then use the questions to simulate an interview for a position at Faith Community Christian School.

Involving parents and other volunteers

The school is part of a larger community. That larger community in turn is part of the school. The responsibility of children's basic nurture rests with parents (Dt 6:7; Eph 6:4). The home inculcates basic attitudes toward God, other people, self, authority, and learning. Parents thus have a major effect on schools and how their children experience them. Moreover, to be Christian communities of learning, schools need parental support and involvement. A school is a community school only to the extent that parents have a meaningful role in its operation. Together, parents and teachers need to set a direction for learning and discuss related issues.

In many Christian schools parents are members of the board, the education or other committee, or parent advisory council. In this way parents contribute directly to setting and implementing the school's overall direction. At the same time, in order for parents and schools to understand each other, many schools also hold orientation meetings for new parents as well as parent-teacher meetings that discuss topics of common interest.

What is also effective in bonding homes and schools are home-school activities that invite parents to shape and participate in the school's social life. Families may also complete assignments before they are discussed in school (for instance, the family might read a story of an 11-year-old boy who shoplifts a CD, and then discuss what a friend who sees this should do; or students might interview their parents about their views on friendship). Where families and schools work together to promote learning, student learning improves (O'Neil 1997; Schaps et al. 1997).

Parents, grandparents, preservice teachers and other volunteers can provide invaluable service to schools. Volunteers can do many tasks for which teachers do not have time. Some can assist individual students with learning difficulties or in the library. Some can organize escorts and transportation for field studies. Some may teach short option courses. Others will pray for specific school concerns. Many are willing to prepare learning materials for students.

The presence of volunteers provides students with opportunities to relate to other adults. Especially students from disadvantaged homes benefit from having other adult role models. Adult volunteers enrich students' school experience and make them realize that adults are interested in their learning and well-being. They experience a community at work. At the same time, volunteers usually become more committed to the school and its program. Parent volunteers gain a deeper understanding of what school is like for their students. Schools do well to show volunteers regular formal appreciation for their work, perhaps during an annual tea.

Schools can observe several cautions to ensure that volunteers contribute to and become part of the school community. They may hold an in-service session for volunteers at the start of the year. Such a session might discuss expectations, set out schedules, and emphasize that teachers count on volunteers during those times. Volunteers work under the direction of a teacher who also reviews the expectations. Sometimes volunteers intimidate students, do their work for them, or are sloppy in carrying out tasks. The school might try to find a more suitable task for them. If necessary, the principal may have to talk to a volunteer gently but firmly, difficult as this is when people give generously of their time.

A school staff can keep parents fully informed of what is happening in the school through after-school informal contact, phone calls, newsletters, open houses, and parent-teacher meetings. A community informed of the school's joys and struggles is a community that is more likely to support the school. Honest communication develops mutual respect and trust, hallmarks of a true community.

ACTIVITY 7-15

Make a list of potential benefits and pitfalls of volunteer involvement in schools. How can schools prevent the pitfalls? Why do elementary schools use volunteers much more extensively than high schools?

Reviewing the main points

1. *For effective learning, schools need to be communities of love, care and respect* where all the stakeholders–parents, students, teachers, staff, board and committee members–have important roles and their voice is heard.

2. *The principal of an effective school is a servant leader*, a catalyst who pulls together the stakeholders in the community to develop, maintain and implement a common vision.

3. Each of the following contributes to a school being a positive community of learning (see also Newmann & Wehlage 1996):

♦ *spiritual unity and fellowship*

♦ *pursuit of a common vision*

♦ *school-wide activities that promote unity of purpose and "lift the spirit"*

♦ *education for character as well as for emotional and social development*

♦ *service learning that is an integral part of the curriculum*

♦ *relatively small school size*

♦ *the principal and teachers working as a team*

♦ *staff development consistent with the school's mission*

♦ *meaningful parental involvement*

ACTIVITY 7-16

Speak with a principal or a superintendent about their views of effective schools. Compare their views with the foregoing list.

REFERENCES

Aristotle. 1985. *Nicomachean Ethics*. Translated by T. Irwin. Indianapolis, IN: Hackett.

Burrett, K. & T. Rusnak. 1993. *Integrated Character Education*. Bloomington, IN: Phi Delta Kappa Educational Foundation.

Frisken, R. 1996. The task of teaching. *Christian Community Schools Curriculum News* 16(1): 3-4.

Frisken, R. 1996. The importance of teaching. *Christian Community Schools Growing Up* 18(1): 3-4.

Frisken, R. 1996. School culture. *Christian Community Schools Curriculum News* 16(2): 3-4.

Goleman, D. 1995. *Emotional intelligence.* New York: Bantam.

Kohn, A. 1996. *Beyond discipline: From compliance to community.* Alexandria, VA: Association for Supervision and Curriculum Development.

Lewis, C., E. Schaps, & M. Watson. 1996. The caring classroom's academic edge. *Educational Leadership* 54(1): 16-21.

Lickona, T. 1991. *Educating for character: How our schools can teach respect and responsibility.* New York: Bantam.

Meier, D. 1996. The big benefits of smallness. *Educational Leadership* 54(1): 12-15.

Molnar, A. (ed.). 1997. *The construction of children's character.* 96th Yearbook, Part II. Chicago: National Society for the Study of Education.

Newmann, F. & G. Wehlage. 1996. *Successful school restructuring: A report to the public and educators by the Center on Organization and Restructuring of Schools.* Madison, WI: Wisconsin Center for Educational Research, University of Wisconcin-Madison.

O'Neil, J. 1997. Building schools as communities: A conversation with James Comer. Educational Leadership 54(8): 6-10.

Porath, M. & D. Matthews. Development in the social/emotional domain: Critical periods and educational facilitation. Unpublished paper presented at the Canadian Society for Studies in Education, June 12, 1997, St. John's, Newfoundland, Canada.

Purpel, D. 1991. Education as sacrament. *Independent Education* Spring: 45-60.

Raywid, M. 1998. Synthesis of research: Small schools: A reform that works. *Educational Leadership* 55(4):34-39.

Schaps, E., V. Battistich & D. Solomon. 1997. School as a caring community: A key to character education. In Molnar, A. (ed.), pp. 127-139.

Schine, J. 1997. *Service learning.* 96th Yearbook, Part I. Chicago: National Society for the Study of Education.

Van Brummelen, H. (ed.). 1986. Serving the Lord wholeheartedly: Spirituality in British Columbia's Christian schools. Langley, B.C.: Society of Christian Schools in B.C.

Willis, S. 1993. Learning through service. Association for Supervision and Curriculum Development *Update* 35(6): 1-8.

Chapter 8

TEACHING IN PUBLIC SCHOOLS[1]

PATRICIA needed time out to think and pray about her teaching vocation. Finding a seat on a park bench overlooking the city, she began to contemplate her situation:

I want to bring my faith to my vocation. But how? Can I weave the Bible into my lessons or should I drop an appropriate word outside of class? Can I design units of study around Christian values? Can I bring Christian books into my class? What about guest speakers I know are Christian? What can I say to parents, or will saying anything about the Christian faith that orients me and shapes my teaching get me into trouble? Should I limit my witness to fellow teachers in the staffroom?

There certainly are opportunities, but which ones are really significant? Am I really acting with integrity? The whole thing raises more questions than I have answers for.

Patricia recalled that it had all seemed more straightforward when she first began teaching eight years ago. She's tried all of

---

[1]This chapter was written by the Task Force on Education of the Evangelical Fellowship of Canada. Its members at time of writing were Brenda Babich, Ken Badley, Gary Duthler, Gary Hartlen, Kathy Hubley, John Janzen, David Knight, Robert Losier, Carla Nelson, Glenn Smith, Harro Van Brummelen, and Aileen Van Ginkel. It was first published and is available as a booklet under the title *Diversity and Faithfulness: Reflections for Christian Teachers on Plurality and Pluralism in Canadian Schools* (Markham, ON: Evangelical Fellowship of Canada, 1996). I made some minor changes for audiences beyond Canada and added four activities.

her strategies for integrating her faith with her vocation, but lately she's been sensing that they're contrived rather than natural, even done on the sly, hoping she won't be found out.

She reflected that her principal takes a very cautious line about religion in the school. The Lord's Prayer had been omitted from opening exercises soon after the school opened. The Christmas Concert has become the "Holiday Concert," and she has been told on more than one occasion to keep her religious views to herself. The principal once told Patricia that her first loyalty is to the Board.

"I think she respected my stand when I told her my first loyalty is to Christ, then my family and then my work. Still, there isn't a day goes by when I don't question how I should think about things that happen in the course of my work.

"I was happy when my pastor asked me to talk about the spiritual challenges of my life as a teacher. I could talk so freely about the incredible privilege of shaping young lives and of being a role model to them. I love the chance to bring a little sunshine into the lives of some sad children. But when I started talking about the really puzzling questions, I wasn't so sure.

"Do I have a right to restrict students' access to pornography on the Internet when the computer club meets at lunch time? How should I approach students from other countries, who don't share the same values as those of us who have lived here all our lives? What about the student I spoke with at lunch who is sure she's lesbian—should I have said what I did? What should I do with the course outline from the Ministry of Education that recommends those meditation exercises? Or the social studies curriculum that continually ignores the role of religion in the lives of people in our nation and around the world? And how will I propose that we begin our work on the new race-relations policy when we meet after school on Monday?"

Patricia teaches social studies in a junior high school in a suburban area outside a large city. Hers is a new school, built eight years ago for a new, upper middle class neighborhood that has recently received a very large influx of Asian immigrants. The school is home to some 650 students.

Patricia's experience will sound familiar to many Christians in Canada as well as elsewhere. That we face diversity on multiple levels is a fact few would contest. During the past thirty-five years,

Canadians, for instance, have seen a dramatic increase in the number of people who have come to Canada with different ethnic origins and different religious beliefs. At the same time, we have watched our neighbours take on varying lifestyles or points of view. The impact of this diversity will undoubtedly continue, especially in our school systems.

Many teachers look at this cultural, religious and ideological diversity—and panic. Looking for direction in a situation so different from the one in which they were educated, they ask, *How can I respond in a Christian manner to this diversity?*

Plurality and pluralism

♦ *"Well, my opinion is just as valid as yours," yelled an angry student, storming out of Roger's classroom.*

Patricia stuck her head in the door. "Are you being pig-headed again, Roger?" she teased. Roger was shaking his head. "I don't understand it, Patricia. Some things are so obviously crazy-wrong—you know it, but students just don't see it these days. You're the ethical genius, Patricia, what's the answer?"

"I'll let you know in the morning," Patricia said, "I don't have time to explore ethical theory right at the moment; I'm overdue for a meeting on copyright policy in the photocopy room."

To begin with, we need a clear definition of the issues and their implications. Keeping the words *plurality* and *pluralism* distinct helps us to get at the heart of the issue. The cultural and religious plurality in modern Western nations is something we live with. It's a given in today's society. Ideological pluralism, on the other hand, is a way of dealing with diversity and plurality. Indeed, it is based on premises that run counter to Christian beliefs about God and about who we are as human beings in God's world.

Cultural plurality refers to the presence of peoples from diverse backgrounds. Such backgrounds include nationality, ethnicity, religion and value framework. For nations such as Australia, Canada and the United States of America the image of a cultural mosaic is appropriate today. For example, among the roughly 200,000 students in one Canadian city, 168 countries are represented. The situation is similar in other major cities.

Religious plurality is also the order of the day. In 1991, 82 per cent of Canadians still identified themselves as Christians. However, many are Christian in name only. Moreover, this percentage has declined during each recent census. Of the remaining 18 per cent, five per cent belonged to a wide diversity of world religions. Thirteen per cent indicated no religious affiliation. While the precise figures differ for other Western nations, the trends are similar.

Unlike *plurality*, the term *ideological pluralism* describes not simply a fact of Western life but a way of dealing with plurality. It functions at the level of one's basic assumptions about the way the world operates. In combination with secularism and relativism, it provides the current consensus of opinion about the role that basic beliefs should play in public life.

Roger's student reflects a prevalent attitude in today's society. We are encouraged to be "tolerant" of all viewpoints and values. We are urged to recognize that there are several ways to believe and to behave, all of which are equally true. A 1994 Canadian survey raised the question, *Is what is right and wrong a matter of personal opinion?* More than half the respondents said *yes*–in every region of Canada   and for every age group. Even 49 per cent of weekly church attendees agreed! Clearly, ideological pluralism dominates the Canadian scene on this fundamental issue.

When more than half the population holds that values are just a matter of personal choice, it is no wonder that Patricia feels tension as she sits on her park bench. If the people she deals with hold to ideological pluralism, then none of her attempts to answer difficult questions will seem better than anyone else's answers.

Throughout much of history, most human beings have found themselves in a lifelong, uniform cultural context. Today in many Western nations, however, we constantly encounter people of different cultures, religious beliefs and lifestyles. Communications technology, such as television and the Internet, as well as rapid transportation put us in contact with other views in a matter of hours and even seconds. And the neighbors on our street may well belong to half a dozen different cultural groups.

What is new is not only the breadth of plurality but also society's response to it. The suggestion now is that plurality is not only accepted as a fact but actually required in intellectual, cultural and religious life. To claim that one group has an exclusive claim to truth is at best viewed as, *That's a unique perspective!* and at worst,

What gives you a corner on the truth?

It is important for Christians to grasp the historical and philosophical move toward this advocacy for diversity that we now call ideological pluralism.

In the 18th century, European philosophy placed its confidence in the power of reason to provide a certain foundation for knowledge. This confidence is often referred to as *rationalism.* The idea that divine revelation is essential was gradually discarded. Since then, the debate has raged on about how to find a rational foundation for "true truth" and a human basis for morality.

But in the last century, cracks began to appear in the trust people were willing to put in rationalism. A new movement, *romanticism,* appeared, which tried to capture the God-consciousness in each one of us. But this hope was lost, too. The painters and poets of our century have depicted the despair of a world gone wrong because it pursued pure reason and worshipped science. But they provided no alternative. There was no hope within or without.

In recent decades, philosophers also have begun to critique the modern world of reason and science. Many of them see no hope for a unique, external, transcendent truth. Indeed, they say, nothing can be known with certainty. History is devoid of purpose. Universal stories or quests for truth must be abandoned. Everything is relative. Truth is elusive, inward and subjective.

For many, this approach to truth is both desirable and normative. Those who hold to the philosophy of ideological pluralism do not just describe a state of affairs (plurality), but endorse a bias for a state of life where relativism reigns. This approach is sometimes called *postmodernism.*

♦ *As she rode home on the subway, Patricia opened a new reference book the librarian had asked her to review. It was a comparative religions text, called* Worldviews: The Challenge of Choice, *written by Ken Badley. She was dozing off when her eye flickered on the word tolerance. It jerked her back to reality. "That's it!" she shouted. The startled woman sitting beside her darted a puzzled look at her. Patricia apologized, then went back to the beginning of the paragraph. She read,*

> Living ethically requires that individuals and whole societies distinguish clearly those things that should be tolerated and those that should be celebrated. Today, many Canadians tend to think that tolerance is a virtue in itself, as if tolerating all differences is admira-

ble. Yet, most of us do not want a society in which beating up people we disagree with or the ancient Chinese tradition of footbinding
is tolerated. As well, too much talk of tolerance undermines the
sense that some of our differences are worthy of celebration. Racial
difference might inspire celebration—not merely tolerance—once
we pause to wonder that there are so many unique kinds of people
in the world. (Badley 1996, p. 28)

*The author outlined a continuum of responses to cultural,
religious and ethical diversity. The continuum ranged from what
can be* celebrated *in a pluralist society (such as personality and
racial diversity), what can be* respected *(such as differing religious holidays) and what can be* tolerated *(such as inconven-
iences due to linguistic differences) to what requires*
assimilation *(such as driving with the same set of traffic laws) or
outright* annihilation *(such as child abuse).*

*"That's the problem," Patricia thought. "My convictions seem
to sound arrogant and impertinent because I don't respond to
differences — especially differences of opinion — with a shrug
of my shoulders." Badley's continuum seemed to be a helpful
way to distinguish things. "Now I just have to figure out what
issue fits into what category. . . ."*

◆ACTIVITY 8-1

Think of situations and views on issues involving diversity that arise
in public school settings where you should respond with (a) celebration, (b) respect, (c) tolerance, (d) assimilation, and (e) annihilation.
Compare your list with that of another person. Try to establish criteria for placing a situation or view in each category.

Public schools in a pluralized society

Before we can talk about how Patricia might apply her changing
orientation to plurality in her classroom, we need to remind ourselves of the role of public schools in Western culture today.

Simultaneous with the loss of faith in transcendent, universal
truth has come the reduction of the social significance of institu-
tional religion. The church is no longer viewed as a structure in
society that helps people believe. A Canadian study of adolescents
asked, *Who would you go to for help in making a decision about*

money, relationships, sexuality, good and evil, school, vocation or a serious problem? Only four per cent indicated they would turn to a priest or a minister.

The Western family has also evolved in numerous ways in the past 30 years. The result is that the school is asked to provide day care services, feed poor children and tutor potential dropouts. Often, it must also integrate immigrant children into the dominant culture. And it must do so in a competitive global community that demands proficiency in languages, mathematics, computer skills and the sciences.

These new demands mean that the local school is being asked to do much more than educate students. It is also asked to bring *believability* and *meaning* to all sorts of subjects, including life itself. In a very real sense, the battle for how people will view life is being played out every day in the classroom.

Increasingly, our societies make a distinction between the public world of facts and the private world of values. In the former we discuss "truth" and issues that are viewed as objective and verifiable. This is what we know. In the latter we find beliefs and issues that are subjective.

What happens when religion becomes a subject in a curriculum? Or when the issue of funding faith-based schools comes up? In a column he wrote in the spring of 1996 for the *Globe and Mail*, Canada's major national newspaper, Michael Valpy articulated a common response:

> Religion in a liberal society belongs in private culture, in the family, and the house of faith. It does not belong in the public school system, which is our most important instrument of socialization, citizenship and community for all.

In Valpy's opinion, the exclusion of religion from the public school "does not compromise the right of Canadians to practice their faiths and raise their children in their faiths." Yet we must recognize Valpy's opinion as an expression of *ideology* or *religion* in its own right.

As human beings, we live out of a basic set of beliefs, core values or ideas that inform and guide our actions. We act in the world around us in terms of a *worldview* with which we make sense of life and which directs how we live. One's religious beliefs are an integral dimension of a worldview.

Therefore, we disagree with those who view the public arena as religiously or ideologically neutral or who think that religion should be kept private. Religion or ideology is the ultimate commitment that provides personal and communal direction to life. It is what is of ultimate importance to a person, community, group or institution. It informs the worldviews that are foundational to any political plan or, for that matter, any human enterprise in the public arena.

Religion deals with spirituality. It is at the heart of our human nature. We are born asking questions like: Who am I? What relationship do I have to other human beings? to the world around me? to God? How can I make sense of the world? Questions such as these must be answered so that we can have a sense of meaning and purpose in our lives.

It is impossible to separate values from ideology and religion, and to remove these from the public domain. According to *Webster's Dictionary*, religion is that which one holds to be of ultimate importance. Thus, education, because it deals with questions of ultimate importance, is inherently religious or value-based. Attempts to remove religion from education stem from the decidedly non-neutral beliefs which presume that religion is irrelevant to public life.

This ideology or religion espoused by Michael Valpy and others is secularism, that is, a view of life or any particular matter based on the premise that religion and religious considerations should be ignored or purposely excluded.

♦   *Lunch time—Patricia has just finished reading Valpy's column in the* Globe & Mail. *She is furious. With ten minutes left before class begins, she dashes to the computer room and fires off a quick e-mail note to Mr. Valpy.*

Dear Sir,

While I deeply respect your right to an opinion, why do you suppose that your secular convictions should be more acceptable in the public school than my religious ones? You've got to be the blindest bigot on the block!

"Not pretty," thinks Patricia, "but at least I feel better! I'll wait until after class to send it, though." Later, Patricia rereads the first paragraph of her letter, and decides to approach it a little differently. She deletes her last line and goes on,

I take it that the views you expressed in your column stem from deeply held beliefs about what is of ultimate importance to you. In that regard, your beliefs are similar to mine: I, too, express my views and live out my life on the basis of deeply held beliefs about what is of ultimate importance to me. In my case, these beliefs have to do with who I am in relation to other people and to God. I can't cut those views out of me every time I step into my classroom, nor would I expect you to do the same to yours if you were to visit my classroom.

Speaking of which, my class is currently studying the role of religion in cultures around the world. Would you care to speak to my class to illustrate the impact that secularism (which, given Webster's definition of religion, is a religion in its own right) has on Canadian public institutions today?

"I wonder if he even reads his e-mail," thinks Patricia as she signs off.

◆ACTIVITY 8-2

With one or two others, draft a possible reply that Michael Valpy might give to Patricia's e-mail, as well as Patricia's (second) response to Valpy.

Many Christian teachers teach in schools that are increasingly pluralized. They teach students who come from a wide plurality of cultural and religious backgrounds. Moreover, they also teach at a time when ideological pluralism shapes the thinking of more and more colleagues, students and parents.

The reactions of Christians to plurality and pluralism run the full spectrum. Some people consciously *surrender* to the ideological pluralism. They give up their own traditions and beliefs. Others *bargain* with the diversity. They try to decide what to keep and what to let go of in order to function in the pluralizing context. Some people *retrench defensively*. They seek to withdraw into a fortress within which all the old norms, doctrines and behaviors can be maintained. Finally, others *react offensively*. They seek to rearrange society and return it to the traditions they perceive to have existed before pluralization took place.

Looking to the Bible, we can discern models for how God's people dealt with plurality. These situations differed with changing times and circumstances.

In Old Testament Israel, neither cultural nor religious plurality was to be tolerated. In fact, God instructed the people of Israel to wipe out the nations who had previously inhabited the land of Canaan. Israel was not be tempted to take up pagan cultural and religious practices. The people of Israel failed to keep faith with God, however, partly because they failed to obliterate pagan practices and were constantly influenced by them. God punished them with destruction and exile.

God's people found themselves in a totally different situation when living in exile. No longer did they have the political boundaries or military might to keep plurality at bay, even if they had wanted to. Nor did they have any priestly leadership to look to, once the temple in Jerusalem was destroyed. All they had was God's Word. For some, like Daniel and Esther, that was enough to sustain them. Others, however, surrendered, and adopted Babylonian culture and religion.

Those who remained faithful to God in exile did not have the means to wipe out plurality. Indeed, God did not even expect them to try. The prophet Jeremiah suggested a surprisingly different approach. In a letter to those who had been exiled in the first stage of deportation (597 BC), Jeremiah wrote, "Seek the peace and prosperity of the city to which I have carried you into exile. Pray to the Lord for it, because if it prospers, you too will prosper" (Jer 29:7). Staying faithful to God without destroying the surrounding pagan culture may have sounded heretical to those who prayed for Babylon's destruction. God's intent, however, was to rebuild Israel into a people that could remain faithful in the midst of overwhelming circumstances.

The situation of God's people in New Testament times was in many ways similar to that of those who had lived in exile. Those who lived under the lordship of Jesus Christ had neither the political nor the temple establishment to back them up. They could not establish cultural and religious uniformity, nor did God instruct them to do so.

Jesus himself showed tolerance and respect for those of foreign cultures. The gospels include many stories of his interaction with non-Jews. This shocked even his disciples. For Paul also, cultural diversity was not an issue. He knew how to relate to those who would hear the good news of salvation in Jesus Christ without having any reference point in the Old Testament Scriptures. Paul's sermon at Mars Hill in Athens (Acts 18) is a good illustration. In it he quoted extensively from pagan literature to make his point to a non-Jewish audience. Paul's defense of the faith before Festus and Agrippa, two dominant political leaders of his day, shows us how he understood his role in the diversity of public life in the first century.

What can we learn from these biblical illustrations of how God's people dealt with diversity? Our situation, as Christians in Western culture, is more similar to that of the Jews in exile and the early Christians in the Roman Empire than it is to the nation of Israel. We no longer have (if we ever did) the social consensus based on shared belief in Jesus Christ. We are no longer able to model all institutions on biblical principles. Yet, we must find ways of living in faithfulness to God within a pluralized society that is dominated by ideological pluralism.

Today Christians from around the world celebrate the fact that, in Jesus, cultural diversity is welcomed. We do not need to convert to Judaism in order to enter into God's family. In fact, the racial and ethnic diversity that we see in the Church today is a gift to all Christians. God is not and never has been a white North American or European male.

Religious diversity is another matter. We are called to witness to the truth of the gospel. We cannot accept the assumptions of ideological pluralism: *All points of view are regarded to be equally valid. All religions lead to God. Sincerity is all you need.* This philosophy of life seeks to accommodate Christianity to other religious traditions. It willfully discards all distinctive doctrines that give faith in Christ a clear identity. It also takes great liberty in reducing other religious traditions to convenient points of view.

Ironically, advocating this type of relativism is outdated in its understanding of objectivity. It is also amazingly arrogant. Pluralism rejects dogmatism and pleads for its point of view based on the premise that we live in a global community and that all religions share a "common core." What is the common objective core when a fundamentalist of one religious faith zealously kills a believer of another tradition in the name of a deity?

It is for these reasons that pluralism is accused of having a flimsy ethical basis for action and of being allergic to questions about what is truth. As C.S. Lewis so poignantly stated,

The God of whom no dogmas are believed is a mere shadow. He will not produce the fear of the Lord, in which wisdom begins and will therefore not produce the love in which it is consummated. There is in this menial religion nothing that can convince, convert or console. There is nothing therefore that can restore vitality to our civilization. It is not costly enough. It can never control or even rival our natural sloth and greed. (C.S. Lewis in Hooper 1970, pp. 142-43)

If we start from the point of view that religious diversity is a fact of life, like Paul did, then we need not see it as a threat or as something good in itself. It is simply an opportunity to talk about and live out the good news of salvation in Christ to those who don't know it.

By combining with secularism, ideological pluralism trivializes and privatizes religion. It makes the opportunities presented by religious diversity exceedingly difficult to meet. But the inability of ideological pluralism to deal with ethical issues may ultimately lead to the growing realization that the Christian faith has something to offer to public life after all. This will happen only if Christians show themselves to be committed to the common good because they follow the Creator who pours out grace on all the cosmos as part of his care for it.

As Christians we will want to articulate that nucleus of values, those "rules of the game" and those crucial institutions that must be for all a source of profound inspiration for life in society and the glue for unity and social coherence.

This common public culture includes a commitment to national Bills of Rights and the United Nations Universal Declaration of Human Rights. There are some fundamental values we will want to uphold, such as mutual respect, mutual responsibility, economic equity, social justice and environmental integrity. The game rules must include civility and a respect for minorities, as well as truthfulness and a desire for personal integrity. They must also reject the view that religious belief is irrelevant to public life.

Our task will also include entering into dialogue with other partners in the diversity of today's society. We are suggesting neither a mere exchange of ideas nor a polemical argument. Dialogue in today's pluralistic environment is a serious, no-holds-barred interaction between competing claims on the level of truth.

The New Testament illustrates this in Paul's second and third missionary journeys. These trips took him into cities whose citizens had worldviews very different from his. On numerous occasions Luke reminds his readers that Paul dialogued with his listeners

(Acts 17:2; 18:4, 19; 19:8-9). He explained his premises by opening people's minds to his ideas (Acts 17:3) and giving them reasons to accept his point of view (Acts 18:4).

Such a dialogue is rooted in the development of full, mutual, intellectual understanding and a respect for differences of nuance and subtlety. This applies particularly to the diverse "lived values" within the culture of all ethnic groups. The dialogue develops attitudes and mentalities within the common public culture that welcome the various cultures and lifestyles within a society. It will also see this variety as an enrichment of human life. However, this dialogue is not merely a tolerant, intellectual assent of shared opinions. Rather, it is a process whereby respectful exchange about differences results in deeper mutual understanding.

◆ACTIVITY 8-3

Patricia's class was studying Canadian West Coast First Nations (Indian) society. One group made a presentation on totem poles, and the subject of religion came up. The students seemed to feel that First Nations religion could be freely discussed and admired, but that it was somehow out of place to discuss their own religious beliefs with similar objectivity.

Patricia pointed out that the same Charter that protects the rights of and freedoms of others also protects the rights of each student. "And the teacher," said one of the students, and added, "What religion are you?"

How would you as a public school teacher use this opportunity? Then suggest ways in which you may legitimately promote the basic values outlined in this section in a public school classroom.

Christian teachers in the public school classroom

So how can a Christian teach in the midst of our diversity as we enter the 21st century? In our increasingly diverse society, how are Christian teachers ever going to explain God's truth? The very orientation to truth, to history and to the meaning of life is in a state of constant flux. It seems students think that nothing can be known for certain. For them, history is devoid of any sense or direction and all truth is relative.

A Christian teacher like Patricia wants to engage in the diversity of her nation's education system. She has a huge task but a noble ambition. Her response to its plurality and pluralism will begin with how she thinks about the issues. Once she understands the basics about pluralism, she can take steps to become involved with integrity in her ever-changing situation. Her process of engagement must be rooted in a commitment to contribute to the development of a public culture.

How can Patricia live the truth of the gospel when faced with the dilemmas of her pluralistic environment?

Part of the answer begins with how she reacts to differences in the school and in the classroom. It is very important that she discern the difference between what people do and say and who they are. She need not reject anyone because of that person's belief system or actions. Far too often, fear comes from a lack of understanding. In that case, one's identity rests on gender, race, language, class, religion and even one's region of origin. Then differences may become inherently threatening.

Patricia could spend time in the community around the school and get to know the people who live there. She might also have someone come and describe the experiences of those who come from different cultural communities. This would provide a good opportunity for her to see how her students react to diversity. She may find it easier to preserve her own Christian identity if she realizes how solid her identity appears to others.

Furthermore, Patricia could expose her students to diverse settings, such as a Sikh temple or a local First Nations reservation or a Christian house of worship. This creates opportunities to discuss the development of the common public culture. She can also ask questions, such as, What are the rights and responsibilities of minorities in the culture? Do we have a utopian view of other cultures? Who is the individual in the culture? What are our stereotypes?

In this context Patricia is building bridges. She does not assume that she really knows the individual who is different. Instead, she asks good questions. She is an active listener. She may invite herself into the home of the person with whom she is developing a relationship. In this venture into plurality in all its facets she will live with integrity, operating from a set of principles that come from God's perspective. She will try to approach situations in the same way that Jesus dealt with his real-world situations—with compassion and integrity.

Patricia will bring into her curriculum discussion of the role of religion in the lives of individuals and cultures around the world. She will lead her students to the questions that deal with ultimate meaning and purpose in life. Without indoctrinating students into her own Christian beliefs, she will share with her students how she answers those questions. She will always respect the ways in which her students answer those questions for themselves.

Above all, Patricia will live in such a way that she puts to the lie the idea that religious belief makes no difference in one's public life. And, by God's grace, she will do so in confidence and joy, remaining faithful to the God who created her, sustains her and calls her into loving service.

♦ *That night Patricia had a dream. She dreamt that her principal was recuperating from a car accident, and she went to visit her in the hospital. They reminisced for a while about the school, and then the principal started saying incredible things:*

> You Christians bring a distinctive flavour into our school and I want to thank you.
>
> Your attitude goes beyond being a good professional. You genuinely look out for the well-being of others, both staff and students. Others come first for you. You don't let the negativism of the staffroom bury you; you model a spirit of joy and hope. Even when you're frustrated, you don't explode. It's not a stoical, grit-your-teeth sort of thing; you have a nice blend of realism and serenity. No matter how crazy it gets around here, you seem confident that everything's okay. Some of the rest of us don't cope with stress quite so well. Your patience has a hidden source or resource within you somewhere.
>
> Because you are kind to others you seem to bring out the goodness in them. In your words and actions there's a gentleness that is not weak or pathetic, but confident and authoritative.
>
> I know I can always rely on you, not that you'll always agree with me, but that you'll be truthful and straight with me. Students and parents have said the same thing; so has the secretary. Last week — the day before my accident — in our difficult interview with Patrick and his mother, you were honest and direct, but you were also amazingly courteous and restrained.
>
> I've enjoyed every minute I've spent sitting in your classroom. You're not afraid to handle sensitive ethical issues or questions of religious significance. Some of us would be too unsure of ourselves

to handle the differences of opinion that come up in these situations, but you respect the students' opinions and aren't afraid to share your own. The kids really respond well to your willingness to share what moves you, what gives your life meaning. Not all of us share your Christian beliefs, but we all could take lessons from you about how to teach about religion without indoctrinating at the same time.

You know what strikes me? You're able to celebrate the differences among us that contribute to the richness of our school experience, and you can respect other opinions even when they clash with yours. Where you're convinced that differences will cause harm or injury to others, you're ready to step in and ask for assimilation into healthier ways of doing things. And you're not afraid to demand annihilation of harmful ways of thinking or acting — like when you marched those students who were using racist and sexist language down to my office. It's funny, you know, I wouldn't use the word "tolerant" to describe your attitude. You're always respectful, but you're not afraid to ask for change when it's needed.

If these things come out of your religious convictions, you have my permission to exercise that in your classroom any day of the week. I couldn't restrict these things even if I wanted to. But why would I want to? We need more of what you bring, not less!

Patricia had little to say in response, except that it was evident that her principal had lots of time on her hands to think. They went on to talk of more personal matters, and Patricia was able to end her visit with a short time of prayer.

When she woke the next morning, Patricia read something that gave her a fresh sense of purpose about her role in the school. Her devotional reading included a passage from Jeremiah 6:16:

This is what the Lord says: "Stand at the crossroads and look; ask for the ancient paths, ask where the good way is, and walk in it, and you will find rest for your souls."

"Okay, Lord," she said, "it's a crossroads out there where you've placed me. Sometimes I don't know which way to turn. Help me to experience your rest in my soul and to be a crossing guard for those at school that are searching for direction."

◆ACTIVITY 8-4

You can walk with God in your classroom no matter where it is located. Think back to the three injunctions that God gives us as believers: the creation mandate, the Great Commandment, and the Great Commission. How do each of these affect you when you teach in a public school classroom?

Reviewing the main points

1. *Cultural and ideological plurality is a fact of life in Western nations.* Like Jesus, Christian teachers welcome cultural diversity and respect students of all backgrounds.

2. *Ideological pluralism, on the other hand, holds that all beliefs and values are equally valid.* This in itself is a "religious" faith that runs counter to Christian beliefs. It also leads to the view that religious views must be excluded from public life.

3. *God calls Christian teachers to witness to the truth of the gospel.* Under national and United Nations Charters of Rights and Freedoms, Christian teachers in public schools have the right to lead students to the questions that deal with ultimate meaning and purpose in life. They may not indoctrinate students into their own beliefs, and must respect how their students answer those questions. However, they may share with students how they answer those questions themselves.

REFERENCES

Badley, K. 1996. *Worldviews: The challenge of choice.* Toronto: Irwin Publishing.

Hooper, W. (ed.) 1970. *God in the dock: Essays on theology and ethics.* Grand Rapids, MI: Eerdmans.

Postscript

Teaching is a rewarding calling, but not without frustration and stress. The irritating behavior of some students may sometimes get to be too much. Demands for curriculum changes or extra-curricular activities on top of your regular teaching and preparation may overwhelm you. It may bother you that not all students or parents like you or agree with your approaches. There are days when your students or you yourself would rather be anywhere but in the classroom. You may develop a case of February doldrums. You may even become somewhat bored with your own teaching. You thought you had prepared a great lesson but it bombs, and you feel deflated. The legal obligation to report suspected abuse gnaws at you since you can't be fully certain that it is occurring.

Such frustrations and the resulting stress are a natural part of teaching. Accept that they will occur and learn to cope with them. First, take time for personal devotions and reflections. Speak to God and a trusted colleague about your frustrations. Think through why they are occurring and how you may be able to overcome them.

Do you need to improve your competence in certain areas of teaching? If so, get some advice and help. Are you overtired? See whether you can change your schedule to make sure you get enough sleep. Find some time for relaxation. Do you feel defeated or overwhelmed? Think about ways to cope with your responsibilities. Talk to someone about your situation. Accept that all good teachers have lessons that fail. Perhaps the only ones who don't, in fact, are ones who play it so safe that little excitement about learning exists in their classrooms (which brings along its own stress!). Keep your students and yourself interested by changing your strategies. Learn to present your views positively to parents. Listen carefully to them, but accept that not all will see things your way. Sometimes tell your stu-

dents how you fell, and, yes, ask them to take that into consideration during that day.

As a teacher you need a support group. If you're a new teacher, it is helpful to be teamed up with an experienced mentor. If not, seek one out. Help build a team of teachers in your school who care for and support each other. Help create an atmosphere where teachers can share their joys and their difficulties. Teaching can become lonely when you isolate yourself. I made that mistake when I began teaching. I had one very difficult class in the public high school where I taught, and I assumed that I should solve the problems myself. I did have to come to grips with the situation myself–but would have benefited a great deal from discussing it with one or two experienced colleagues. When you face difficulties or ethical dilemmas, discuss them with a colleague you can trust. God did not create us just as individuals. As teachers, too, Christ has apportioned grace to each of us in a special way, not only to carry out our God-given roles with our students, but also to support and build up each other in love (Eph 4).

Teaching as a journey

Teaching is a journey, a journey to which the Master calls you. He tells you something about the desired destination of those he entrusts to you on the journey: *responsive discipleship*. He also gives you guidelines. Some of these are:

♦ *Tell the next generation the praiseworthy deeds of the Lord, his power, and the wonders he has done. (Ps 78:4)*

♦ *Act justly, love mercy, and walk humbly with your God. (Mic 6:8)*

♦ *Let the little children come to me. (Mt 19:14)*

♦ *Teach them to obey everything that I have commanded you. (Mt 28:20)*

♦ *Look not only to your own interests, but also to the interests of others (Php 2:4)*

♦ *Set an example by doing what is good. In your teaching show integrity, seriousness, and soundness of speech. (Tit 2:7-8)*

But the Master leaves most decisions in teaching up to you. He wants you also to be a *responsive* disciple. Which highways, roads, or trails do you take? Which turns do you make at crossroads? Which means do you use to make progress? Where do you linger? Who do you keep with your group and who do you send forward or hold back?

The journey of teaching is a peculiar one, however. You usually make more progress toward your destination by walking or riding a bicycle than by taking an express train or a jet. A successful journey involves allowing your group, under your guidance, time to explore the byways. You deliberately seek out some barriers that your group has to overcome. You help them sample and make use of the resources along the way, not so much to speed up the journey as to improve it.

You do not allow your group members to be passengers who just give each other an impersonal greeting at the start and end of the journey. Instead, you have them interact so that they become a company of travelers whose various abilities contribute to the communal goals. You guide your company so that they can cope with personal and group failures and frustrations. Then you stand back to rejoice in success. In the end, you have not traveled as far as you might have. Yet, you have brought your group–and your-self–much closer to your destination than you would have had you sped from one point to another. In the process, you have enriched each member of the company. You yourself have become a wiser, more insightful, more loving travel guide and companion.

However, not all journeys are successful ones. Some are un-happy. Perhaps the chemistry of your group constantly undermines progress. Perhaps your group members have little or no interest in the journey. Perhaps you do not have a clear vision of your ultimate destination, and your group makes little headway. Perhaps you do not know enough about the terrain of the journey, or have little that is worth sharing. Perhaps you do not have the patience or the ability to deal with the human dynamics in your group. Perhaps you set out to be a friend but forget that you are first of all a guide. Perhaps you cannot relate well to children at your group's age level. Perhaps your comments and reactions cut down members of the company rather than build them up.

Whether or not any of these apply to you, ask yourself why you want to set out on the journey of teaching. A requirement for a successful journey is that you have ideals, a vision of how the journey can impact the members of your company in positive ways. If you have never before embarked on a journey of teaching, spend some time with groups of children and teenagers, if not in a school, then in a church, camp, or recreational setting. Do you enjoy being with and leading groups? (That differs from working with individual children!) Are there children of certain age groups with whom you relate well, or others with whom you feel uncomfortable or lose patience? Do you respect children and teens even when they have values that differ from yours, or when they belong to different socioeconomic or ethnic groups, or when they declare a homosexual orientation? Do you enjoy working with children with special handicaps? Are you flexible enough not to be unduly baffled by unexpected situations–and able to deal decisively with them? Are you strong enough to set high expectations and enforce rules in a loving but firm way? Above all, are you able to love people with whom God has called you to work, to love them as you love yourself?

Teachers and learners are on a pilgrimage together, a pilgrimage that focuses on the Kingdom of God. To embark on such a pilgrimage, Christian teachers must have clear goals, as described earlier in this book. But, more than that, they must ask themselves whether God calls them to go on this particular pilgrimage. "To each grace has been given as Christ has apportioned it," I have stated before (Eph 4:7). If Christ in his grace has given you the primary gifts needed to become a teacher, be grateful and rejoice in a worthy and fulfilling calling. You may still find some classes difficult. In the end, however, the journey will be rewarding both for your students and for yourself. There are many teachers who have taught for many years and still say, "I actually get paid for doing what I love doing most!" These are the ones whose journeys will change many of their students in indelible, praiseworthy, and gratifying ways both for this life and for eternity.

If self-analysis or advice from others shows, however, that in one way or another Christ has not given you the grace to be a teacher, try to be thankful for other gifts and rejoice in a different worthy and fulfilling vocation. Airline reservation clerks unhappy in their position may affect individual passengers for a few moments. But teachers not suited for teaching often become not only unhappy themselves but each year again affect the lives of many

students in unpleasant and even harmful ways. They may exasperate children–something Paul warned against (Eph 6:4). If you find
yourself in such a situation, find another calling, for their sake and
yours.

On your pilgrimage of teaching, set out to discover and understand Truth with your pilgrims. At length, when you walk with
Christ's Spirit, the journey of Christian teaching leads, as Parker
Palmer puts it, not to us mastering Truth but to Truth mastering us
(1983, p. 59). Thus your role as teacher is to walk along roads with
your students where together you may practice obedience to the
Truth that is Jesus Christ. That is what ultimately makes teaching
such an exceptionally rewarding vocation.

◆For further reading

A rationale for Christian schooling that highlights the impossibility
of religious neutrality in education is Richard Edlin, *The Cause of
Christian Education,* 2nd ed. (Vision Press, P.O. Box 1106, Northport,
AL 35476; 1997).

For a descriptive agenda for Christian schooling developed by a
group of scholars who worked under the auspices of the Calvin Center for Christian Scholarship, see Doug Blomberg and Gloria Stronks
(eds.), *A Vision with a Task: Schooling for Responsive Discipleship*
(Baker Books, P.O. Box 6287, Grand Rapids MI 49516-5287; 1993).
John Van Dyk's *Letters to Lisa: Conversations with a Christian
Teacher* (Dordt Press, 498 Fourth Avenue NE, Sioux Center, IA
51250; 1997) presents issues for Christian teachers in an informal,
sensitive way.

A companion volume to *Walking with God in the Classroom* that develops the foundation and practice of curriculum in much more depth
is Harro Van Brummelen's *Steppingstones to Curriculum: A Biblical
Path* (1994). Like this volume, it is published by Alta Vista College
Press, P.O. Box 55535, Seattle, WA 98155.

For reading about enculturating students into their tradition in
meaningful ways, see Thomas Groome's *Christian Religious Education:
Sharing Our Story and Vision* (HarperCollins, 151 Union Street, San
Francisco CA 94111; 1980), and John Bolt's *The Christian Story and
the Christian School* (Christian Schools International, P.O. Box
8709, Grand Rapids MI 49518-8709; 1993).

Robert Pazmino writes mainly for church education, but his books are insightful: *Foundational Issues on Christian Education* (1988), *Principles and Practices of Christian Education* (1992), and *By What Authority Do We Teach?* (1994). All are published by Baker Books.

Paul Kienel is the editor of *Philosophy of Christian School Education* (Association of Christian Schools International, P.O. Box 35097, Colorado Springs, CO 80935; 1995). The book deals more with Biblical bases and practices for education than philosophy per se.

For two Australian collections of essays on topics of interest to Christian school educators see Ian Lambert and Suzanne Mitchell (eds.), *Reclaiming the Future: Australian Perspectives on Christian Education* (1996) and *The Crumbling Walls of Certainty: Towards a Christian Critique of Postmodernity and Education* (1997). Both are published by the Centre for the Study of Australian Christianity, Robert Menzies College, Macquarie University, P.O. Box 1505, Macquarie Centre NSW 2113, Australia.

A book written for Christian teacher educators that contains chapters on teaching Christianly relevant for classroom teachers is Harro Van Brummelen and Daniel Elliott (eds.), *Nurturing Christians as Reflective Educators* (Learning Light Press, 1156 Camino Del Sur, San Dimas CA 91773; 1997).

Christian Educators Journal is a quarterly journal of fairly short articles on approaches and issues in Christian schools (1828 Mayfair Drive NE, Grand Rapids, MI 49503). *The Journal of Education and Christian Belief* has more in-depth articles and is published twice annually (Paternoster Press, P.O. 300, Carlisle, Cumbria CA3 0QS, United Kingdom). *The Journal of Research on Christian Education* provides a forum for research findings about Christian schooling (School of Education, Andrews University, Berrien Springs MI 49104).

Finally, a detailed bibliography of published materials related to Christian schooling is available via e-mail attachment from myself at vanbrumm@twu.ca.

REFERENCE

Palmer, P. 1983. *To know as we are known: A spirituality of education.* San Francisco: Harper & Row.

Index